外国建筑师中国作品选

SELECTED WORKS SINCE 1980

INTERNATIONAL ARCHITECTS IN CHINA

刘尔明　羿风　主编

LIU ERMING/YI FENG

中 国 计 划 出 版 社

中国大百科全书出版社

CHINA PLANNING PRESS

ENCYCLOPEDIA OF CHINA PUBLISHING HOUSE

图书在版编目(CIP)数据

外国建筑师中国作品选／刘尔明，羿风主编，－北京：
中国计划出版社，1999.6
ISBN 7-80058-777-0

Ⅰ.外… Ⅱ.①刘…②羿…Ⅲ.建筑艺术－世界－现代－
图集Ⅳ. TU-881.1

中国版本图书馆CIP数据核字（1999）第21188号

First published in China in 1999 by CHINA PLANNING PRESS,
Building 3, 2 Yue Tan Bei Xiao Jie, Beijing 100037

Printed in China by Shenzhen ARTRON Color Printers Ltd.

Desinged and edited by Liu Erming & Yi Feng

Distributed by Xinhua Bookstore, Beijing, P. R. China

ISBN 7-80058-777-0

出　版

中国计划出版社　　中国大百科全书出版社
（北京市西城区月坛北小街2号3号楼）　（北京阜成门北大街17号）
新华书店北京发行所发行
深圳雅昌彩色印刷有限公司印刷
开本889×1194 1/16 印张11
1999年6月第1版 1999年6月第1次印刷
印数：1-4500
ISBN7-80058-777-0/TU·147
定价：180.00元

序　言

本世纪以来，外国建筑师在中国的部分城市陆陆续续地设计了一些建筑，近20年的设计在规模、类型和水平上都超过了历史上任何时期。本书的编者将中国改革开放后20年间外国建筑师在中国设计的建筑及方案有代表性地收集并予以介绍，这对于中国的建筑师和业主以及对中国建筑业有兴趣的外国建筑界同行，都是一件很有意义的工作。

20年来，外国建筑师在中国的建筑设计是在我国经济快速发展和实行改革开放的大环境下产生的，这与中国改革开放前20年(60年代和70年代)形成了巨大的反差，在那段时期，由于天灾人祸和闭关自守等原因，几乎没有外国建筑师在中国设计建筑；我国的建筑创作活动也不多，中国的建筑师在离开了世界建筑发展的主流环境中独自摸索。受巴黎美术学院（Beaux Arts）影响的当代中国建筑始终难以摆脱学院派的影响，中国的现代建筑从未有过革命而只有渐进式的演变。

改革开放后，中国的建筑师走出国门开阔眼界，外国建筑师频频来中国承担建筑设计和规划，中国建筑界对外交流增加，中国建筑的创作活动进入了历史上最活跃时期。迄今为止，外国建筑师在中国国土上所设计的建筑已有不少投入了使用，这些“洋楼”是中国的建筑师和老百姓所能看见和感受的场所，在设计建造过程中，大多数项目有国内建筑师配合，使一批设计单位和建筑设计师们从中学习到当今世界的先进设计思想和技术，增加了对现代建筑的理解及当今世界各种建筑流派的认识。

世界经济全球化的趋势使建筑设计行业“服务”的国界越来越模糊。比较典型的城市巴黎和柏林有许多非本国的世界著名建筑师设计的建筑，法国前总统密特朗有将巴黎建为世界文化之都的雄心，柏林即将成为德国的新都，也决心使柏林重新成为世界著名的大都会之一。这些都是发达国家大城市的做法，它们不怕外国建筑师的“入侵”，相反，巴黎由于拥有了贝聿铭设计的鲁佛尔宫新馆而更吸引人，每年所增加的游客数就是对法国最好的回报。柏林目前正在建造的波茨坦广场也可能会起到类似的作用。中国上海的浦东、深圳的新市中心有不少外国建筑师参加了设计，能否为这些城市的旅游业增加回报现还难以预测，但对中国建筑师和老百姓带来更新的观念则是不容置疑的。

建筑是一种文化，建筑的国际交流也是一种文化的国际“交流”，21世纪这类交流的机会将会更多。目前大多数是单向的、先进的国家到落后的国家交流，外国的建筑师来到中国“交流”，福斯特设计的香港机场和汇丰银行所体现的高新技术；SOM在上海设计的金茂大厦所象征的现代化中国特色的摩天楼；李名仪的深圳市中心规划设计所追求的生态建筑和以人为本的思想等，这些外国建筑师设计的实例不仅仅是物质的成果，也是文化交流的体现。在同属于发展中国家的印度，有了勒·柯布西埃和路易·康的建筑范例，成长出以柯里亚为代表的几位国际认可的建筑师。外国名建筑师在中国优秀建筑的建成，是否会催促和激发中国建筑师早日达到国际水平？我期望在今后10～20年时间内中国也有若干位国际同行们普遍认可的国际级大师的出现，更期望在几十年之后能编出一本“中国建筑师在国外”，我期待着那一天的早日到来。

许安之

中国建筑学会副秘书长

Foreword

By Xu Anzhi

In the 20th century many architects from foreign countries have designed several buildings in China but the last two decades alone have featured an unprecedented amount of stunning architectural examples both in size, scope and variety. The editors of this volume present us an impressive collection of representative works in China designed by international architects. This undertaking is highly valuable for Chinese architects and clients, as well as their foreign counterparts.

Designs by international architects active in China during the last two decades were produced in a period of rapid economic growth and the implementation of reform and open-door policies in China. This is in stark contrast to the preceding two decades of the 60's and 70's, during which time, almost no foreign architects made any design in China due to devastating natural disasters, political turmoil and self-alienation from international contact. Architectural imagination came to a standstill, and Chinese architects were probing their way in isolation away from the main streams of world architectural development. Modern Chinese architecture never succeeded in freeing itself from the influence of Beaux Art traditions and therefore experienced no revolution but gradual evolution.

Since the implementation of the reform and open-door policies, Chinese architects began to travel abroad and expand their horizon; meanwhile, foreign architects became increasingly involved in the design and planning activities of Chinese projects. Architectural composition in China entered its most productive era in history. To date, many of the buildings designed by foreign architects have been put into use. These "foreign buildings" are places seen and experienced by Chinese architects and ordinary people. The design of such buildings were often assisted by Chinese architects, who whereby gained knowledge of advanced design philosophies and techniques current in the world, as well as comprehending of various modern architectural trends outside the country.

The globalization of world economies made makes national boundaries less restrictive for international design services. Typical examples are cities like Paris and Berlin; both have a large number of buildings designed by foreign architects. Former French president Mitterand had the ambition to make Paris the cultural capital of the world; Berlin will soon be the German capital again and it is also determined to become a world famous metropolis. Major cities in developed countries do not fear the "invasion" of foreign architects. Quite to the contrary, Paris becomes more attractive for tourists because of I. M. Pei's creation for the Louvre. The increase in the number of tourists each year is the best return for France. The Potzdamer Platz currently under construction may play a similar role. The development of Pudong, Shanghai and the new city center of Shenzhen involved many foreign architects. Their impact on tourism remains to be seen; however, it is unmistakable that they have brought new concepts to Chinese architects and the general populace alike.

Architecture is a part of culture, and architectural exchange is cultural exchange. There will be more exchange opportunities in the 21st century. At present, most exchanges are unilateral - from the advanced countries to developing countries. Often the foreign architects have come to China to get involved in Chinese projects: witness Foster's high-tech design of the Chek Lap Kok International Airport and the Shanghai-Hongkong Bank Headquarters in Hong Kong, SOM's high-rise Jing Mao Mansion with a metaphor of Chinese culture in Shanghai, and John Lee's ecological and human approach for the new city center in Shenzhen. These striking examples by foreign architects are not only architectural products, but also product of cultural exchange as well. Being a developing country, India has produced a number of internationally acknowledged architects such as Correa because of the presence of foreign architects like Le Corbusier and Louis Kahn. Will the realization of good designs by foreign architects urge and stimulate Chinese architects to reach the international level earlier? We look forward to the emergence of Chinese designers that are widely acknowledged by their international colleagues, and perhaps, a volume of "Chinese Architects Abroad", may someday introduce works by Chinese architects designed for foreign clients.

目　录

Contents

夏邦杰建筑师事务所
ARTE JEAN MARIE CHARPENTIER & ASSOCIATES

夏邦杰建筑师事务所由巴黎建筑师协会前任主席、法兰西建筑科学院院士夏邦杰先生1993年创立。事务所的历史可追溯至1969年夏氏创立的设计公司。事务所总部设于巴黎，致力于创新而富有想像地解决特定的建筑与城市设计问题。

事务所在项目前期研究、城市规划、景观、建筑及室内设计、建筑技术、投资控制及项目监理等诸方面具有丰富的经验，采用最先进的计算机技术有效快捷地服务于设计的全过程。在欧洲、非洲、柬埔寨、中国、土尔其、阿联酋等地均有项目。该事务所在机构总部、办公楼、公共建筑、文化性建筑及城市设计等方面均有创造性的成果和作品。

90年代以来，该事务所积极参与了上海地区许多重大项目的设计与竞赛，这些项目包括：上海大剧院、浦东展览中心、花木兰广场、房地产培训中心、浦东中央广场规划、钱家塘居住区规划及万里试点小区规划等等。

Arte Jean Marie Charpetier & Associates was founded by Jean Marie Charpentier, a member of the "Academie d'architecture" in France and the former president of the "Ordre Architects de Paris". The firm is developed from the practice that Mr. J.M. Charpentier set up in Paris in 1969. Based in Paris, the firm has a team of international architects, engineers and urban planners who share a common goal that is to solve specialized architectural and urban design problems with innovation and imagination.

Their experience in programming, urban planning, landscaping, architectural and interior design, building technology, cost control, project and construction management has served private and public sector clients throughout the world. They employ the latest computer technology at every stage of the design process from inception to completion, to provide design and production information to clients and consultants with speed and efficiency, whatever their geographical location. The firm has constantly diversified and extended its activities through working with different cultures in different parts of the globe and has experience in many European countries, Africa, Cambodia, China, Turkey, United Arab Emirates and in the French Territories in New Caledonia.

Since 1990, the firm actively involved in many projects and competitions in China. These projects include the Grand Theater Opera, Pudong Exhibition Center, Real Estate Educational Complex, Magnolia Plaza, Central for Pudong City Hall, Planning for Wanli District and Qianjiatang Neighborhood etc.

The depth and breadth of their experience is illustrated by a portfolio of diverse and innovative solution in the fields such as company headquarters, office buildings, business parks, shopping centers, cultural and art centers, residential housing, interior design and urban design.

上海大剧院

剧院位于人民广场市政府大厦西侧，建筑高度40米，总面积62803平方米，是一包括剧院、餐厅、办公、排练及商业等设施的综合体。整个建筑地下2层，地面6层，顶部2层，共10层。内设大、中、小三个剧场，大剧场观从厅约1800个座席，拥有目前国际上容纳面积最大、功作变换最多的舞台设备，可满足国际、国内大型芭蕾舞团、歌剧团及交响乐团的轮流演出。中、小剧场规模分别为600和250座，满足室内乐、小剧场话剧和时装表演等需要。

剧院采用简洁独特的弧形屋顶造型，透明的玻璃外墙，使建筑宛若一座轻盈而飘逸的水晶宫，兀立于高层林立的城市环境之中。为上海这一国际性大都市增添了浪漫的现代建筑诗篇。1998年建成后，它成为上海的标志性文化建筑。

Shanghai Grand Theater

Located in the western side of the City Hall in the People's Square, the theater complex consists of spaces for theaters as well as restaurants, administration offices, workshops and a retail arcade. With a total floor area about 62,000 square meters and 40 meters in height, it has 2 underground levels, 6 levels above the ground and 2 levels in the top. Three theaters are in different scales. The main one is equipped with the most advanced stage facilities which provide almost limitless variation of stage area to meet performance requirements of world's largest orchestras, operas and ballets groups. It's auditorium provides1,800 seats. The two other theaters, with 600 and 250 seats separately, are suitable for chamber music, contemporary drama and dance etc.

The highlight of the design is the unique curving roof. With the transparent curtain wall, the building looks like a light and soaring crystal palace, which gives greater importance to the building amidst the surrounding high-rise flowers. It adds the most romantic and exciting poem of modern architecture to city of Shanghai, an international metropolis.

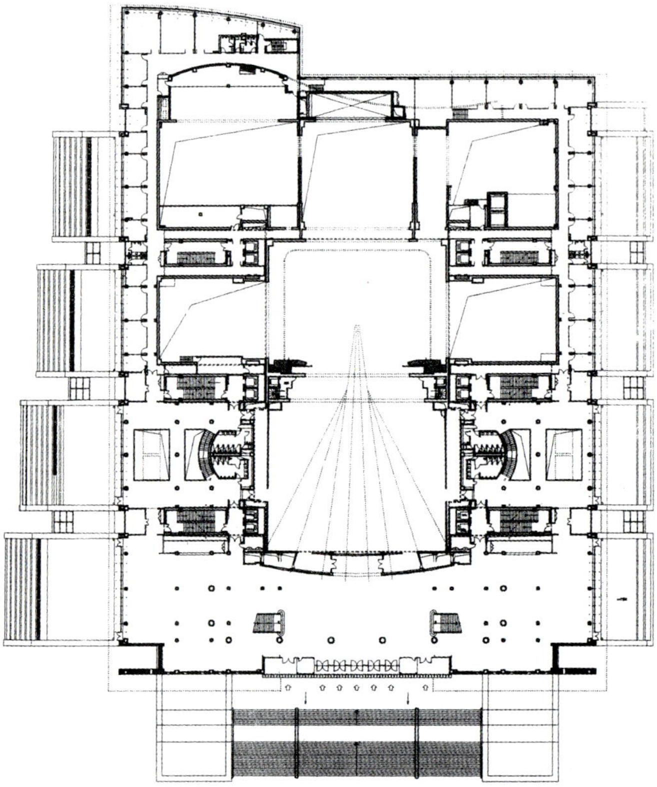

二层平面 Second floor plan

外观 Exterior view

夜景 Night view

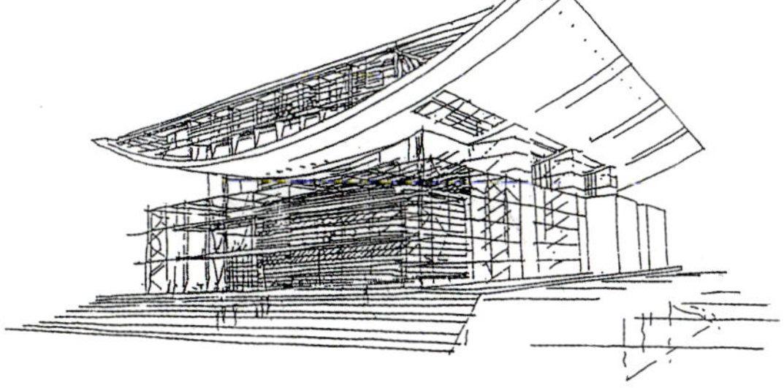

草图 Sketch

大堂 Lobby view

舞台 Stage view

观众厅 Auditorium view

AMP 建筑设计公司
AM PARTNERS, INC.

AMP建筑设计公司成立于1985年，公司员工75人，主要承接商业、居住性建筑设计。经过不断发展，公司已成为一个国际认可的全职设计公司，在夏威夷、洛杉矶、香港及上海均设有分部。

公司大部分项目集中于中国大陆，正建的项目有：广州的商业办公综合楼、北京一栋包括13栋高层、400个居住单元的居住、办公综合体及珠海的一个会所建筑。

公司总裁Charles Lau生于香港，1973年赴夏威夷，毕业于夏威夷大学，并曾在该校建筑系任教。在成立AMP之前，Charles Lau曾在当地几家事务所工作，由此奠定了其国际设计经验。

Charles K. C. Lau, AIA, is the founding partner of AM Partner, Inc., a 75 member multi-national architecture and design firm with world-wide commissions for commercial and residential projects. Mr. Lau founded AM Partners in 1985 and serves as the firm's president and business development director. From its modest inception, AMP has grown to become an internationally recognized full service firm with offices in Honolulu, Los Angeles, Hong Kong and Shanghai.

Much of the firm's current portfolio of work is centered in The People's Republic of China, with construction in progress on several world-class projects: a commercial office tower in Guangzhou, comprised of international retail shops, numerous food and beverage outlets, commercial office suites and executive apartments; a health club, residential and office complex in Beijing and a 400 unit residential development consisting of 13- high-rise buildings and a clubhouse in Zhuhai City.

Mr. Lau was born and raised in Hong Kong. He moved to Hawaii in 1973 where her completed his formal education. He holds a degree in architecture from the University of Hawaii, where he served as a professor in the School of Architecture. Mr. Lau was principal designer for several Hawaii-based firms prior to establishing AMP, which enabled him to gain the international experience that reflected in the firm's design philosophy.

广州 Keep Mount 广场

该工程建于亚洲最大的地铁站之上，容纳办公、商业和居住空间，总面积20000平方米。塔楼在6层高的裙房之上，裙房的中庭和地铁总站相通，内设商店和餐厅。裙房立面材料采用玻璃、钢及石材。27层高的办公楼坐落在裙房之上，酒店式公寓位于最顶层，住户可以直接到达停车场、商场和街道层面上。

Guangzhou Keep Mount Plaza

This dynamic project, rising dramatically above the largest subway station in Asia, provides nearly 20,000 square meters of office, retail and hospitality space. The tower structure is located atop a six-storied atrium cored podium which opens to the main subway station level below and features retail and restaurant spaces. The podium level in glass, steel and stone. Suspended above the lively, open entrance and repeated in larger scale atop the office tower, sits a gemstone-like crown which will feature a multi-level restaurant and private membership club. The 27-floor office tower rises from the podium roof level and executive serviced apartments on the uppermost floors. Tower occupants have direct access to parking, shopping and to the street level below.

外观 General view

上海温莎花园

这是一片豪华出租公寓的设计和规划项目。包括60幢钢筋混凝土和砖结构建筑，为外籍人士提供的欧陆风格的别墅共有6种户型。公共设施包括会员俱乐部，内设物业办公室、便利店、快餐店、酒吧、游戏室、壁球和网球室、桑拿房、淋浴及更衣设施。其它设施还包括家政服务、储藏及室内外游泳池等。

Shanghai Windsor Park

The project consisting of the master plan and architectural design of an exclusive luxury rental community located in Shanghai. The community includes 60-reinforced concrete and masonry structures. The European-style executive villas, designed for expatriates, have a range of six unit types. Common amenities include a membership club with front desk, property management office, convenience store, snake, bar/sports bar, game room, squash/tennis facility, sauna, shower and locker facility, support facilities including housekeeping, storage, and support spaces plus outdoor and indoor swimming pools.

外观 General view

外观 General view

外观 General view

珠海住宅区

住宅区规模为400个居住单元，占地53014 平方米，包括13幢沿中心庭院布置的8层建筑物。庭院内瀑布、游泳池和娱乐设施穿插于自然景观之间。同时在规划之中的还有10幢3627平方米住宅。在坡地上规划了独立别墅和一个俱乐部，使其获得私密的景观。

Chief Zhuhai Residential Development

This proposed development of a 400-unit residential community on a site of 53,014 square meters in Zhuhai city, The project consists of thirteen 8-story high-rise buildings arranged to form central courtyards with waterfalls, swimming pools and recreation areas interwoven with the natural landscape. Also planned are ten 3,627 square meters 2, 3, & 4-Bdrm. Single family villas and a clubhouse facility set on a gently sloping bluff that allows privacy and a southern view exposure.

鸟瞰 Overall view

安什＋艾伦建筑设计公司
ANSHEN + ALLEN, INC.

安什＋艾伦建筑设计公司于1940年成立，在医疗、科研和商业建筑设计领域具有丰富的历史和经验。公司在旧金山、洛杉矶、巴尔的摩、撒拉索塔和伦敦设有事务所，拥有巨大的设计资源，在建筑、规划和室内设计多方面为客户提供优质的服务。公司目前的业务遍布全世界，远至北美，东西欧、亚洲和中东地区。

公司的设计享有国际声誉，所获的奖项超过65次，其中包括美国建筑师学会加州分会的最高荣誉：1997年度“最佳事务所”奖。公司作品发表逾300次，其中包括主要专业杂志如：建筑、建筑实录、进步建筑、现代保健、建筑评论、医院发展、世界建筑和I' ARCA中的专题介绍。

公司提供的服务包括可行性计划，工程选址，总平面规划，工程计划，医院规划，建筑设计，建筑概预算，室内和平面设计等方面。

Founded in 1940, Anshen + Allen's richly diverse history of experience includes healthcare, academic technology, and commercial building design. With office in San Francisco, Los Angeles, Baltimore, Sarasota, and London, Anshen+Allen offers enormous resources available to support the highest standards of client service and seamless delivery of architecture, planning, and interior design services. The firm's current projects span the globe, serving clients throughout North America, Eastern and Western Europe, Asia, and the Middle East.

Anshen+Allen has an international reputation for commitment to design excellence. The firm has received more than 65 design awards, including the America Institute of Architects, California Council's highest honor, "Firm award," in 1997. Anshen+Allen's work has been published more than 300 times, including features in such leading design journals as Architecture, Architectural Record, Progressive Architecture, Modern Healthcare, Architectural Review, Hospital Development, World Architecture, and l'ARCA.

Services the firm provides include: strategic planning, site selection, master planning, programming, medical planning, architectural design, project feasibility, interior and graphic design.

天津世界贸易中心

中心是集办公、住宅、商业和娱乐空间于一体的综合性建筑，总建筑面积229000平方米。位于天津市中心重要地段，9层裙房上建有两座塔楼，分别为一座60层的办公楼和一座20层的住宅楼，享受着海河的无限风光。

Tianjin World Trade Center

This proposed mixed-use complex of office, apartments, retail and entertainment space on a prominent block in Central Tianjin offers commanding views of the Haihe River from two, sleek 60-storey office and 20-storey apartment towers rising above a 9-level retail and entertainment base.

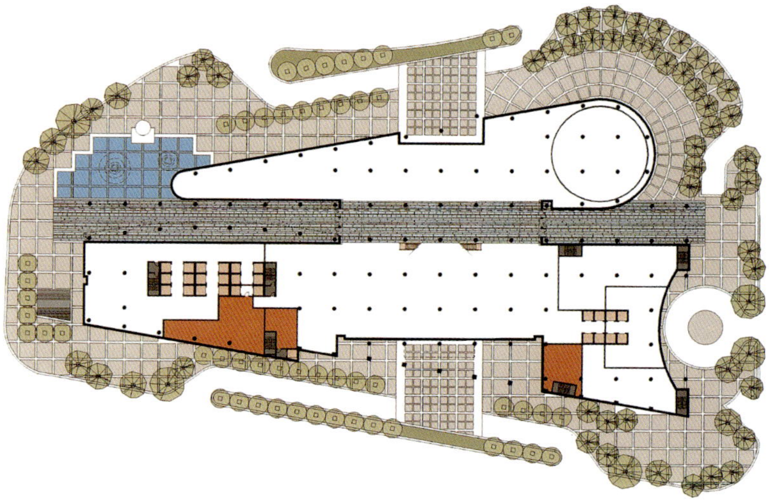

首层平面图 Ground floor plan

入口透视 Perspective view from entrance

外观 General view

上海 Way To Fund 国际金融大厦

这是一项国际竞赛的获奖项目。基地位于苏州河与黄浦江交汇地带，紧邻四川北路的传统商业区与城市中心新建的商业区。该综合性建筑包括两座分别为20层与25层的商住塔楼，自然形成上海外滩和浦东新区之间的门户。

为了加强传统的沿江发展模式，同时又为今后发展树立良好典范，大厦的设计强调自身的水滨地位，结合桥和河岸等元素，创造出宁静而富有生机的城市环境。两座塔楼布置在北端，使得沿河一侧形成一条步行大道。位于南部和西部的步行公共广场将活力引入建筑，并使塔楼和附近街区连为一体。

建筑运用了桥、门和塔的元素作为设计语言，以反映上海作为水滨城市所特有的文化和场所感。南立面柔和的曲线与苏州河的河道走向一致，开放性的入口大堂将塔楼、苏州河岸及商店区结合起来。其它共享的设施还包括展览厅、会议中心、互动式儿童博物馆、俱乐部及健身中心。

Shanghai Way To Fund International Finance Building

Winner of an international design competition, the mixed-use complex combines 20-story and 25-story live-work towers with retail to create a gateway transition between Shanghai's historic Bund and emerging Pudong business districts. The site occupies a pivotal position in the city near the intersection of Suzhou and Huangpu rivers and marked a transition from the historical Sichuan Bei retail district to a newly emerging business district in downtown Shanghai.

Intended to reinforce historical waterfront development patterns while establishing a precedent for sensitive future growth, this design enhances and celebrates its riverfront location by incorporating the bridge and rivers edge as sources of vitality, tranquility, recreation, leisure, and civic life. Placement of the two towers to the north creates a public promenade running the length of the site along the river. Pedestrian-oriented public plazas to the south and west draw life into the heart of the complex, creating a physical connection and encouraging movement between the towers and the surrounding district.

The building's vocabulary of bridge, gateway, and pagoda elements physically reflect the sense of place and culture of a Chinese waterfront city. The gently curving south facade traces the course of the Suzhou River. An open public lobby links the towers and the site to the Suzhou river and retail district. Shared amenities including an

透视图 Perspective view

平面图 Floor plans

正立图 Front elevation

侧立面 Side elevation

青岛国际酒店

为酒店设计的三个方案以探讨其发展的各种可能性。

低层方案中，客房沿着与海岸平行的三条不同标高的地形布置，形成两条线型开放空间。其中一条是内有商店的有顶公共广场，另一条是仅供客人使用的内部花园平台。

第二方案沿一系列绿化平台布置，平台最终通往一个巨型庭院。除顶层客房外，所有客房都以内廊方式布置以获得紧凑的总平面。从海上望去，建筑优美的轮廓线犹如三层贝壳，唤起大海的意象。

在高层方案中，来访者由一个大型的门廊进入。门廊作为画框收入广阔的天空和海景，又将人带到建筑的中心：一个三层高自然通风的庭院。设计中还运用了自然的气候调节手段，如培植茂密的植物、使空气自然流通的渠道和智能型的遮阳设施等。主要屋顶设花园，客人可欣赏黄海全景及远山。

Qingdao International Hotel

Three proposed schemes for a hotel and complex bordering the Yellow Sea explore a wide range of comparative development options. The low-rise scheme organizes guest rooms in three bands of varying height sited parallel with the beach front to define two linear open spaces, including a covered public galleria enlivened by retail activities and a second, more private garden terrace for the exclusive use of hotel guests. The second scheme is organized around a series of planted terraces leading to a grand, wind protected courtyard. Except for the uppermost guest room levels, rooms are arranged in a double-loaded configuration to create a more compact footprint. When viewed from the waterfront, the graceful curvature of the structures of the structures is designed to evoke the nautical imagery of three descending shells. In the high-scheme, visitors enter through a monumental portal that frames an expansive vista of water and sky and leads to naturally ventilated atrium, but wind protected three-story tall atrium sky-courts that hinge the building together. Other bio-climatic design principles include lush planting within each of the sky-courts, natural wind ducting, and strategically placed shading devices to create an environmentally responsive high-rise building. The major roof surfaces topped with garden terraces are accessible to hotel guests and visitors, each offer panoramic views of the Yellow Sea and distant mountains.

草图三 Sketch 1

草图二 Sketch 2

草图三 Sketch 3

B+H 国际建筑师事务所
B+H ARCHITECTS INTERNATIONAL INC.

B+H 建筑师事务所成立于 1953 年，长期以来在商业性与机构性建筑设计方面的成功与创新，使该公司在加拿大建筑设计界处于领导地位。

事务所先后成功地设计了BCE广场、加拿大广播中心、多伦多伊顿中心、第一加拿大中心、多伦多自治中心、多伦多会议中心扩建、皮尔逊国际机场第三空港等。目前正为一批令人激动的项目进行设计，这些项目包括将世界上最高的独立式构筑物多伦多 CN 塔的基座改造成引人注目的商业、娱乐综合体。

在海外B+H建筑师事务所以B+H国际建筑师事务所进行运作。自 1992 年在上海开设事务所以来，已成为在中国最活跃的加拿大事务所。目前在上海、北京及香港的分部雇用了15名以上加拿大本地和中国当地建筑师。

事务所设计的厦门高崎国际机场候机楼及位于浦东的新上海国际大厦两个项目已建成。其它正在建设或设计的项目包括：北京首都国际机场新候机楼（设计咨询）、上海新世界中心、上海美国学校、深圳社区购物公园、CAAC 浦东大厦、上海宾馆、中国建设银行计算机结算中心、上海长宁区中心医院、海口美兰国际机场候机楼、长沙机场候机楼及杭州萧山国际机场等。

总之，事务所80余位成员在5位董事的领导下，致力于以优质的设计服务于客户。服务范围包括建筑设计、城市总体规划、空间规划及室内设计。

Bregman + Hamann Architects was founded in 1953 and has developed into a leading force in Canadian architecture with a long history of successful and innovative projects covering the entire range of commercial and institutional developments. These projects include such notable Toronto buildings as BCE Place, Canadian Broadcasting Center, Toronto Eaton Center, First Canadian Place, Toronto-Dominion Center, Metro Toronto Convention Center Expansion, and Pearson International Airport's Terminal Three.

Currently, the firm is working on a number of exciting projects including transforming the base of Toronto's CN Tower, which is the world tallest freestanding structure, into a landmark retail/entertainment complex.

Overseas, the firm operates as B+H Architects International Inc. and, since the 1992 opening of its office in Shanghai, the firm has established itself as the most active Canadian architectural practice in China. Currently, B+H employs over 15 Canadians and Chinese nationals in permanent offices in Shanghai, Beijing and Hong Kong.

Two B+H projects, the Xiamen Gaoqi International Airport Terminal and New Shanghai International Tower (Pudong District, Shangha), have already been completed. Other projects currently in construction or design include the Beijing Capital International Airport's New Terminal (where the firm is providing on-going design consultation), New World Center (Shanghai), Shanghai American School, Shenzhen Community Shopping Park, CAAC Pudong Tower (Pudong District, Shanghai), Shanghai Hotel and Tennis Facility, The People's Construction Bank of China's Bank Computer Clearance Building (Beijing), Changning District Central Hospital (Shanghai), Haikou Meilan International Airport Terminal, Changsha Airport Terminal, and Hangzhou Xiaoshan International Airport.

In total, the firm has approximately 80 staff members directed by five partners, all of whom are committed to design excellence and client services. Services offered include architectural design, urban and master planning, space planning and interior design through B+H Design Consultants Inc., specifications, contract documentation, and contract administration.

新上海国际大厦

大厦共39层，于1997年竣工。位于陆家嘴金融区中心的浦东南路，与黄浦江对岸的外滩历史建筑遥相呼应。由7层裙房、一座办公塔楼和3层地下室组成。底部裙房坚实雄伟，塔楼形体高耸挺拔，外包银绿相间的反光玻璃。裙房后部是一个由顶部自然采光的巨大中庭。

裙房的主入口在由反光不锈钢材料构成的天棚之下，其造型与屋顶平台上直升飞机升降场的结构相呼应。大堂四周为银行营业厅、证券交易所、航空售票处，楼上是商务中心、会议厅、展览和餐厅等设施。

大厦采用了无立柱的办公楼层设计，以满足不同种类办公室需求的高效布局。平面以1.5米为基本模数，可以利用0.75米的网格布置顶棚和灯光。层高3.6米，因此用户可以根据自己的装修需要提升楼面。9至20层和22层至38层为商业、金融和贸易办公空间。地下层内设有停车及其它辅助设施。

New Shanghai International Tower

Completed in 1997, the 39-storey New Shanghai International Tower combines the classicism of a solid and majestic stone podium with a soaring tower clad in a combination of green and silver reflective glass with stainless steel spandrels. Situated on Pudong South Road on a 6,784 square meter site, it is a centerpiece of Pudong's Lujiazui finance and trade zone and sensitive to the historic building sited across the Huangpu River on the Bund. The Tower is comprised of a seven-level podium, office tower and three basement levels. A large atrium topped with a skylight is situated at the rear of the podium. The tower configuration and column-free office floor allow for the variety of office layout.

The podium is primarily accessed by an entrance located behind a mirror-finish stainless-steel canopy that relates to the design of the rooftop helipad structure. The main lobby is surrounded by a ring of banking, stock exchange and airline ticketing offices and upper-floor business center, conference and exhibition facilities and restaurants.

The tower configuration, with its differing profiles, provides for a variety of efficient floor layouts. Based on a 1.5-metre planning grid, floors can be subdivided into 0.75 meter for ceiling and lighting connections. A floor-to-floor height of 3.6 meters allows for the installation of raised flooring. The 19th to 20th and 22nd to 38th floors contain offices of trading, finance and business enterprises. The levels below grade hold shipping and receiving facilities, parking and other support functions.

外观 Exterior view

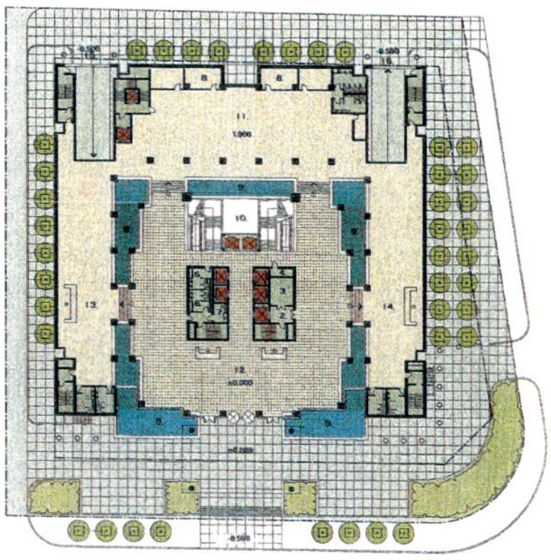

首层平面 Ground floor plan

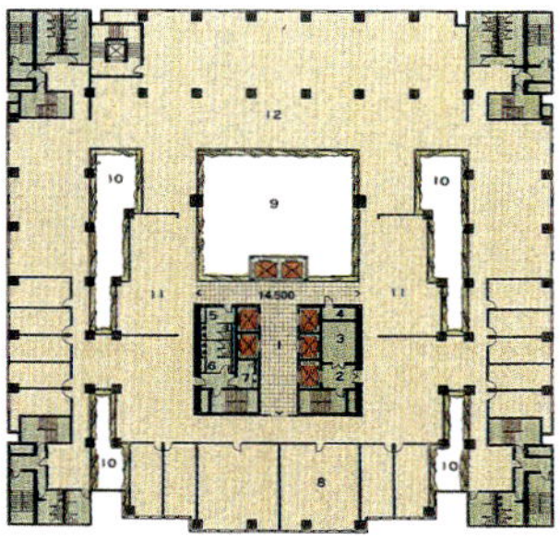

四层平面图 Fourth floor plan

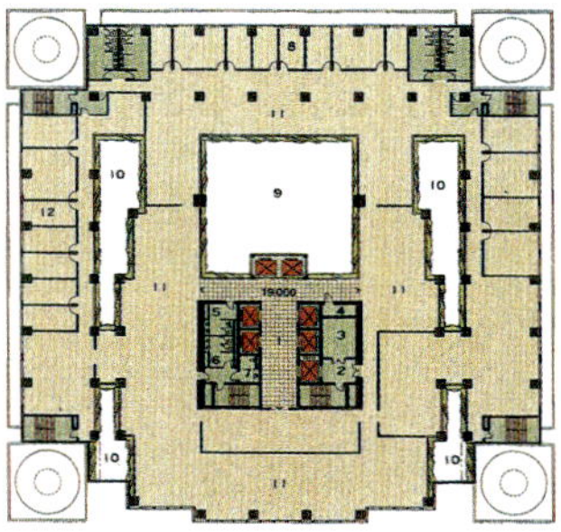

五层平面 Fifth floor plan

厦门高崎国际机场候机楼

这是一座拥有最新技术的候机楼，共有13个直接登机口和12个远程登机口。其设计具有内在的灵活性，可以适应不断变化的国内外旅客比例和数量的要求。屋顶借鉴传统中国建筑形式，巨大的顶棚遮盖住整个出发区，而下层的到达区向上部开放，在中庭里布置了所有旅客使用的主要垂直交通楼梯和扶梯。中庭的夹层内设有商店和旅客休息空间，中心区设票务、托运、航空公司办事处、保安、远程登机休息厅、商店、快餐及其它旅客服务设施。到达区设行包领取、食品储藏、建筑维护和货运服务等设施。航站楼的南部设有两层停车库。

机场设施实现了最合理的总体布局，飞机和旅客流线简单明确，具有最大的灵活性和适应性便于今后发展和增容。建筑形式运用了厦门地区的传统语汇，又完美地满足了功能要求，使其达到国际先进水准。

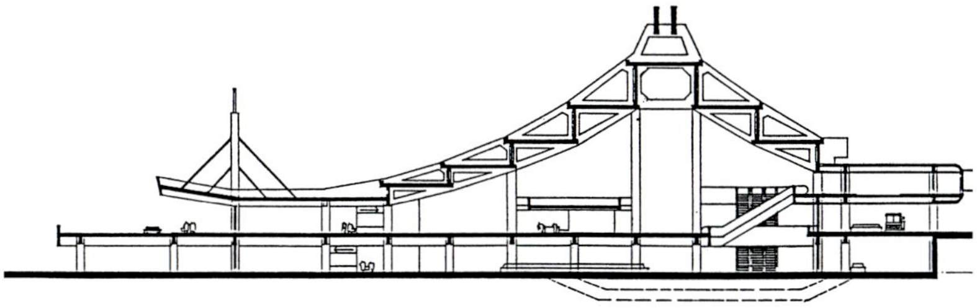

剖面 Section

Gaoqi International Airport Terminal, Xiamen

This state-of-the-art facility has a linear design with 13 direct aircraft boarding gates and 12 remote aircraft boarding positions. It has built-in flexibility to accommodate a varying ratio of domestic to international passengers in response to the country's rapidly expanding air travel requirements. The roof, recalling a traditional Chinese profile, provides a generous canopy over the departures area, while the arrivals level below is deliberately opened up to this space. The resulting atrium contains all the major vertical circulation stairs and escalators for passengers. A mezzanine for retail and a number of departure lounges overlook this space. The central expanse houses ticketing, checked baggage, airline offices, security, remote boarding lounges, shops, food service, and other passenger service. The arrivals level houses baggage claim and related services, food storage and preparation, building maintenance, and storage and truck service. Two levels of parking are located south of the Terminal.

外观 General view

The intent of the concept is that the Great Hall and its processing functions be expressed differently from the airside piers and their boarding function. The Great Hall is expressed in architectural concrete, with a main column, beam and vierendeel truss structure on an 18.0 metre by 18.0 metre bay system. This gives a gradually ascending series of roofs with filtered sunlight through clerestory windows. The remaining concrete structure is on a 9.0 metre by 9.0 metre grid. Brise soleil with horizontal concrete slats are used on the large east and west windows of the hall where low angle sun requires control. The piers, on the other hand, are deliberately modernist, with metal cladding and circular windows, in order to relate more to the airside and aircraft functions - 'high tech' like the aircraft themselves.

The facility achieves the most rational site arrangement, simple aircraft movement and passenger flow, and ease of expansion and maximum flexibility. The physical design recalls the regional architecture of Xiamen, while satisfying functional requirements in an elegant style, appropriate for a world-class facility.

内景 Interior view

上海新世界中心

中心位于上海著名的淮海路商业区心脏地带，高58层，包括一座五星级酒店以及商业零售、商务公寓、办公和公共停车设施，另外还带有一个多层公共开放空间。沿淮海路的4层裙房限定了街道空间，同时又为街道增添了活力和作为步行街的空间节奏。公共开放空间为大厦的使用者和附近社区居民提供了一个安静的处所。这座标志性建筑蕴涵着古典的优雅气质，通过对现代技术和材料的运用，建筑在表现未来的同时也体现出它对历史和文化传统的尊重。由于中心的主要功能是五星级酒店，因此其材料和氛围的处理亦体现出相应的典雅与华贵。

Shanghai New World Center

Located in the heart of the Huaihai Road special development precinct, the 58-storey New World Center is located along Shanghai's most prestigious and fastest-growing shopping street, Huaihai Road. It includes a five-star hotel (365,840 square feet), retail (269,000 square feet), business apartments (199,060 square feet), office space (145,260 square feet), public parking garage (118,360 square feet), and multi-story public open spaces. Along Huai Hai Road, the four-story podium will provide a definition of the street, enhancing the life and rhythm of the street as a promenade. The public open spaces, to be used for both active and passive use, will provide a place of quiet repose for both the building's users and community. This landmark design reflects a classical elegance, and through the use of modern construction techniques and materials, it will celebrate the future while recognizing its history and context of the people and their culture. As the Center's main use will be as a five-star hotel, its material and aura will celebrate luxury and elegance.

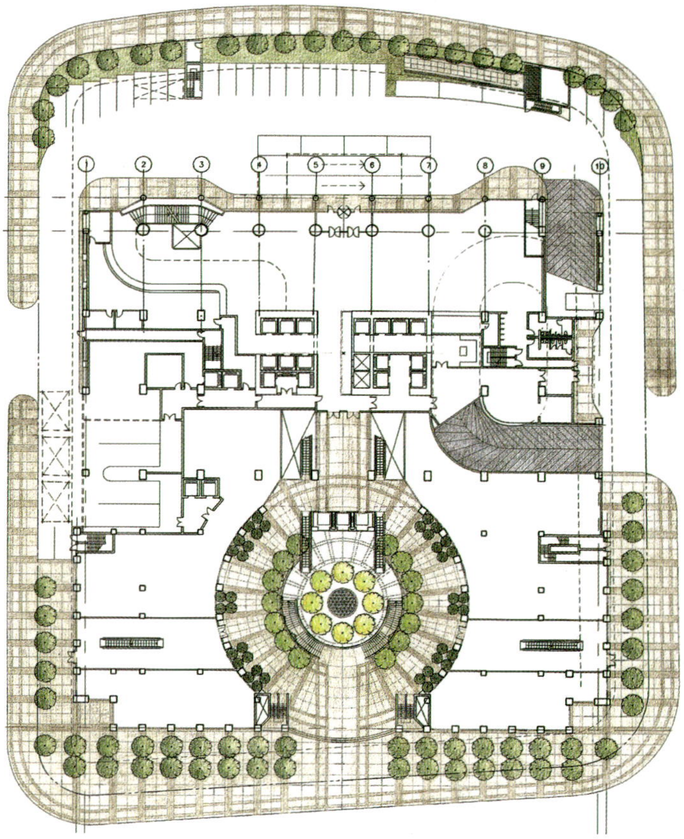
首层平面 Ground floor plan

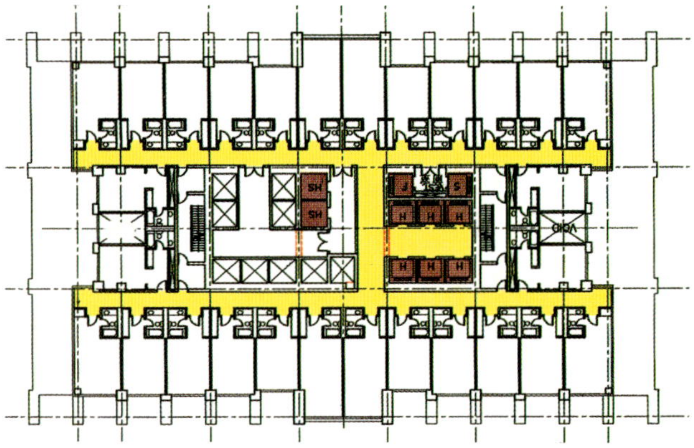
客房层平面 Hotel floor plan

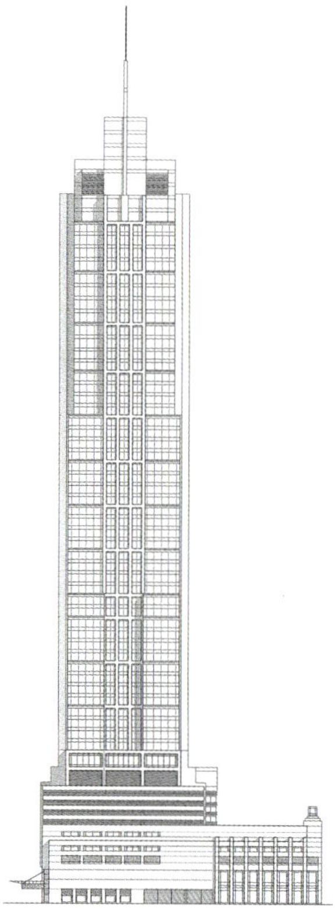
西立面 West elevation

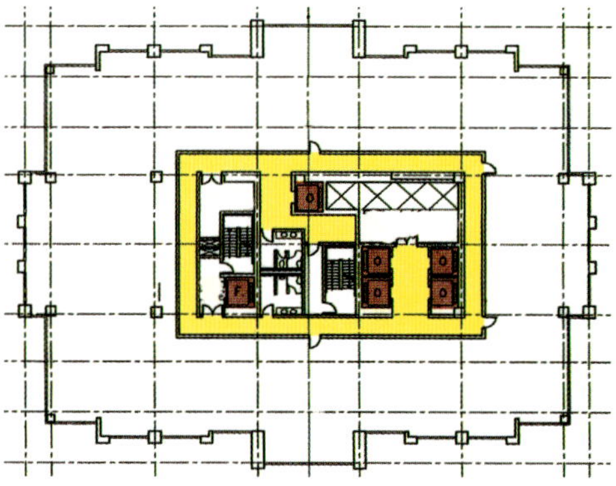
办公层平面 Offie floor plan

透视图 Perspective view

上海弘扬花园

该工程分两期实现，基地面积3.5公顷，包括居住和商业功能。除了为该工程作总体规划之外，还包括为其中的第一期工程，一座6万余平方米的住宅进行建筑单体设计。

Shanghai Hong Yang Garden

The firm is preparing the Master Plan for this two-phase residential and commercial complex situated on a 3.5-hectare site, as well as the design of Phase I which consists of a 60,600-square meters residential component.

模型 Overall view of Model

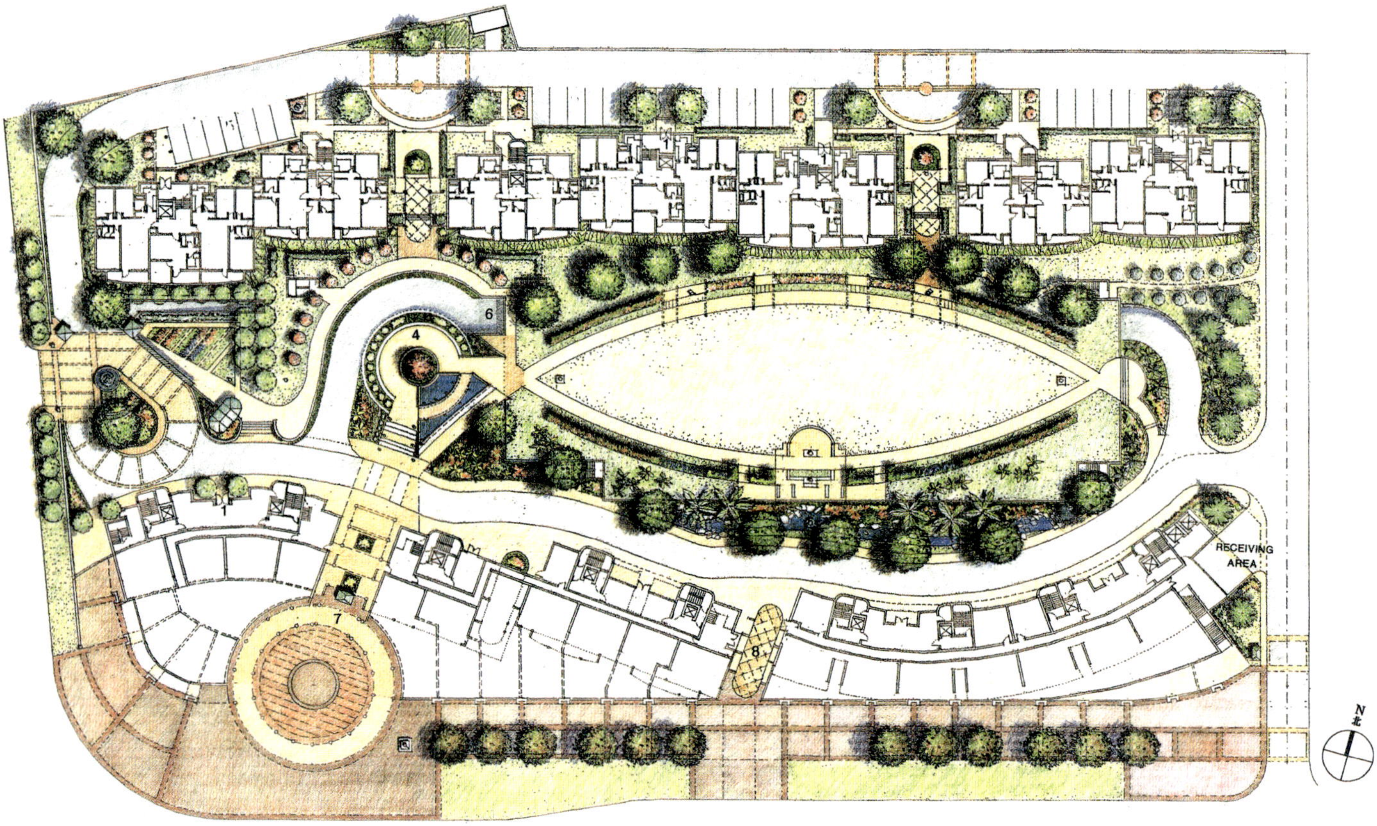

首层平面 Ground floor plan

透视图 General view

上海桃林花园住宅区

住宅区项目位于浦东住宅建设黄金地带，包括1260个居住单位。绝大部分公寓为11至18层，其中另有一幢27层高的塔楼和一座6层高带平台的豪华连排式住宅。设计的特色之一是其中大多数单元都享有南向的宽敞起居和餐厅空间。另外，在这片6.6公顷基地的轴线中心位置设有一个独特的下沉式瀑布花园，形成整个小区环境的焦点。

Shanghai Tao Lin Garden Residential Development

This 1,260-unit luxury residential development has been designed as the jewel of residential construction in the Pudong District. The majority of the apartment buildings will be 11 to 18 storeys, while there will be also be a one 27-storey tower and one 6-storey luxury townhouse complex with terraces. Most units will have spacious living/dining areas with large southern exposures as a special design feature. A primary amenity of the development will be its unique landscaping featuring a sunken garden and waterfall to accentuate the focal points along the major axis of the 6.6-hectare site.

总平面 Site plan

鸟瞰 Aerial view

福斯特建筑师事务所
FOSTER AND PARTNERS

福斯特事务所创立于1967年，目前在世界范围内共有480位设计人员，其中在伦敦的事务所共有385人。事务所的工作由一个董事会负责，福斯特爵士任主席。事务所自创立以来，已取得140次奖项，赢得了40次国内外设计竞赛奖。事务所设计项目和规模非常广泛，从城市扩建改造到单体建筑、室内设计、家具和产品设计、企业形象设计和会展布置。总部位于伦敦，事务所目前在格拉斯哥、柏林、法兰克福、香港、新加坡都设有办公处。

他们相信杰出的设计来自与业主的密切配合，除建筑和城市设计两个主项以外，事务所还有其它的专业支持。他们强调模型的重要性，它不仅是设计的工具同时又是与业主交流所需的手段。除了通常的缩尺模型以外，事务所还常常制作一些1:1的模型，这是事务所讲求细节的原则的一部分。事务所有一个综合的幻灯和照片资料馆，这样设计者可以向业主分析以往方案的每一个细节、解释其设计方法和发展过程。事务所坚持认为建筑和室内设计是不可分割的两个部分，因此对建筑室内的每一个细节，甚至紧急出口的标志的设计都进行具体的控制，几乎每一幢设计的建筑物的室内都由同一个设计组完成，因而能够对室内设计的各项要求和内容作出全面的控制。

在福斯特与合伙人事务所设计的重要建筑当中，有位于Nowish的圣斯伯雷视觉艺术中心、香港的汇丰银行、伦敦的皇家学院撒克勒画廊、伦敦第三国际机场、东京世纪塔、巴塞罗那通讯塔等。规划项目包括伦敦的国王十字、格林威治、康城、柏林、杜尔斯堡、鹿特丹和巴塞罗那等。目前正在设计中的工程有：法兰克福的商业银行总部；香港赤腊角新机场；瓦伦西亚会议中心及柏林新国会中心等。

公司创始人诺曼·福斯特1935年生于曼彻斯特。1961年从曼彻斯特的建筑与城市规划学院毕业后，获亨利奖学金前往耶鲁，成为乔那森·爱德华学院的研究员，并获得建筑硕士学位。1983年被授予皇家建筑金奖，1990年在女王生日庆典中被授予骑士身份并由女王亲自提名为1997年荣誉奖。自1991年以后，他被授予欧洲建筑密斯·凡·德·罗奖，法国建筑学院金奖；1994年美国建筑师学会金奖；MIPIM年度人物奖；巴塞罗那国际声誉奖等。

诺曼·福斯特是英国皇家建筑师学会会员；伦敦皇家艺术学院的会员；皇家西英学院院士；美国建筑师学会及众多国外专业机构的荣誉会员。并任伦敦建筑协会的副会长，皇家艺术学院委员会委员，以及英国皇家建筑学会教育与巡回评估委员会成员。

Foster and Partners employs about 480 staff worldwide with about 385 located in their London office. A Board of Directors leads the practice. Of the senior directors in the firm, Sir Norman Foster is chairman. Foster and Partner has, since its inception in 1963, received over 140 awards and citations for excellence and won 40 national and international competitions. Projects range in scale from masterplans for regeneration and expanding cities to individual buildings, interior design, furniture and product design, corporate graphics and exhibitions. Based in London, the practice currently has offices in Glasgow, Berlin, Frankfurt, Hong Kong, and Singapore.

They believe that design excellence can only be achieved through active collaboration with the client. In addition to the prime skills of architecture and urban planning, the firm is supported by a substructure of other disciplines. They attach importance to models, both as design tools and as a means of communicating ideas to the client. In addition to scale models of buildings they regularly produce full size mock-ups of components as part of their policy of testing everything. They maintain a comprehensive slide and photographic library. They recognize the importance of keeping a detailed visual record of every stage of every project. This enables the studio to analyze past schemes with clients in detail, explain its design methods and demonstrate the evolution of the design. They maintain that architecture and interior design are indivisible and they retain control of all details of the interior of their buildings down to fire exit signs. There is hardly a building completed by their practice in which the interior has not also been designed by their teams. The studio is capable of handling the full range of interior design requirements.

Amongst Foster and Partner's major buildings are Sainsbury Center for Visual Arts in Norwich; the Hongkong and Shanghai Bank in Hong Kong; the Sackler Galleries at the Royal Academy in London; Stansted, London's Third International Airport; the Century Tower in Tokyo; the Torre de Collserola, a communications tower in Barcelona; and etc. Masterplans include King's Cross, Greenwich, Cannes, Berlin, Duisburg, Rotterdam and Barcelona. Recent projects include a headquarters for Commerzbank in Frankfurt; the new Hong Kong airport at Chek Lap Kok; a Congress Center for the City of Valencia and a new German Parliament at the Reichstag, Berlin.

Norman Foster was born in Manchester in 1935. After graduating from Manchester University School of Architecture and City Planning in 1961, he won a Henry Fellowship to Yale University, where he was a fellow of Jonathan Edward College and gained a Master's Degree in Architecture. He was awarded the Royal Gold Medal for Architecture in 1983, in 1990, was granted Knighthood in the Queen's Birthday Honours and appointed by the Queen to the Order of Merit in 1997. Since 1991, he has received the Mies van der Rohe Award for European Architecture; the Gold Medal of the French Academy of Architecture; the American Institute of Architects Gold Medal for Architecture 1994; MIPIM Man of the Year Award and the 'Premi a la millor tasca de promocio international de Barcelona's for the international promotion of Barcelona .

Norman Foster is a member of the Royal Institute of British Architects; a Member of the Royal Academy of Arts, London; a Royal West of England Academician; Honorary Fellow of the American Institute of Architects and many other Foreign Professional Institutes. He has been Vice-President of the Architectural Association in London, Council Member of the Royal College of Art and a Member of the Board of Education and Visiting Examiner for the Royal Institute of British Architects.

香港汇丰银行大厦

大厦位于皇后像广场前端，这是香港最引人注目的地段之一，占有中环商业办公区唯一的开放空间，距水边400米。背后是花岗岩构成的陡峭山坡连接太平山顶。

建筑采用钢柱结构悬挂体系，分为三段。钢柱由两层高的衔架连接于建筑的5个点上，而楼层则从衔架上开始悬挂，由底部的8层减至顶部4层，每段上升至不同高度，28层、35层及41层，交错的楼层高度使室内空间具有多种宽度及高度、花园式平台及生动活泼的东西立面。

方案探讨了公共与私有空间之间的关系，银行有公共底层、内部顶层及构成半公共和半私有空间的中段。在街道层面上，建筑底层为12米高的步行大厅，完全为公共空间，由此一对自动扶梯可直达主要营业大厅（半公共）及10层高的中庭。银行主体由沿西立面玻璃电梯井布置三组高速电梯，来访者由类似低层建筑内的自动扶梯每两层高度停留。建筑顶层仅一个跨度进深，是银行高级职员办公室构成的半私有领域。

银行生动的外观将钢结构及透明的面板结合一起，以表现内部空间的丰富、多样。1985年投入使用10年后，建筑的灵活性由于需要增加一新的交易厅而得到证实，在传统办公楼内通常不可能增加如此大且具有完善设施的建筑体量，而汇丰银行却能以最小的代价与最短的时间（不足6周）在其总部大厦内插入新的交易大厅。

Hongkong and Shanghai Banking Corporation Headquarters

The building stands at the head of Statue Square. This is one of the most spectacular sites in the Colony; it presides over the only substantial open space in the central business district and overlooks a 400 meters stretch of level land leading to the waterfront. Steep granite rock formations rise up behind, culminating in the Hong Kong Peak.

The building is suspended from steel masts, arranged in three bays. At five points up the building, the masts are connected by two-story trusses from which the floor clusters are suspended, diminishing from eight stories at the base to four stories at the top. The bays, too, rise to varying heights: 28 stories, 35 stories and 41 stories. This staggered profile creates interior spaces of varying width and depth, garden terraces and vigorous east and west elevations.

The tension between public and private was explored in this project. The Bank has a public base, private summit and a central section composed of semi-public/semi-private space. At street level a 12-meter high pedestrian concourse runs clear beneath the building. This is a wholly public space, from which a pair of escalators rise up to the main banking hall (semi-public and its ten stories atrium. The main body of the Bank is reached by three sets of lifts which move at high speed up and down the west elevation I glazed lift-shafts. Visitors are set down at each of the double-height levels, and complete their journey (as in a low-rise building) by means of escalators. The topmost levels, only a single bay deep, are the private or semi-private domain of senior Bank personnel.

The Bank exterior is a vigorously modeled combination of structure and transparent panel to express the rich mixture of spaces within. Ten years after its opening to the public in 1985, the flexibility of the Bank was put to the text by the need for a new dealer room. Normally it would not be possible to locate such a large volume with high levels of servicing within a traditional office tower. But the Bank was able to insert its new dealer room into its own headquarters, with a minimum of disruption, and in less than six weeks.

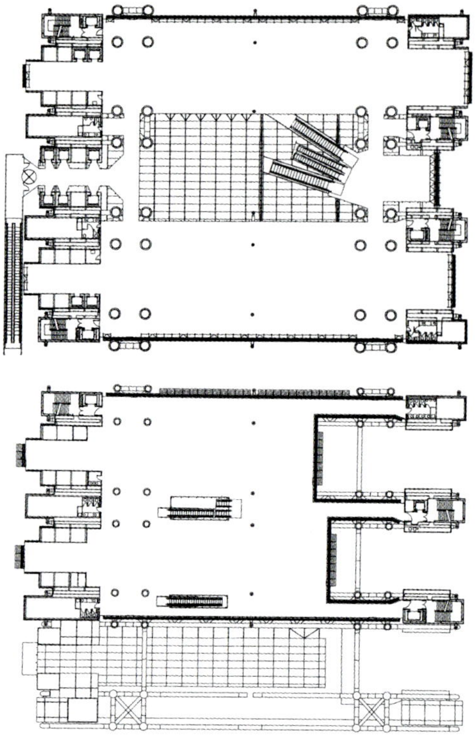

平面 Floor plans

外观 Exterior view

室内中庭 Interior view

香港红勘火车站改造及扩建

为满足中港两地火车运行大量增长的要求，并使大量人流高效地通过相对紧凑的空间，新的扩建将现有火车站完全重组，使规模扩大一倍，将目前每年5000万人次提高至2014年的8700万人次。

设计以一新的轻型结构将原有建筑向东延展。利用车站原有基座结构及基础，新建筑由一个引人注目的轻质波浪形屋顶覆盖，通过北面的带型天窗及通高的镀膜玻璃幕墙采光，使车站各层采光得到最好的控制，并尽量减少太阳辐射。

在原有结构中插入新的夹层，为本港旅客提供到达站台的最快捷径。并首次与更复杂的外埠旅行流程相隔离，夹层减少必要的转层，大大加快了换乘的速度与效率。新的加建亦为埠外乘客提供了通道及设施。

车站的布局进行了极大的简化。扩大的中央大厅分成外埠离境、外埠到达及本港旅客三个明确的区域。这些区域采用全空调，放大的座席区及新的车站营运、移民与海关设施均按国际机场标准设置。

站台、公共步道及中央大厅与一系列中空大厅相连，为使自然光线到达下层站台，中空大厅穿过建筑所有楼层，集中于中空大厅的电梯与自动扶梯将相关楼层连为一体。为达到目前国际标准，站台区经彻底重整，改善采光、标志、地面及整修墙面，增加通风及点状供冷。建筑内均专门设计了作为票务及零售空间的场所，这些紧凑的单元与屋顶咖啡厅等紧密结合，从屋顶咖啡厅并可俯览中央大厅。

Hung Hom Station Renovation and Extension, Hongkong

To meet the demand of massive increase in rail travel between Hong Kong and mainland China, The new extension has doubled the size of the existing rail terminal and completely reorganized it, to allow vast numbers of people to flow efficiently through a relatively compact space. The project increases the station's current capacity from 50 million passages per annum, to 87 million by 2014.

The original Railway terminal, has been extended to the east with a new lightweight pavilion structure. This new extension uses the station's original podium structure and foundations. The new building, covered by a striking lightweight wave form roof, is naturally lit by north-facing linear roof-lights and a full-height glazed curtain wall. These admit maximum controllable light to all levels of the station, with minimum solar gain.

A new mezzanine inserted into the original structure provides domestic passengers with very swift and easy access to the platforms, and for the first time separates from the more complex process of international travel. The mezzanine reduces the necessity to change levels and greatly increases speed and efficiency of movement. The new extension provides access, circulation and processing facilities for international passengers.

The station layout has been greatly simplified. The enlarged concourse area is divided into three distinct zones- International Departure, International Arrival and Domestic Travelers. These zones are air-conditioned and served by enlarged seating areas, as well as new Station Operations, Immigration and Customs facilities, all provided to international airport standards.

室内 Interior view

The platform, public walkways and concourses are connected by a series of atrium voids, which penetrate through all levels of the building allowing natural light to reach the platforms below. The new escalators and lifts, concentrated in these atrium spaces, link the respective levels. The platform areas have been completely refurbished with improved lighting, signage, floor and wall finishes, together with increased ventilation and spot cooling, raising them to current international standards. Within both buildings, new purpose-designed cabins accommodate ticketing and retail. These compact units incorporate rooftop cafes which offer views across the concourse.

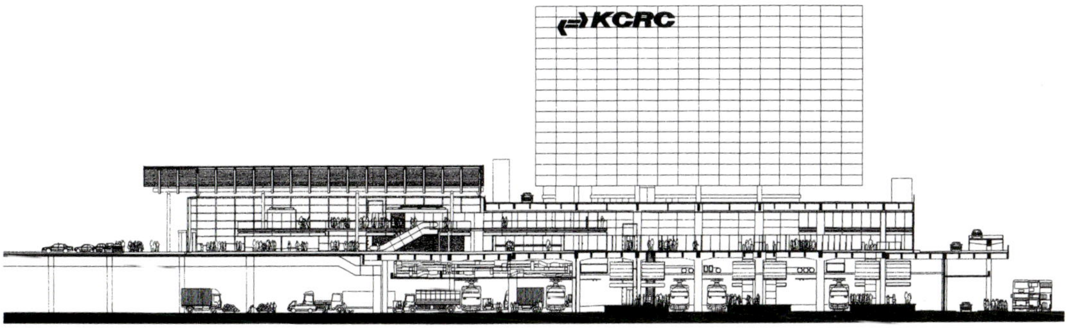

东西向剖面 East-west section

外观 Light roof

香港国际机场地面运输中心

地面运输中心通过往返于机场的各种地面与轨道交通与机场到达或离境的旅客相连。贯穿机场面宽，位于其东端，并在道路层面及地面以下三层与空港直接相连。

中心的核心是地铁机场快速干线站，40%旅客在他们到达或离开香港将利用这一干线。铁路为城市与空港之间架起快速与方便的通道。无论旅客是离境或到达，铁路与空港一气呵成。而乘客车、出租车或公共汽车的乘客，只需通过向下的缓坡坡道作层面转换。

地面中心的混凝土屋顶座落于道路层面上，离境旅客在机场入口顶棚处下车，因而地面中心在地上看到的仅仅是一个屋面。屋面之下，机场快线火车进港与出港在另一个不同的层面上。在屋面上第一层，出港旅客从机场快线下车直奔离境大厅。而其下层的入境旅客从到达厅直通机场快线火车。这种布局与入境旅客与出境旅客分层设置的方式密切相关。

通过中庭连桥建立空港与站场之间的联系，中庭的镀膜玻璃顶反射机场的动态景观。地面中心本身有一个200米长、引人注目的两层通高的中庭，通过中庭可看到空港，这种视觉上的不断联系作为一种空港导向手段是非常重要的。

地铁机场快线站之下是地面中心的公共车、出租车站场，进港旅客可由大厅通过坡道直达，出港旅客可在机场快线中环或九龙站进行行李检查，行李通过火车特殊行李箱运至空港，这些行李自动下到地面运输中心的底层，再转至主要的旅客空港行李系统。

Ground Transportation Center, Hong Kong International Airport

The Ground Transportation Center building at Hong Kong International Airport connects air travelers arriving and departing from Hong Kong with all means of road and rail transport to and from the airport. The building runs the length of the front of the airport at its eastern end. It links directly to the terminal at road level and at three further levels below ground.

At the core of the complex is the MTR Airport Station of the Mass Transit Railway's Airport Express Line. Forty per cent of all the 80 million passengers expected to use the airport will use this rail link when arriving and departing from Hong Kong. The rail connection offers both swift travel between city and airport and convenient transit once at the airport. Whether passengers are arriving and departing, they experience no change in level between airport terminal and railway link. Those arriving and departing by car, taxi or coach are required only to change levels via ramps sloping gently downwards.

The building's concrete roof sits at road level, where vehicles drop departing passengers under the airport entrance canopy. Thus the Ground Transportation Center is only visible from above ground as a roof form. Beneath the roof, Airport Express Line trains arrive and depart on separate levels, one on top of the other. On the first level beneath the roof, departing air passengers alight from the Airport Express Line and proceed to the Departure Hall. One level below, passengers arriving from airplanes access the train directly from the Arrivals Hall. This arrangement relates directly to the configuration of the airport terminal, which process arrival passengers one level below departures.

Connections, both ways, between terminal and station, are made via atrium bridges whose glazed roofs give dramatic views of the airport. The Ground Transportation Center itself has a 200m-long gazed double-height atrium, through which the airport terminals are visible. This constant visual connection, as a means of orientation, is a key element throughout the airport.

Below the MTR Airport Station is the Ground Transportation Center's coach and taxi collection area for arriving air passengers, accessed via ramps from the airport's Arrivals Hall. For departing passengers only, baggage can be checked-in either at the MTR Central Station or Kowloon Station in the City. Their luggage is delivered to the airport in special baggage containers in cars at the rear of the train. These baggage are automatically lowered to the basement of the Ground Transportation Center where it is transferred to the main Passenger Terminal baggage system.

中庭内景 CAD interion perspective of glazed atrium

香港新国际机场

香港新国际机场作为香港唯一的机场于1998年7月6日投入营运。它构成香港壮观的门户，巨大、轻盈、飘逸的形象令人印象深刻，同时它又是友好而亲切的。尽管它是世界上最大的空港，其尺度并没有给人一种恐惧或震撼感。设计赋予了它易于理解、易于接近的特质：庄严而非势不可挡。

"Y" 型的平面形式在总体设计任务书中已明确规定。由于拱顶能将分散的建筑体量连为整体，设计迅速确定了单一的、波浪型的单向筒形拱顶。事实上，在仔细规划的柱网上采用模数制建造的统一屋面，不仅使以后的加建更加容易，而且使设计更易于实施。采用重复连续的格网至少是基于快捷、方便维护、保养的考虑——这对于不断处于使用状态的机场是十分重要的。

由于拱顶方向在整座建筑内保持连续不变，拱形屋顶本身即具有导向作用，宽阔的拱形波浪亦可漫射及限定光线的形状——白昼采用自然光线，夜晚则人工照明。照明系统利用拱顶形状主要布置于屋面上，增加了空间的多样性与戏剧效果，并且使整个空港导向明确。拱形屋顶在离境层最为引人注目，天蓬下巨大的中庭空间中的光线、场景气氛缓解了旅行前的紧张。

新机场延续发展了福斯特在1991年建成伦敦第三大机场——斯坦斯特机场中首创的设计理念。其特征包括：轻型屋面、解放设备空间、广泛应用自然光，将环境气候控制设备与行李处理及运输设施统一布置于中央大厅之

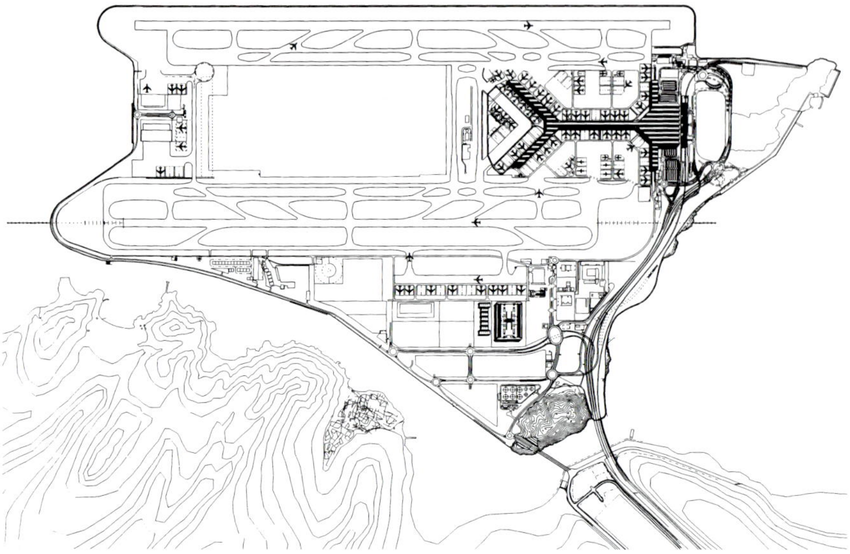

总平面 Site plan

鸟瞰 Overall view

下，使建筑中的流线与运动尽可能自由。

离境层登记台之后设有商业区。一旦通过安检，所有旅客将穿越东厅——机场商业中心。商业中心之后，空港收窄成一个长厅，最后在西端成“Y”型的两叉，漫长的“Y”型大厅连接了机场的 38 个登机口。

新机场周围的自然景色是壮观的，旅客在空港内任何一处均可享受外部宽阔的景色，玻璃面的最小高度均大于 4 米，并清除视觉范围内各种障碍以减少景观遮挡。设计强调利用周围环境导向远远超过空港建筑本身导向：旅客可看到大地、海面，放眼远处的道路、桥梁和近处的飞机起降。这种考虑与许多空港采用封闭的“盒子”或通道的作法大相庭径，旅行变为一种愉悦的过程。

空港之下为 6 米高、32 米宽的通道，沿通道设机场内部穿梭火车。当空港第二期扩建完成时，通道内将设有火车及高速行李转运系统。第1期行李处理采用全自动化系统，各航班可在柜台进行行李登记，行李则可快速、准时转换至航班。这种快速处理过程由集中于地面下的行李“高速公路”网络完成。

赤腊角机场空港的规模与建造是大胆与空前的，其所有要素及空间构成一个具有逻辑性与统一性的整体。其外观是雄伟的，但在气氛上却是近人与友好的，它是人类建筑与工程史上的里程碑，单一的、富有诗意的雕塑形式描绘了 21 世纪建筑动人而壮丽的场景。

Hong Kong International Airport

The new terminal forms a spectacular gateway to Hong Kong: grand, light, airy and impressive, and most importantly- friendly. For, although it is the largest airport in the world, its scale will not daunt those who pass through it. Its design ensures that it is easy to understand and accessible: it may be imposing but it is not overwhelming.

The Y-shaped plan form of the new airport was firmly written into the masterplan design brief. The architects were quick to identify the single, undulating, roof with its barrel vaults all travelling in the same direction, as the element which would unify a potentially fragmented building, which making an overall aesthetic statement. Logistically, too, it was established that the unified roof, built in modules on a carefully planned grid, would make it easier to extend the building later, and would enable the design to be realized more quickly. A repeating grid was adopted in many other design elements, not least to give quick and logical access to services for maintenance-an important consideration for an airport which is constantly in use.

Since the direction of the vaults remains constant throughout the building, regardless of the divergent directions that the 'prongs' of the Y-shaped plan take, the roof is itself an aid to orientation. Its broad ripples also serve to filter and shape light -natural by day and artificial by night. The lighting system, located mainly in the roof, takes advantage of the vaulted space, and adds to the variety and drama of the spaces which lead easily one to another, throughout the airport. The arch of the vaulted roof is experienced most strikingly on the departures level where the light, serene atmosphere of the great atrium beneath its canopy eases the tension that often precedes travel.

The new airport extends and develops an innovative concept pioneered by Foster and Partners at Stansted, London's third airport completed in 1991. It is

旅客入口处 Kerbside drop off zone

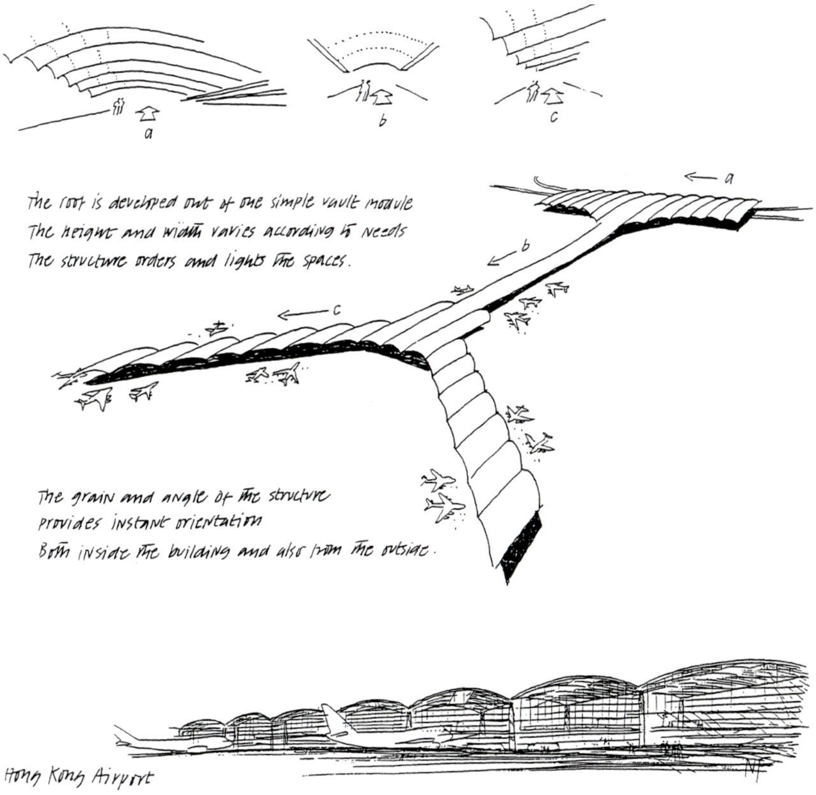

构思草图 Concept sketch

characterized by a lightweight roof - kept free of obtrusive service installation - extensive use of natural light, and the integration of climate - control service beneath the main concourse together with baggage handling and transportation. As important, is the clarity and logic of its traveler - friendly planning, whereby movement through the building is made as free as possible.

Departing travelers alight at the Ground Transportation Center at the eastern end of the terminal before entering the building via one of the atrium bridges. Their initial, dramatic view of the airport evokes a sense of occasion and the unimpeded view along the concourse is a powerful aid to orientation. Assisted by a carefully devised signage system, passengers are able easily to navigate their way through this vast but innately logical building.

Beyond the check-in desks, on the departure level, there is a land-side shopping area. Once through passport control and security, all passengers pass through the East Hall, the commercial hub of the terminal. Beyond this space, the terminal narrows to a long concourse, finally dividing into the two 'prongs' of the Y at its western end. It is from this long Y-shaped concourse that the airport's 38 boarding gates are accessed.

The new airport's natural setting is spectacular. To the south is the backdrop of the landau mountains, while to the north, across the water, are the New Territories, also with mountains in the distance. Wherever passengers are within the building, they can enjoy unimpeded views out - the glass sides of the terminal are purposely left clear up to a minimum height of four meters, and clutter throughout is eliminated so that sight lines are never blocked. The design accentuates natural orientation far beyond the airport itself: you can see the land, the water, and glimpses of the road and rail bridges in the distance, from the terminal; and you can see the aircraft. This elemental approach, so different from the claustrophobic boxes and tunnels through which characterize so many airports, brings pleasure and a sense of occasion back to flying.

Beneath the building there is a 6 meter high, 32 meter wide tunnel, along which the airport's internal shuttle trains run. Within the tunnel there is space for both the train and a future high-speed baggage transfer system, planned to service the terminal as it expands in its second phase. The Phase 1 baggage - handling system is fully automatic and allows airlines to check in bags at any counter and still deliver them swiftly to any flight, while meeting exacting passenger transfer times. This rapid processing is achieved by a web of routes converging on a kind of baggage 'superhighway' beneath the floor.

Chek Lap Kok is a supremely confident building on an unprecedented scale. All its elements and spaces work together with logic and harmony so that, although it is monumental, it is still is human and friendly in its atmosphere. The quality of workmanship in its construction, and the attention to detail, make it beautiful and easy to use. It is a landmark in engineering and construction, wholly contained in a single, poetic sculptural form --an exciting vision for the 21st century.

离境大厅 Interior departure concourse

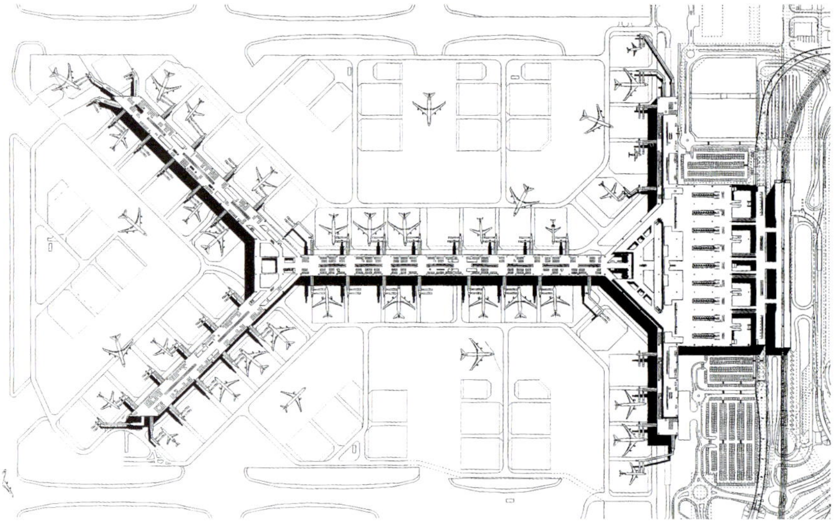

到达层平面 Arrival level

离境登记区 Check-in zone

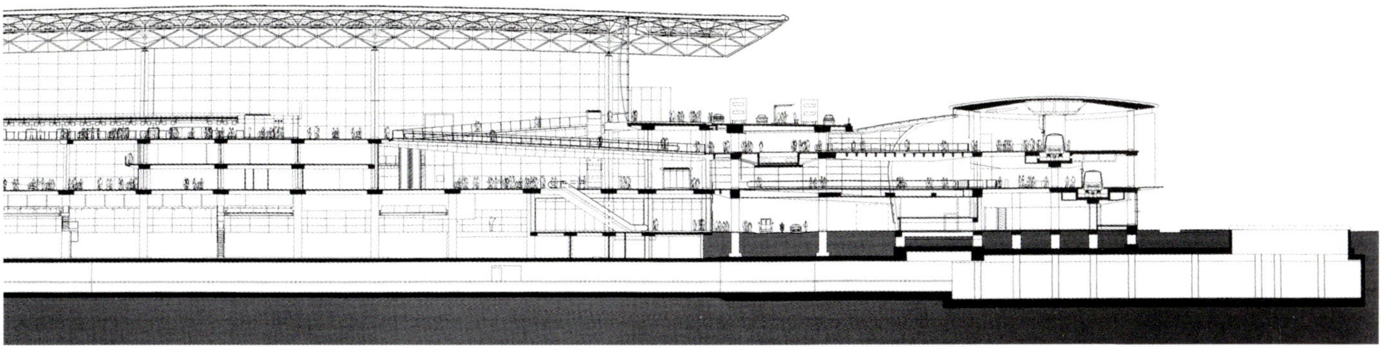

空港及地面中心剖面 Part section through processing terminal and ground transportation center

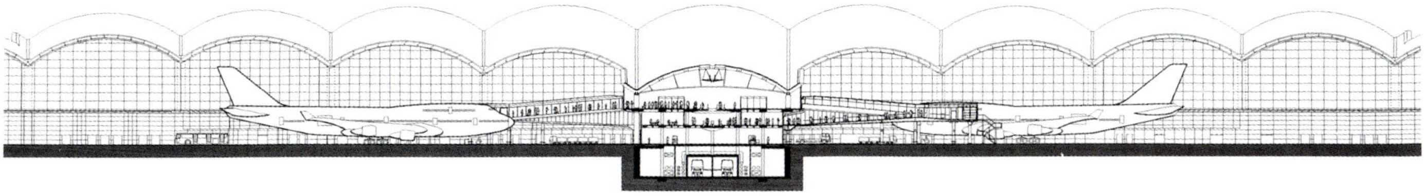

中央大厅往东剖面 Section through concourse looking east

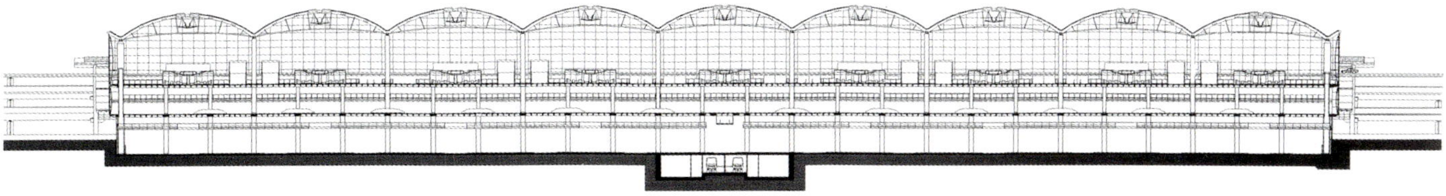

空港过厅剖面 Section through processing terminal

路面下客区进登记台坡道 Ramp from drop off zone to check-in desks

中央大厅剖面 Section through concourse

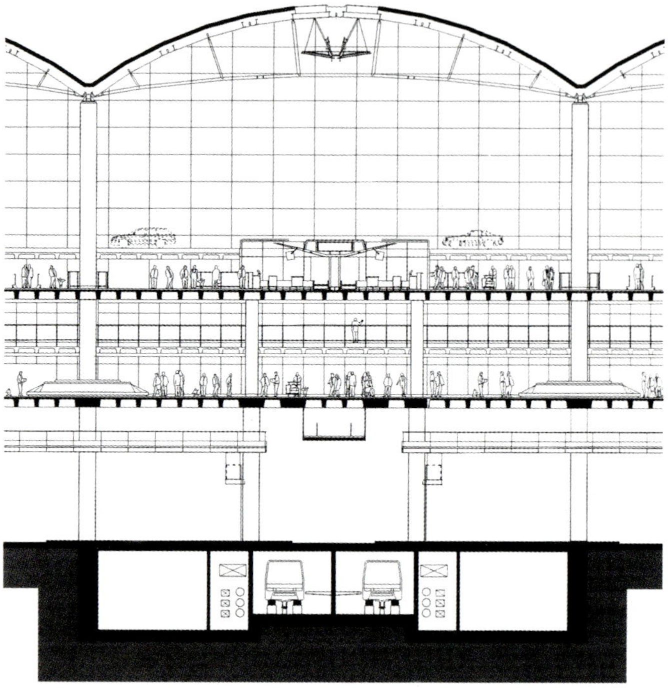

空港过厅剖面 Section through processing terminal

中央大厅 Central concourse

离境厅休息区 Departure lounge seating

中央大厅立面局部 Concourse part elevation

行李到达厅 Baggage reclain hall

离境大厅 Interior departure concourse

福克斯及福勒建筑师事务所
FOX & FOWLE ARCHITECTS

福克斯及福勒事务所为一建筑、室内设计及规划设计事务所，共有50余人，总部位于纽约。为客户提供包括各种规模项目的可行性研究、项目分析及选址到设计与使用评价等一整套服务。

事务所由小罗伯特·F·福克斯及布鲁斯·S·福勒在1978年创立。从一开始事务所的业务呈现出多元化，大量工作集中于办公楼、公司及机构室内设计，文化设施、居住建筑、综合体设计及更新改造项目。在小罗伯特·F·福克斯及布鲁斯·S·福勒的亲自领导下，事务所声誉日渐，并以高质量、高度责任感及整体性著称。

事务所采用合作设计的过程，这一过程中包括客户的积极参与以寻求满意的方案，遵循“建筑师是设计的领导者，而非独裁者”的设计哲学，使其产品具有原创、永恒性，并表达客户理想，而丰富人类的体验。事务所作品的基本特点正如美国建筑学会对布鲁斯·福勒的评价：“其作品独特而与众不同，依靠形式、比例及细节使其作品充满了生气和场所感......”。

在“绿色”这一术语广为人知之前，事务所一直坚持对环境负责的设计，将可持续建筑与专业实践的每个方面结合起来。并努力使项目成为环境的一部分，包括节能指标、可持续材料应用、尽量利用自然采光及提高室内空气质素等。

1995年，事务所被纽约市选为四家有资格进行“绿色”项目设计的单位之一。事务所目前正联合一批全国的专家进行几个环境领域主要项目。最引人注目的是1999年准备完工的Four times square的Conde Nast大厦。除此之外，事务所定期对包括辅助人员在内的所有员工进行培训，因而所有员工具有在日常生活中应用可持续建筑原理的知识。

Fox & Fowle Architects is an architectural, interior design and planning firm of 50 people, based in New York City. The firm provides a complete range of services-from feasibility studies, program analysis and site selection through post-occupancy evaluation-for projects of every size and scope.

Robert F. Fox, Jr. And Bruce S. Fowle formed the firm in 1978. Since its inception, its practice has been diverse, with much repeat work in the planning and design of investment grade office buildings, corporate and institutional interior, cultural and institutional facilities, residential buildings, mixed use, and adaptive reuse and renovation projects. Under Bob Fox's and Bruce Fowel's tutelage and with their "hand-on" approach, the firm has developed a reputation for quality design, responsiveness, and integrity.

The firm employs a collaborative design process that involves the active participation of our clients in seeking solutions consistent with their needs programmatic, economic and aesthetic. "We are design leaders, not dictators" is their design philosophy. This approach produces consistently original, yet timeless, designs that express the identities and aspirations of our clients and ultimately enrich the human experience. The essential character of the firm's work is aptly described in the words the American Institute of Architects wrote to present Bruce Fowle to its College of Fellows: the "work is distinct and unique; the reliance on form, proportion and detail has achieved warmth and a sense of place. This basic, purist approach to design will allow it to endure."

Long before the term "green" entered the popular lexicon, Fox & Fowle has maintained a commitment to environmentally responsible design and to the integration of the principles of sustainable architecture into every aspect of our professional practice. We have always striven to have our projects be environmental "good neighbors" that integrate energy conservation measures, utilize sustainable materials and processes, and maximize materials and processes, and maximize natural light and indoor air quality.

In 1995, we were selected by the New York City Department of General Services as one of only four architecture firms qualified to design "green" projects for the city of New York. We are currently collaborating with teams of specialists from across the country on several major leadership projects in the environmental arena, most notably the Conde Nast Building at Four TIMES Square, which is currently under construction and scheduled for completion in 1999. We also provide a regular program of in-house training sessions for our staff- professionals and support staff alike, so that all members of our firm have the knowledge they need to apply the principles of sustainable architecture within the context of their daily work.

中国工商银行上海分行大厦

大厦是最早在浦东经济开发区兴建的项目之一。其塔楼部分包括两个层次：一个是静态的，另一个则是曲线的动态的元素，象征着银行在本地区的存在和发展的远景。两者的结合象征着一个有活力的金融机构所必须具备的素质——稳定和持续发展。两种要素的并置不仅赋予银行以特征，而且界定了上部办公楼的平面形状，亦陪衬了底部的曲线型银行营业厅和其他较小尺度的功能要素。在城市设计层次上，曲线形的南立面同浦东大道的走向相呼应。

设计在现代的外形中揉合了一些中国建筑的特色。如：直面和曲面的交替，主体与裙楼的处理，屋顶凉亭的光影变幻以及底层的小桥流水。

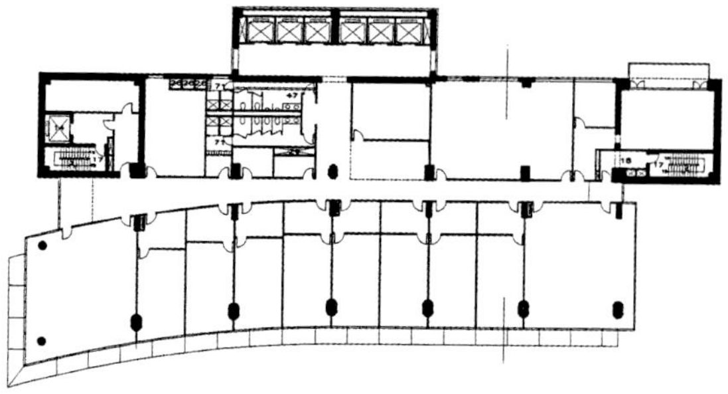

二十七层平面 Twenty-seventh floor plan

Industrial and Commercial Bank of China, Shanghai

The new regional headquarters for the Industrial and Commercial Bank of China, one of China's leading banks, is one of the first new buildings to be contracted in the Pudong. District of Shanghai, a major economic development zone now being developed across the Huangpu River form the center of Shanghai and widely promoted as "the new Wall Street of Asia."

The tower portion of this building consists of twin slabs. One serves as a more static background element or foil for the other -a curving, more dynamic element symbolizing the Bank's presence in the region and its outward vision. Together they symbolize all those quantities necessary to a vital financial institution-stability and progressive growth. These juxtaposed forms not only characterize the bank, they give shape to the office floors and act as a foil for the curved banking pavilion and other smaller scale program elements at the building's base. At an urban level, the curved south facade responds equally to the bend in Pudong Avenue, Pudong's main thoroughfare.

Certain characteristics of traditional Chinese architecture are here woven into the otherwise modern idiom of this project. The interplay of flat and curved surfaces, the elevation of the structure on a low podium, the interplay of light and shade at the roofline pergola, and the shallow pool at the ground level, crossed by bridges.

The project was designed by FFGL, a joint venture of Fox & Fowle Architects, P.C, as primary architects with Rithard Gluckman architects and En-Chuan Liu. Construction documents and construction were carried out by East China Architectural Design Institute in Shanghai.

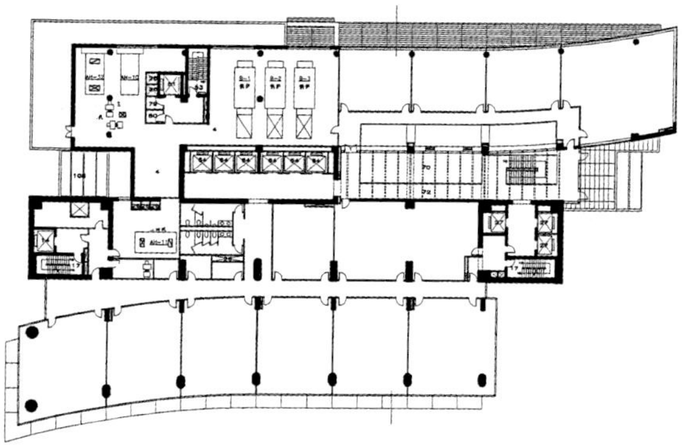

七层平面 Seventh floor plan

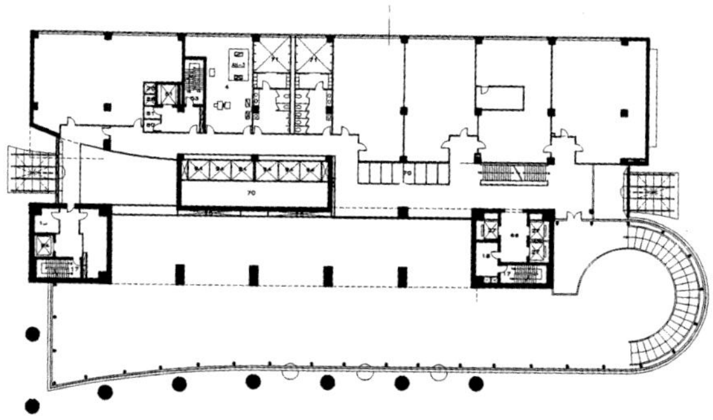

二层平面 Second floor plan

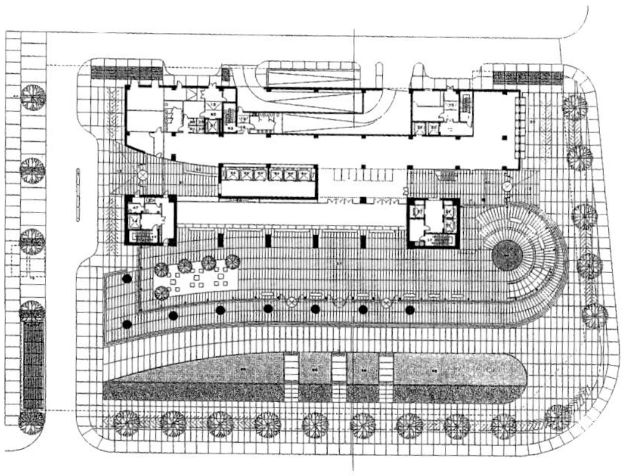

底层平面 Ground floor plan

模型 Model, view from north

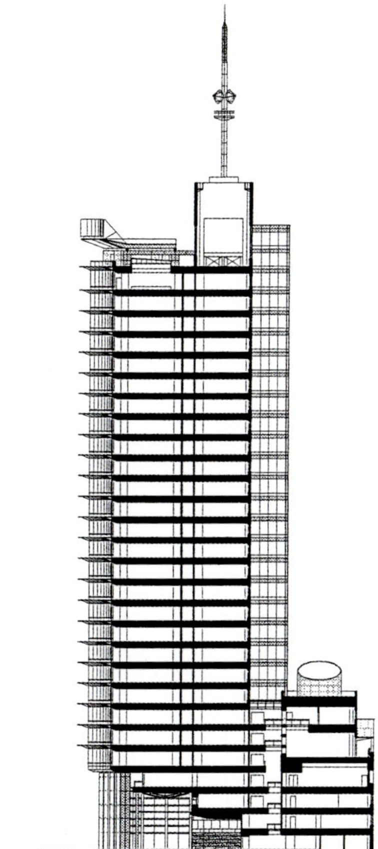

剖面 Section

模型 Model, view from south

上海嘉华大厦

大厦是由上海嘉华公司和中国工商银行兴建的办公楼，高22层。位于苏州河和黄浦江交汇处以北的旧城区。新大厦采用现代风格，与周围形成对比。L形的体量，两侧用花岗岩饰面，中间为弧形玻璃幕墙。在大厦的中间，一系列中庭从门厅升到屋顶，通过弧形的玻璃幕墙可俯瞰黄浦江景色，而角部的塔楼作为外滩的北端标志。大厦的内部空间围绕着一系列重叠的中庭组织，这些富于戏剧性的室内空间为每层提供一个交通枢纽和活动焦点。中庭分为几个部分，每一部分服务的主要功能为：1～4层为银行办公室；5～7层设餐饮、娱乐和会议设施；8～11层为出租办公空间；12～17层为旅馆；18～22层则为办公空间。

Shanghai Jahwa Tower

The Shanghai Jahwa Tower, a 22 stories office building for two leading Shanghai corporations, Shanghai Jahwa and the Industrial and Commercial Bank of China, will be located in an historic area of Shanghai just north of the confluence of Suzhou Creek and the Huangpu River. This area is in the process of being redeveloped as an extension of the Bund, the world famous riverfront promenade of Shanghai. A modern structure is adopted, in contrast to its historic neighbors, composed of an "L" shaped armature with granite-clad facades flanking a transparent curved glass facade. At the center of the building a series of atria rise from the lobby to the roof level. The curved glass curtain wall overlooks the adjacent Huangpu River, while a tower at the corner of the building serves to mark the north end of the Bund. Internally, the building is organized around a series of superimposed central atria. These dramatic internal spaces will offer the occupants of each floor a central circulation and activity focus. The atria occur in segments, each serving the primary function that surrounds it: bank spaces and offices on floors 1-4; dining, entertainment, and conference facilities on floors 5-7; tenant office space on floors 8 - 11; hotel rooms on floors 12 - 17; and office spaces on floors 18-22.

模型 Model

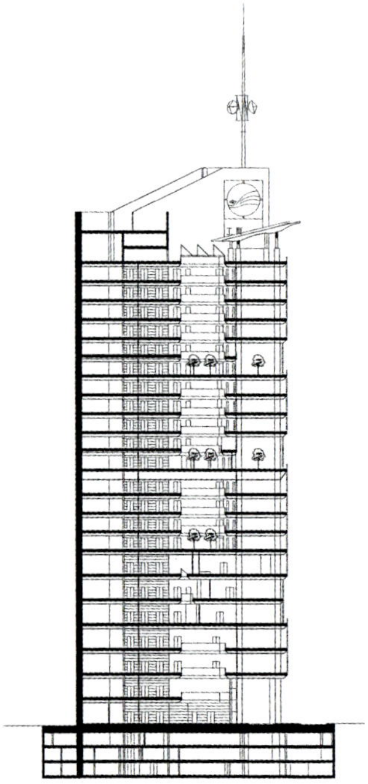

剖面 Section

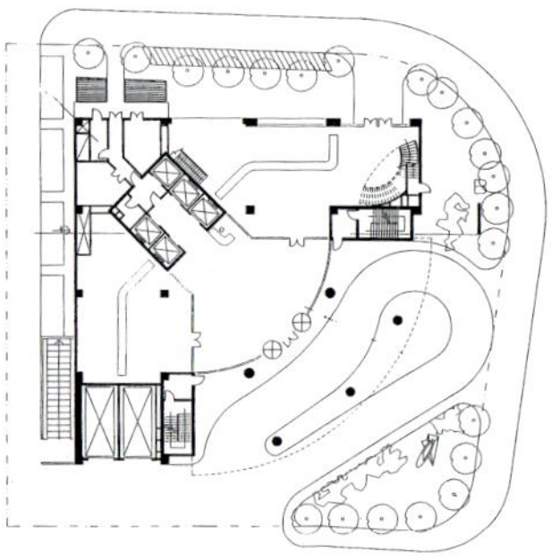

首层平面 Ground floor plan

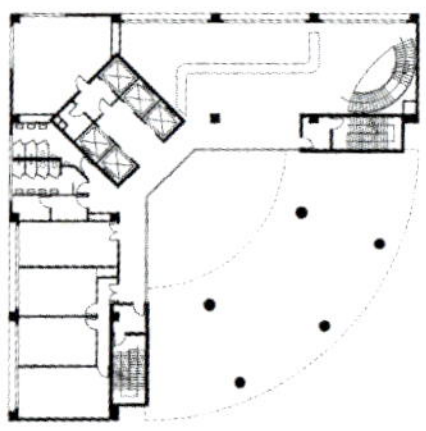

二层平面 Second floor plan

五层平面 Fifth floor plan

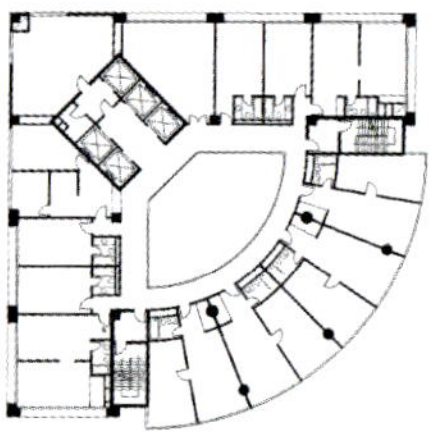

标准层平面 Typical floor plan

迈克尔·格雷夫斯建筑师事务所
MICHAEL GRAVES ARCHITECT

自1964年迈克尔·格雷夫斯在美国新泽西州的普林斯顿建立自己的事务所以来，就一直走在建筑设计的前沿地带。《纽约时报》的建筑评论家保罗·戈登伯格认为，"格雷夫斯是美国本土长期以来首次出现的真正最具原创力的声音"，他的建筑和室内设计超过100次奖项，他本人因此也享有国际声誉。

他在美国完成的工程有：人类公司总部；美洲克朗和汤姆森电气公司等，其它建成的工程包括：波特兰大厦、那帕谷克罗斯·贝吉斯酒厂及奥兰多迪斯尼世界的海豚和天鹅酒店等。他设计的公共文化机构有丹佛中心图书馆和辛辛那提的端佛本音乐中心。

随着更多工程的完成，格雷夫斯的国际名望越来越高，其中在日本的重要工程有：Tajima Kasumi 总部Onjuko 市政中心及横滨的住宅楼等；在欧洲的工程包括法国迪斯尼公园的纽约酒店，比利时安特卫普的酒店和办公大厦以及位于海牙的文化部办公大厦。

格雷夫斯的家具、装饰和工艺品设计同样出名。他为多个品牌设计过家具，为阿莱西公司设计过桌上用品和装饰品，为沃尔卫克公司设计过地毯，还为TAJIMA设计过地砖花饰。

格雷夫斯的作品出现在许多书籍杂志当中，其中包括1972年牛津大学出版社出版的《五位建筑师》；1979年英国学院出版社出版的《迈克尔·格雷夫斯》；1983年Rizzoli出版的《迈克尔·格雷夫斯：作品1966—1981》；1990年普林斯顿建筑出版社出版的《迈克尔·格雷夫斯：作品1982—1989》以及1994年恩斯特出版社出版的迈克尔·格雷夫斯设计作品专辑。收录了1990至1994年间作品的最新专辑也于1995年由Rizzoli出版。

迈克尔·格雷夫斯在辛辛那提大学和哈佛接受建筑学教育。1960年，他获得罗马奖学金在美国的罗马学院学习，目前他是这个机构的赞助人。他自1962年起在普林斯顿大学教学，目前是该校的舍尔默建筑学荣誉教授。

Michael Graves has been in the forefront of architectural design since he began his practice in Princeton, New Jersey in 1964. Paul Goldberger, architectural critic of the New York Time, he said that 'graves...is truly the most original voice America has produced in some time." He has received over 100 prestigious awards for his designs in architecture, interiors, and has come to enjoy an international reputation.

Among his completed projects in the United States alone are: corporate headquarters for Human, Crown America, the Distance Company, and Thomson Consumer Electronics. Other built projects include: the Portland Building; the Clos Pegase Winery in the Napa Valley; the Walt Disney World Dolphin and Swan Hotels in Orlando; and the Aventine hotel and office building complex in La Jula, California. Public cultural institutions include the Denver Central library; and the River-bend Music Center in Cincinnati.

Graves' practice has become highly international, with the completion, for example, in Japan of major projects such as the Tajima; headquarters for Kasumi; a town hall at Onjuku; residential towers in Yokohama; and the Fukuoka Hyatt Regency Hotel and office building, among many. In Europe' project include the Hotel New York at Disneyland Park Paris; a hotel and office building in Antwerp, Belgium; and an office building for the Ministry of Culture in The Hague.

Graves is also well knows for his design of furniture, furnishings, and artifacts, including furniture for various manufacturers, table top items and decorative accessories for Alessi, carpets for Vorwerk; and floor tiles for Tajima.

Graves' work appears in many periodicals and books, including Five Architects, published in 1972 by Oxford University Press; Michael Graves, published in 1979 by academy Edition; Michael Graves: Building and Projects 1966-1981, published in 1983 by Rizzoli; Michael Graves: Building and Projects 1982-1989, published in 1990 by the Princeton Architectural Press; and Michael Graves Design Monograph, published in 1994 by Ernst 7 Sohn. A new monograph covering architectural projects from 1990-1994 was published by Rizzoli in 1995.

Michael Graves received his architectural training at the University of Cincinnati and Harvard University. In 1960, he won the Rome Prize and studied at The American Academy in Rome, of which he is now a trustee. Graves is the Schemer Professor of Architecture at Princeton University, where he has taught since 1962.

厦门邮政电信大厦

大厦包含办公、邮政中心及多种公共服务功能，面对位于西南部在其基地以内的公共绿地。公共绿地内设有一座类似灯塔的圆柱形建筑，以标志两条道路——海滨路和湖滨南路的交汇点。此圆柱形建筑的内部设有旋转楼梯，引人穿越一系列关于中国邮政历史的展览，最终到达可以俯瞰港区、鼓浪屿和厦门中心区的顶部观景台。

大厦的入口是一个巨大的多功能大厅，将建筑的底部融入庭院绿地，使公众能够自由地来往其间。塔楼60层，6层裙房占基地的整个面宽，内部设有邮件中心、营业大厅和停车场等。在裙房顶部设有一个供文化娱乐的平台，正对屋顶阶梯形的露天观众席。塔楼由强调不同形式、色彩和材料的元素组成，立面上不同的开窗方式反映出内部功能的变化，由独立的纪念性立柱支撑的大面积开窗结构则与城市尺度和环境相协调。

Xiamen Postal and Telecommunications Building

The Postal and Telecommunications Building, which includes offices, a postal depot, and a variety of public services, is oriented to its own public garden occupying the southwestern third of the site. Within the garden, a tall cylindrical structure, reminiscent of a lighthouse, marks the intersection of two major city roads-Haibin and South Hubin. A spiral ramp inside leads visitors upward through an exhibition of postal history of China to an observatory overlooking the harbor, Gulangyu Island, and downtown Xiamen.

The entrance to the post office and a grand multipurpose hall extend the base of the building into the garden. An orangerie-like structure, the main hall allows the public to move freely between building and garden.
The 60-story office tower rises above a 6-story plinth that extends the width of the site and contains the postal depot, service, and parking. A cultural and entertainment pavilion on top of the plinth faces a rooftop terrace for outdoor events. The tower is composed of individual elements accentuated by a variety of forms, colors, and materials. Different types of fenestration express the variety of internal building functions. Large pavilion-like window structures supported by monumental single columns relate to the urban scale of the context.

模型 View from northwest

构思草图 Sketch

外观 Exterior perspective view

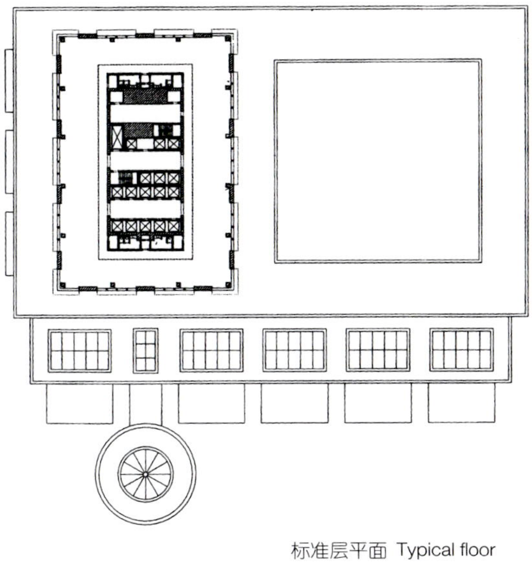

标准层平面 Typical floor

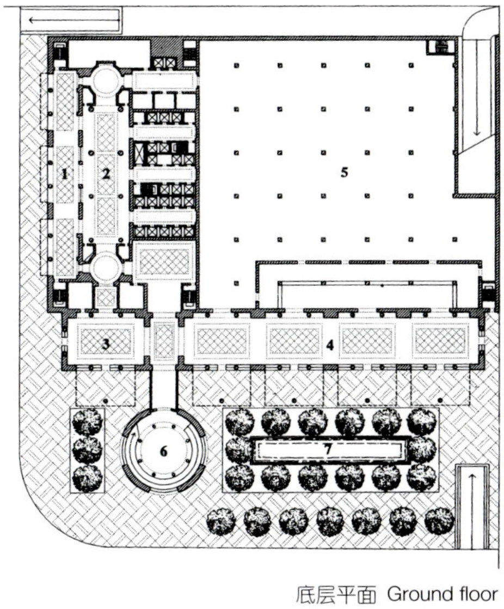

底层平面 Ground floor

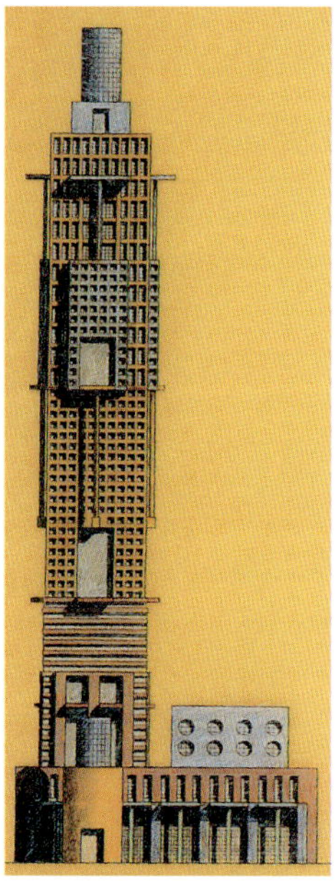

东立面 East elevation

南立面 South elevation

多功能厅室内 Interior of the multipurpose hall

上海福建兴业银行大厦

大厦为19层高的综合性建筑。位于上海的历史区段，临近法院和海关大楼，面向外滩。塔楼的下面10层为银行业务、商业零售以及高级办公空间。大厦另有供出租的办公楼层及两层地下停车场。这些功能在建筑的体量和设计手法中均获得体现。

Shanghai Fujian Xingye Banking Tower

This new bank tower is a 19-story mixed-use building. It is located in the historic district of Shanghai near the Courthouse and the Customs Building, and faces the Bund. The lower ten floors contain banking facilities for Xingye Bank's operations as well as commercial retail and Class A office space. The tower contains tenant office space. There are two levels of parking underground. These several functions will be expressed in the massing and eventual architectural design of the building.

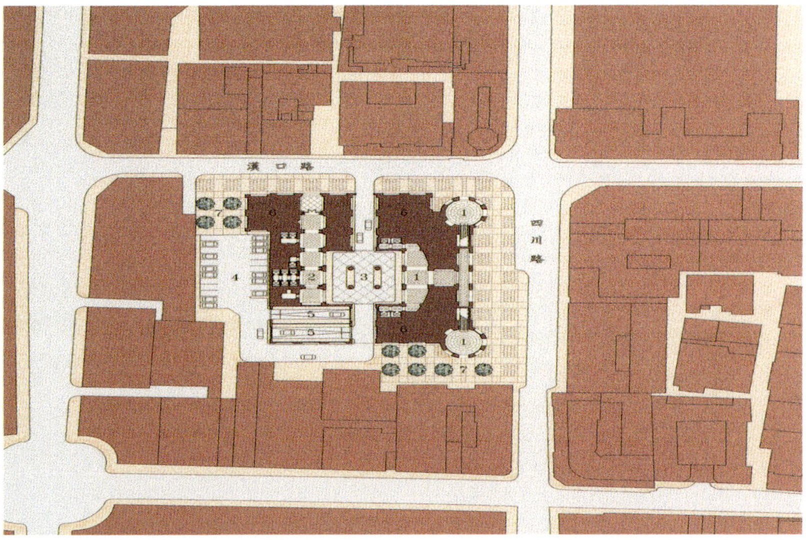

A方案总平面 Site plan (Scheme A)

A方案外观 Exterior view (Scheme A)

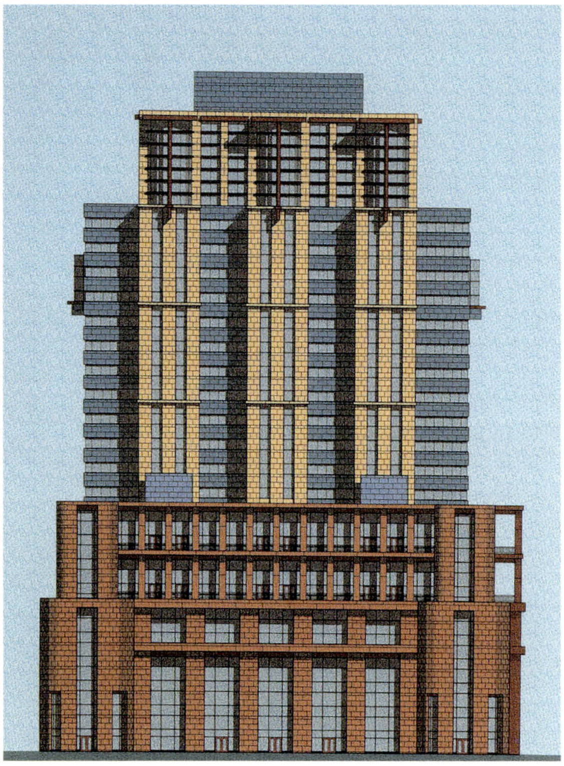

人口立面 Front facade

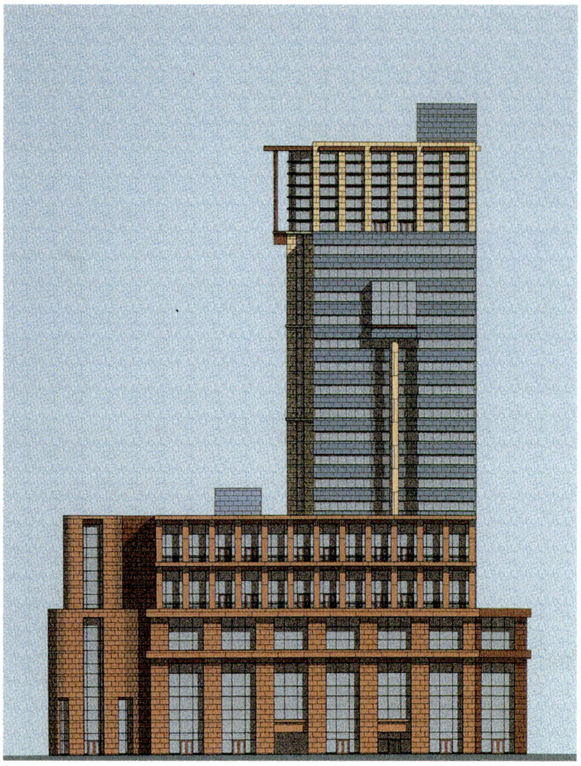

A 方案侧立面 Elevation (Scheme A)

立面研究 Facade study

B 方案外观 Exterior view (Scheme B)

B 方案侧立面 Side elevation (Scheme B)

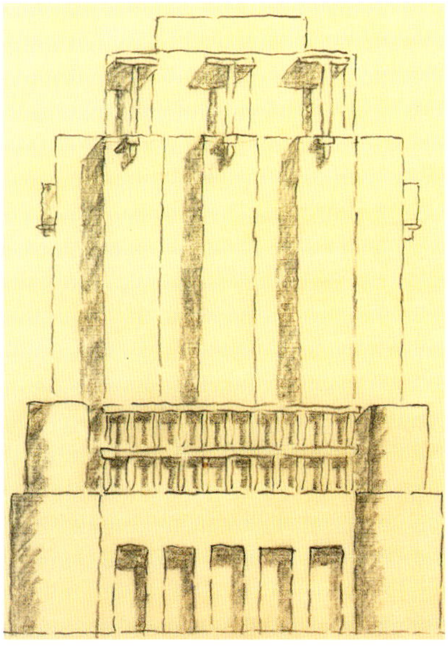

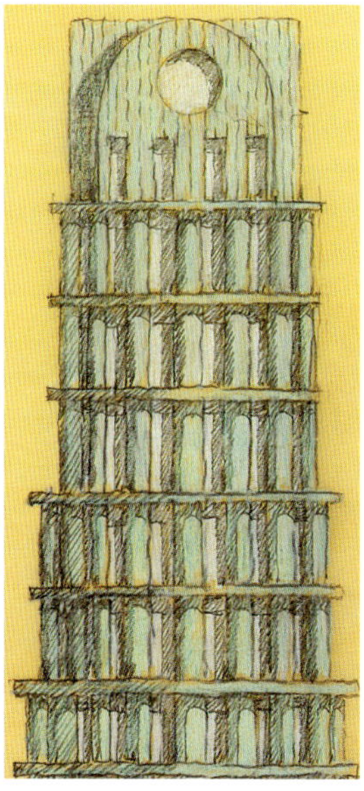

立面研究 Facade study

厦门江头大道办公楼与住宅

江头大道是厦门市的城市主要干道，就江头大道上开发建设高层办公楼与住宅这一问题，厦门市政府组织了一项国际设计竞赛。该基地包含九个独立的地块，每个地块上将建造一座塔楼，塔楼的底部四层包含商业零售功能，可以从江头大道的步行廊到达，停车和附属设施设于地下层。

厦门享有“海上花园”的美誉，因此环境设计至关重要。方案中每个塔楼都有一个面对庭院的中心观景点。沿东侧布置了一系列传统的中国式庭院，庭院主要供住户使用，相对私密和幽静。而与办公塔楼相连的西侧花园则采用了西方古典园林规整的几何式设计手法。

三组塔楼面对四个主要朝向形成门户。纪念性的开窗形式、阳台和遮阳篷都与周围的城市尺度一致，多种多样的开窗手法反映了内部使用功能和人的尺度，自然材料和色彩的运用进一步加强了人和城市尺度之间的关系，使每一座塔楼成为整体构图的一部分。

Office and Housing Development Jiang-tou Boulevard, Xiamen

The City of Xiamen sponsored an international design competition for the master plan of a high-rise office and housing development on Jing-to Boulevard, the major thoroughfare of the City. The site consists of nine separate parcels of land, each of which is to be developed as a tower. The first four stories of the towers contain retail and commercial space accessible from pedestrian arcades along Jiang-to Boulevard. Parking

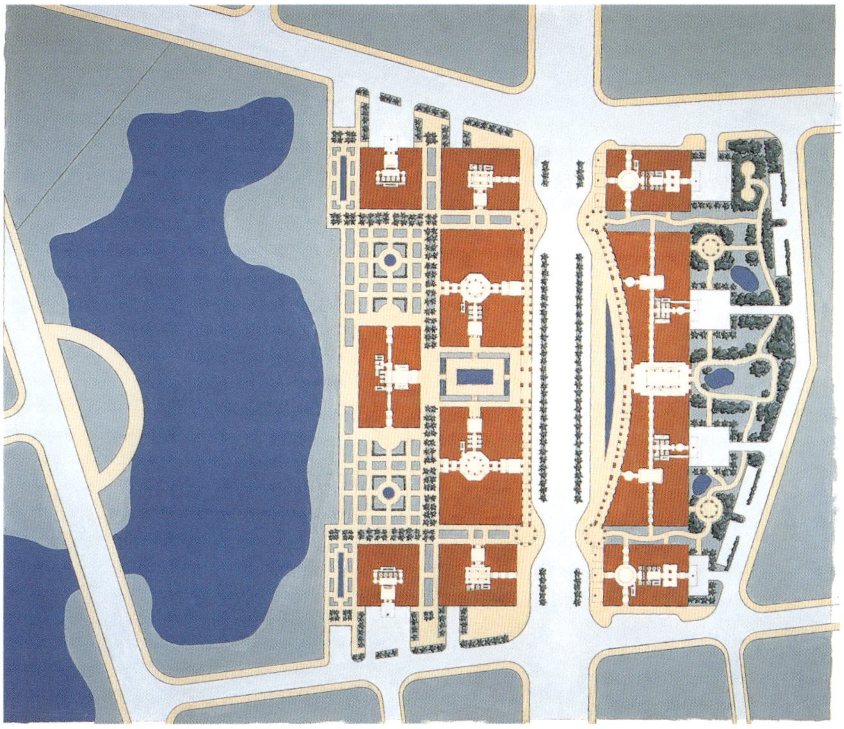

总平面 Site plan

外观 General view

and service are provided underground.

Because Xiamen describes itself as a "garden on the sea", the relationship between buildings and landscape was a major organizing principle of the project. Each tower provides a focal point from which to view a garden. The free forms of traditional Chinese gardens is adopted to create unexpected turns in the landscape along the eastern border. Primarily used by the residential tenants, these gardens are more intimate than the western gardens adjacent to the office towers, which are characterized by the geometric formality of European classical gardens.

Three pairs of towers on the site create gateways facing the four primary directions. The towers' monumental windows, balconies and awnings relate to the development's urban scale. Various fenestration techniques express the human-scale functions within, orienting one within the huge expanse of floor upon floor. A palette of natural materials and colors further develops the relationship between these two scales, allowing each tower to be read as a composition of individual parts.

模型全景 Overhead view of model

西侧外观 View from west

东立面 East elevation

西立面① West elevation Ⅰ

西立面② West elevation Ⅱ

模型 Model

模型 Model

模型 Model

模型外观 View of model

模型 Model view

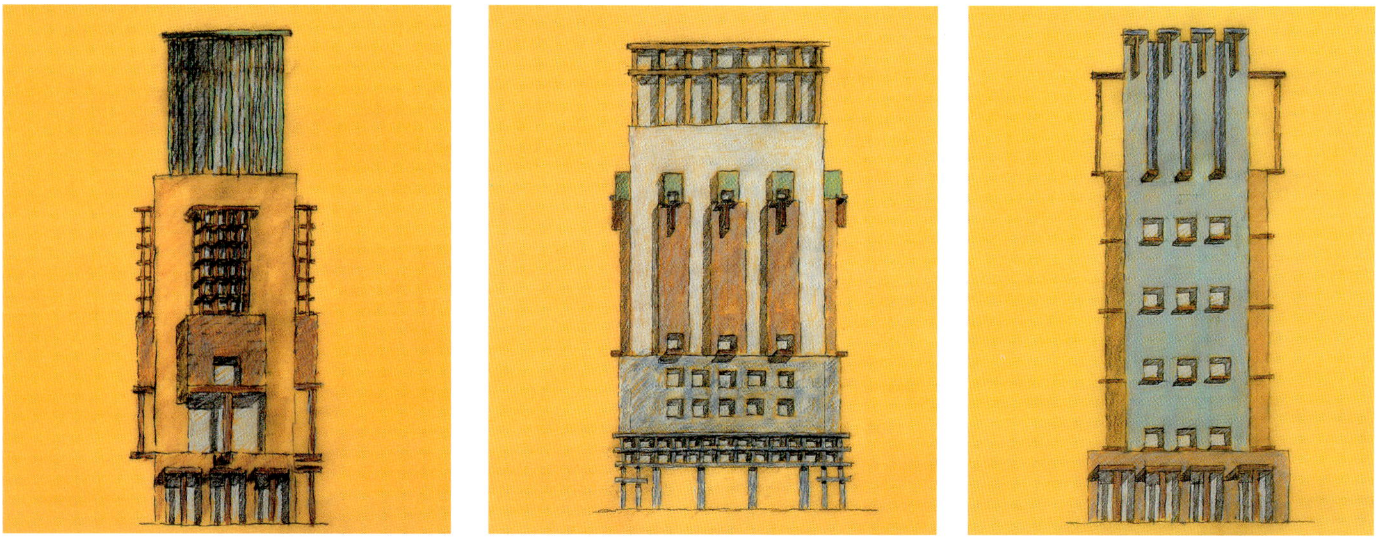

立面研究 Facade study

JMGR 建筑工程设计公司
JMGR, INC.

JMGR建筑工程设计公司创建于1900年，现有专业人员70多人，多年来为世界各地的业主提供综合性的建筑设计、室内设计及工程设计服务。公司的建筑设计以总建筑师负责与参与，高质量的专业性服务和创新的设计方法赢得很高的声誉。

近一百年来，公司专业从事于医疗建筑的规划和设计。承接的各类医疗建筑工程项目包括：专业医疗诊所、实验室及大型教学医疗中心。公司的唯一宗旨是：以创新的设计，融合现代化技术，最好地体现业主的意图，并确保工程的进度及经济预算。

在过去的19年里，JMGR在亚洲、欧洲和南美洲建立了良好的信誉，特别是在中国、德国、比利时和委内瑞拉。JMGR 目前在中国有总数超过百万美元的设计合同，项目的总面积超过13万平方米。在设计中，将中国现实和国际现代化标准相结合，并与中国设计院的成功合作，使公司能更有效地完成这些项目。

公司在美国孟菲斯拥有一支来自多个国家的工作组，包括来自中国、南非和阿根廷，这些人员都曾在他们原来的国家工作过。公司拥有实力强大的建筑师及工程师队伍。其服务范围包括：建筑总体规划、设施分析、任务计划、项目管理、建筑设计、室内设计、医疗设备规划、建筑结构设计、暖通设计、给排水设计、电气设计、施工管理及计算机辅助管理等。

In continuous practice since 1900, JMGR has a staff of 70 professionals and support personnel, providing comprehensive architectural, engineering and interior design services to its clients around the world. The practice has acquired a reputation for principal participation, quality professional service, and innovative design.

Over its nearly one hundred years in practice, JMGR has acquired a recognized specialty in the planning and design of a wide range of health care facilities, with diverse project types including specialized clinics, major medical centers and ambulatory care centers. A single design philosophy emphasizing responsiveness to client input, innovative design incorporating current technologies, and conformance to budget and schedule constraints has led to a history of repeat clients and a reputation for providing functional, efficient and timeless planning and design solutions.

JMGR has solved planning and design problems for small and large scale projects across the US and abroad. As a firm doing business internationally for 19 years, JMGR 's experience reflects an excellent track record of project performance in Asia, Europe and South America, particularly within China, Germany, Belgium and Venezuela.

JMGR 's current projects in China are multi-million dollar contracts, collectively totaling over 130,000 square meters. Their approach to these projects has been to team with a Chinese design institute to deliver these facilities through the most efficient means possible. The design of all five of JMGR 's current projects in China have reflected cutting edge, modern design that presents a positive image and a bold statement about China's emergence into the global marketplace.

JMGR also offers the added benefit of an International team of architects working within their Memphis office in the States. The Memphis-based professional staff includes individuals from China, South Africa, and Argentina. JMGR 's in-house staff of architects and engineers have a full time commitment to the planning and design of new construction and renovation of medical facilities, offering clients a single source for Facility Master Planning, facility analysis, functional programming, project management architecture, interior design, medical equipment planning, mechanical engineering, plumbing engineering, electrical engineering, structural engineering, construction administration and computer aided facilities management.

上海东方医院

将中国传统建筑精华与现代国际标准相结合是设计的主要挑战。方案强调自然采光，主要病房朝南布置于基地北侧，70% 室内空间自然采光。病房弧线型布置、护士站居中使得走廊房间监护视线最好。附属空间设于北侧，既相对隐蔽，又方便使用，深切护理单元分散布置于两护理单元的中部。

护理单元两端布置增加了将来使用的灵活性，并使建筑水平线性展开，突出于周围高层林立的环境之中。挂号及探视人员主入口位于南侧，员工则由西侧专用入口进入，内部各科室联系方便，便于交通分类及对病人活动区域的控制与隔离。

为使建造过程中医院正常使用，新建筑围绕现有医院建设，一期强调诊室、病房及护理单元建设，保留现有建筑，一期完成后，老建筑将拆除作为开放的公共空间。医院总建筑面积 48700 平方米，650 床位。

Shanghai East Hospital

Incorporating the best of traditional Chinese design with modern international standards was the main challenge in developing the design. To properly address the inclusion of natural light, an important cultural element in Chinese medicine, the structure is located on the northern side of the site, allowing for maximum sunlight to radiate into the southern-facing patient rooms. 70%of all interior spaces within the hospital provide natural light.

Patient rooms are arranged in a curved form with the nurses station located near the center allowing excellent views into each of the rooms and of the corridor. Support spaces are located on the north, out of view of the patient units, but with convenient access to staff. Intensive care units are decentralized and located in the center area between two patient units.

Locating two inpatient nursing units side by side on each floor increases the flexibility for future use and maintains a lower profile to achieve a linear building design, thus giving greater importance to the structure amidst the surrounding high-rise buildings. Inpatient admissions and visitor traffic enter the building on the south side at the main entrance, while staff enter the building from the west at a dedicated entrance. Inside, the circulation system has been carefully designed to provide good communication between departments, separation of traffic types and control of patient flow. Outpatients can access outpatient services, diagnostic and treatment areas from the atrium lobby, while inpatients access functional areas from the main elevator core of the patient tower. Inpatient entrance points to diagnostic and treatment departments are separate from the outpatient entrances.

To maintain hospital operations during construction, the new building will be built around the existing hospital. The first phase will address clinic space, patient rooms and nursing units constructed directly above the existing structure. Upon the completion of phase one, the older building will be removed allowing the space and mass of the original building to become open, public areas. With a total area of 48,700 square meters, the hospital has 650 beds.

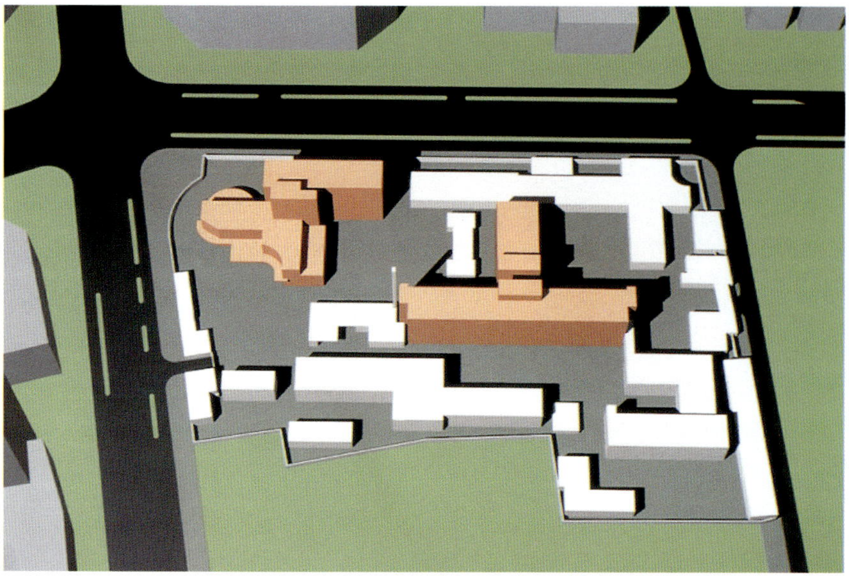

现状 Existing buildings

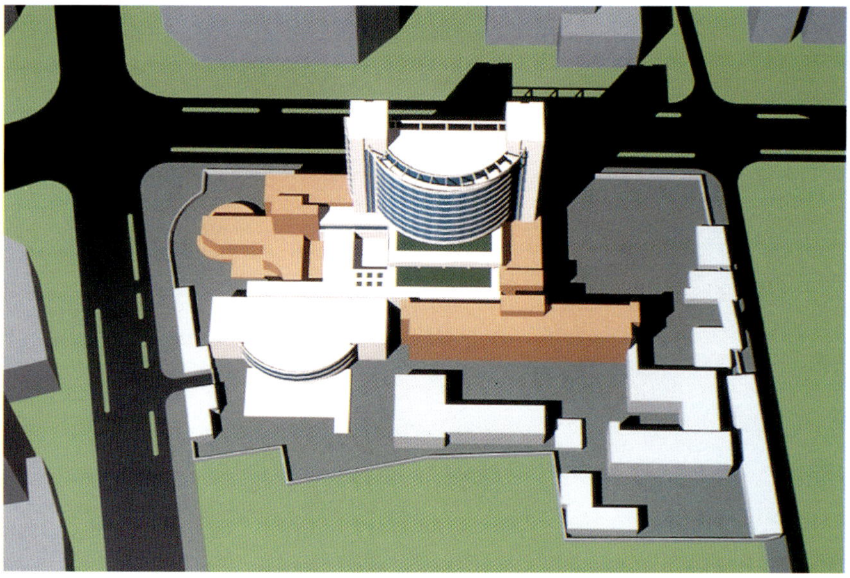

第 1 期 Phase I

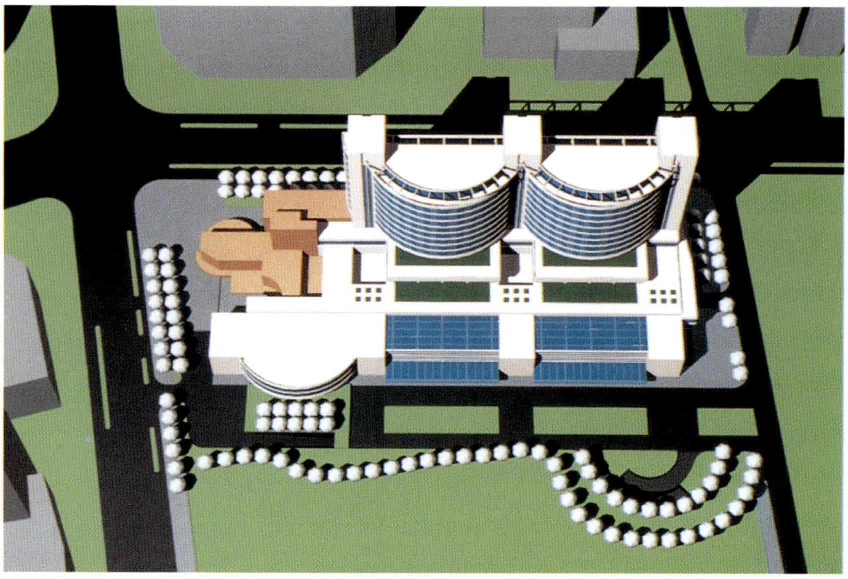

第 2 期 Phase II

外观 Exterior view

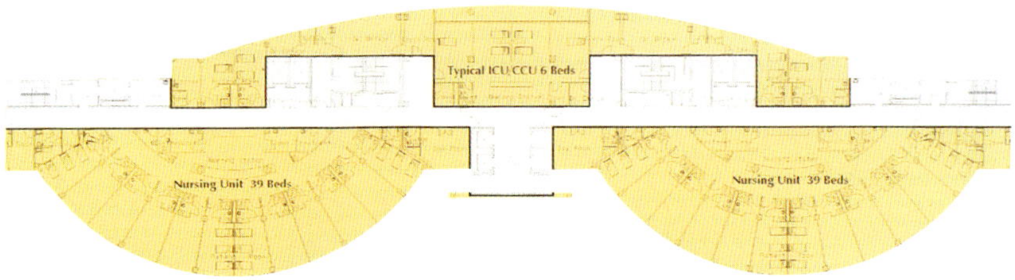

标准层平面 Typical floor

一层平面 First floor

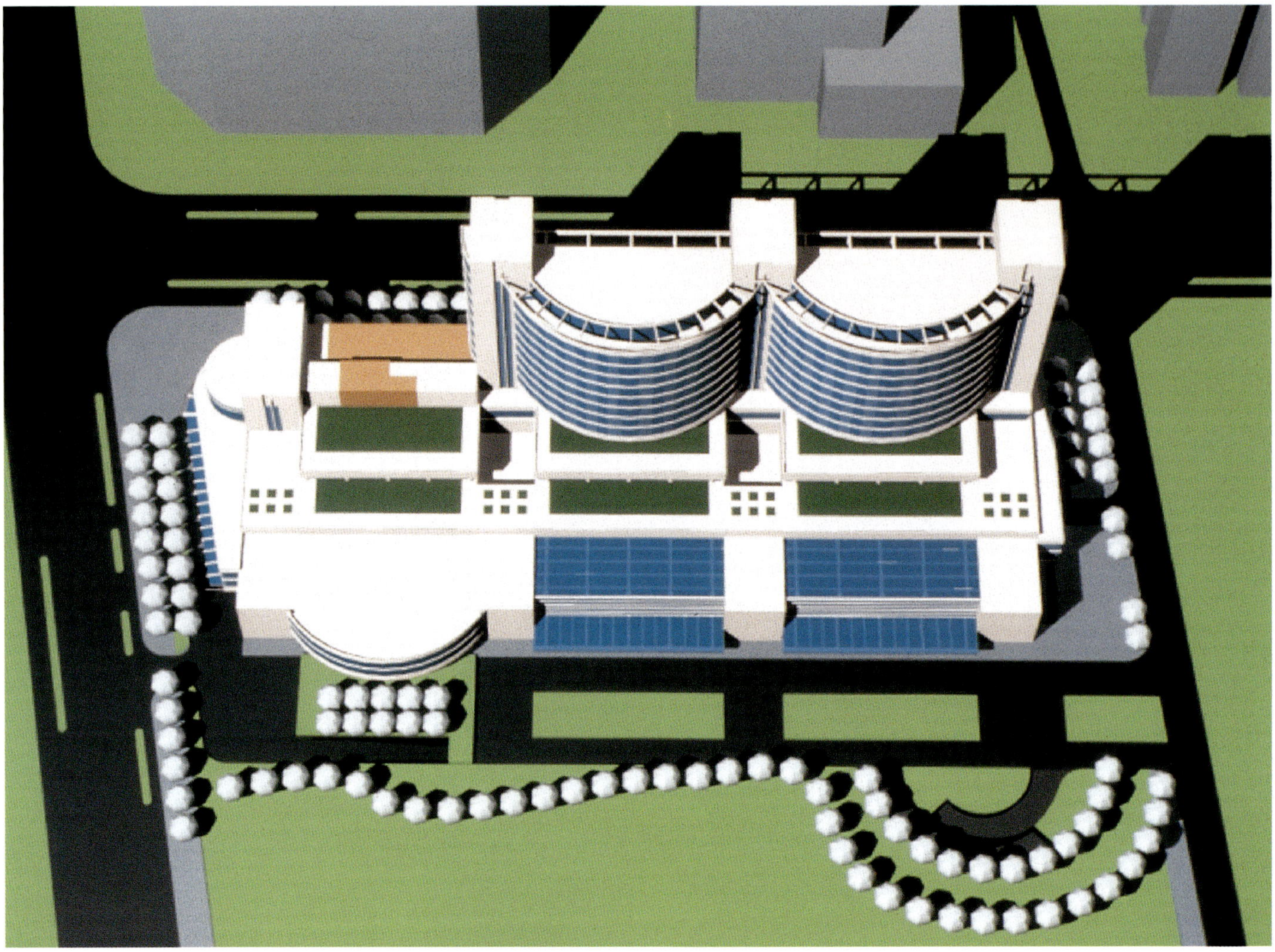
鸟瞰 Exterior overall view

中庭剖面 Cross section of atrium

中庭 Atrium view

成都华西医科大学第三附属医院

医院位于成都新区主要干道交叉路口，总建筑面积50000平方米，600床位。方案充分利用基地，有效地组织内部功能。建筑退后路口，临街留出占基地40%的面积作为绿地。结合用地形状，方案采用双弧形布局，以留出南侧将来布置康复设施。建筑置于基地西北侧，既创造最大的室外空间，又使病房得到充分的阳光。

门诊部沿弧线采用多层布置，单元划分，便于灵活使用。以三层中庭与医院四层中央大厅相连，各楼层功能区流线及导向清晰、直接。诊室及病房之间的中庭不仅为室内提供自然采光，亦是沿主要步行通道导向节点。中庭几层通高的处理丰富了保健与医疗建筑的空间。

不同人口及内部交通组织将门诊与住院、应急服务、传染病区、洁净区、供应区等流线区别对待。除此之外，交通流线设计亦便于各科室之间的联系。

The Third University Hospital of West China University Medical Sciences

Located near an important intersection in a newly developed area of Chengdu, the design balances the best use and arrangement for the site with the most efficient functional arrangement of the facility. By drawing the building away from the intersection, ample open space is provided near the street allowing 40% of the site to be preserved as greenspace. Responding to the site configurations, the building incorporates a double curve arrangement which preserves space to the south for a proposed rehabilitation facility. Located on the northwest side of the site, the structure creates maximum open space and, therefore, optimizes the availability of sunlight to individual patient rooms, a requirement in the cultural traditions of Chinese medicine.

Outpatient clinics are arranged in a series of multi-level structures curving along the central axis of the facility and are configured in a modular concept that permits flexibility by use from one clinic to the next as work loads or patient needs change. Similar to a western "mall" concept, the clinics are located on three floors of open circulation space, stemming from the hospital's central four-story atrium lobby. Patient circulation and orientation are clear and straightforward and the flow between floors and functions is apparent and logical. The skylit atrium between the clinic wing and inpatient wing provides natural light and also serves as an orientation point along a major pedestrian circulation route. The creative use of design elements such as atrium and mall space provide a dynamic image and emphasize the wellness aspect of health care.

Separate entrances and design of the interior circulation systems provide for the separation of outpatients from inpatients, emergency services, infectious clinic, clean supplies and food, and other similar requirements. In addition to proper separation of traffic types, the circulation system has been carefully designed to provide good communication between departments.

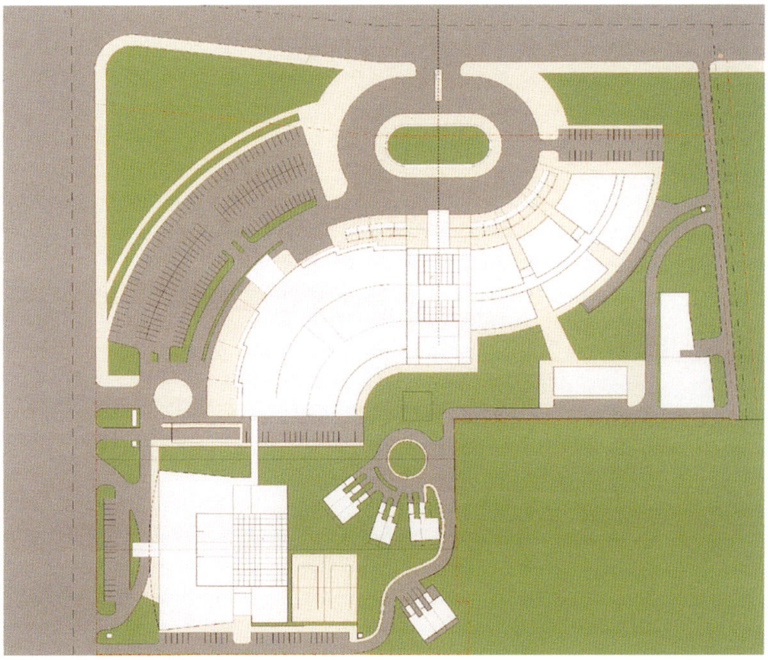

总平面 Site plan

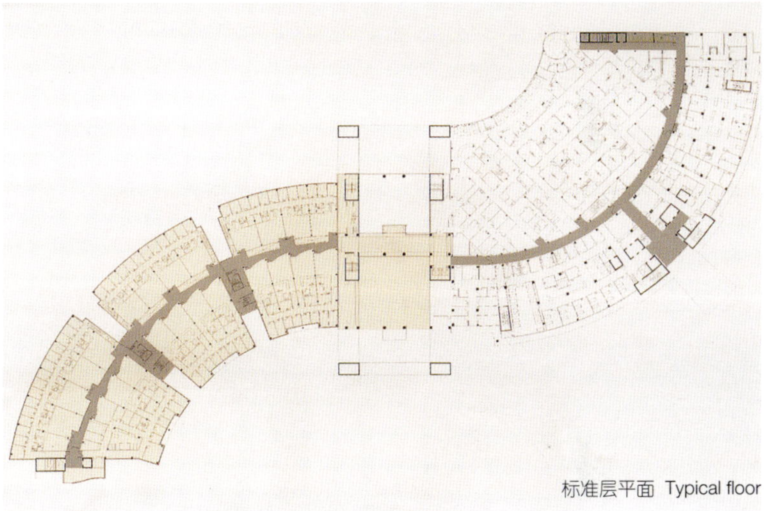

标准层平面 Typical floor

门诊部室内 Exterior view

外观 Exterior view

门诊部室内 Interior view

黑川纪章建筑与都市研究所
KISHO KUROKAWA ARCHITECT & ASSOCIATES

黑川纪章生于1934年，1957年在京都大学建筑系毕业，1964年在东京大学建筑学研究生院完成博士课程。26岁时，他成为60年代新陈代谢运动的发起人之一，开始了他在世界舞台上的第一幕。此后的37年里，他的活动不仅遍及欧洲和北美，甚至扩展到东欧、非洲和亚洲，成为真正世界级的建筑师。

黑川一直倡导设计应该完成从机器原理时代到生命原理时代的过渡，他借助于新陈代谢、形态学、共生学、信息科学、关系学和互感空间等关键性概念来解释生命的原理。1959年以来，他的作品倍受世人瞩目，在此期间获得的奖项有：法国建筑学院金奖，美国加州理工大学理查德·纽特拉奖，保加利亚、索非亚"第五届国际建筑双年大会"最高金奖，美国建筑师学会洛杉矶分会太平洋地区奖。他在日本的奖项有：多次日本营造学会奖，日本建筑学院奖，日本艺术学院奖等等。

他在日本的主要工程有：国立人类学博物馆、国立文乐剧院、名古屋市艺术博物馆、广岛市当代艺术博物馆、和歌山现代艺术博物馆、Ehime科学博物馆等；国外工程有：德国柏林日德中心、中国中日青年中心、澳大利亚墨尔本中心、法国太平洋大厦、马来西亚吉隆坡国际机场、新加坡共和广场等。

黑川纪章1976年成为英国皇家建筑师学会荣誉会员，他是第一个获此殊荣的日本建筑师。1990年成为保加利亚建筑师联盟荣誉会员；1990年成为法国建筑学会会员；1994年成为国际建筑学院院士；1988年获保加利亚索非亚大学荣誉博士；1998年获美国加州纽波特亚太大学荣誉博士头衔。

黑川纪章不仅是一位杰出的建筑师，同时又是一位热忱的教育家，每年他都在世界各地讲学，其中包括美国的哥伦比亚大学、普林斯顿大学、田纳西大学、荷兰的德尔夫特理工大学、中国的同济大学和清华大学以及日本的早稻田大学等。除此之外，他还担任布宜诺斯艾利斯大学、清华大学、同济大学、乔治亚理工大学等校的客座或荣誉教授。

他的著述有：《城市设计》、《建筑论文Ⅰ》、《共生哲学》、《建筑论文Ⅱ》、《建筑诗歌》及《黑川纪章笔记》等，其中《共生哲学》获1991年日本文学最高奖，被译成英文并获美国建筑师学会优秀作品提名。众多国家的出版社出版过黑川纪章的作品。

Kisho Kurokawa was born in Nagoya in 1934 and graduated from the Department of Architecture, Kyoto University in 1957, and the Doctor's Course in the Graduate School of Architecture at Tokyo University in 1964. At the age of 26, as one of the founders of the Metabolism Movement in 1960, he made his debut into the world. For 37 years his activities have spread not only to Europe and the United States, but to East Europe, Africa and Asia, making him a truly international architect.

Kurokawa has been advocating the paradigm shift from the Age of Machine Principle to the Age of the Life Principle. The key concepts he has been using since: Metabolism, Metamorphosis, Symbiosis, Information, Relation, and Intermediary Space, all express the principle of life. Since 1959, his works have been regarded as highly distinguished. Through his activities, he has received: Gold Medal from the Academy of Architecture, France; Richard Neutra Award from California State Polytechnic University, USA; Grand Prix with Gold Medal at "The Fifth World Biennial of Architecture, Sofia, Bulgaria; AIA Los Angeles Pacific Rim Award (first awarded). In Japan, he has received: Takamura Kotaro Design Award (Building Constructors Society Award) many times; Mainichi Art Award; Prize of Architectural Institute of Japan; Prize of Japan art Academy.

His major works in Japan are: National Ethnological Museum, National Bunraku Theater, Nagoya City Art Museum, Hiroshima City Museum of Contemporary Art, Museum of Modern Art-Wakayama, Ehime Prefecture Museum of General Science. Overseas his projects include: Japanese-German Center of Berlin, Germany, Chinese-Japanese Youth Center, China, Melbourne Central, Australia, Pacific Tower, France, Kuala Lumpur International Airport, Malaysia, and etc.

Kurokawa has became the Honorary Fellow of the Royal Institute of British Architects (RIBA) as the first Japanese architect in 1976, and the Honorary Fellow of the American Institute (AIA) in 1981. He is also the Honorary Member of the Union of Architects in Bulgaria, (1990), member of Order des Architecture, France (1990), and a member of the International Academy of Architecture (1994). He is awarded the Doctor's Degree of Philosophy (honoris causa) by Sofia University, Bulgaria (1988), and the Doctor's Degree of Humanities (honoris causa) by Newport Asia Pacific University, California, USA (1998).

He is not only a superb architect, but also a very enthusiastic educator for the next generation. Every year, he lectures at universities all over the world, such as Columbia University, Princeton University, and University of Tennessee in the U.S., Delft University of Technology in the Netherlands, Tsinghua University and Tongji University in China, and Waseda Uiversity in Japan. Furthermore, he has acted as honorary and visiting professor at many universities such as Tsinghua University and Tongji University, China; Columbia University, USA; Musashi Institute of Technology, Japan and etc.

His publication includes: "Urban Design", "Thesis on Architecture I", " Philosophy of Symbiosis", "Thesis on Architecture II", "Poems of Architecture", "Kisho Kurokawa Note" and etc. The "Philosophy of Symbiosis" was awarded the Japan Grand Prix of Literature, and was revised in 1991. It has been translated into English and was cited excellence from the AIA. His woks are published and exhibited all over the world. Of his sketches from the1960s became a permanent collection of museums in several countries.

北京中日青年中心

此项目由中日两国政府支持，其目标是为中、日和其他国家的年轻人提供一个国际间交流的适宜空间，以促进科学、文化、体育和其他活动的交流。中心包括文化设施，以及学生训练、体育和宿舍设施。

方案的构思来自中国传统的天圆地方的概念。剧场、水池和宿舍取圆形作为基本形，而方形象征大地或观实世界。设计师用这个方案来阐述一个双重代码，将传统的中国象征语言同现代的纯几何语言结合起来。与此同时，由非对称和不连续轴线为代表的的自由平面的构成，类似日本庭院中的不规则布置的石头和茶室建筑的风格，反映了日本的空间美学。(方案阶段与北京建筑设计院联合设计)。

Chinese-Japanese Youth Center, Beijing

This project was supported jointly by the Chinese and Japanese governments. The Center provides cultural facilities, as well as training, sporting and dormitory facilities for international exchange between youth from China, Japan, and other nations, to promote scientific, cultural, athletic and other types of activities.

The design concept comes from classical Chinese cosmology, which conceived of the heavens as round and the earth as square. The theater pavilion, pool, and dormitory take the circle as their basic form, while the squares symbolize earth, or reality. The designers envisioned the scheme as manifesting a double code, combining a traditional Chinese symbolic language with the modern university of a perfect geometry. At the same time, a free configuration of forms in plan, characterized by broken axes and asymmetry, represents a Japanese spatial aesthetic, akin to the irregular placement of stones In Japanese gardens, ands the style of tea-house architecture. (collaboration with the Beijing Institute of Architecture on this project in the schematic design phase.)

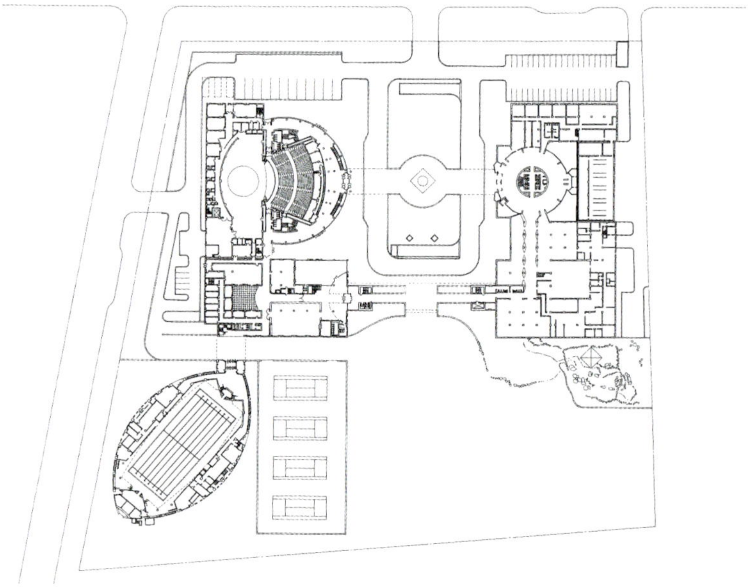

一层平面 First floor

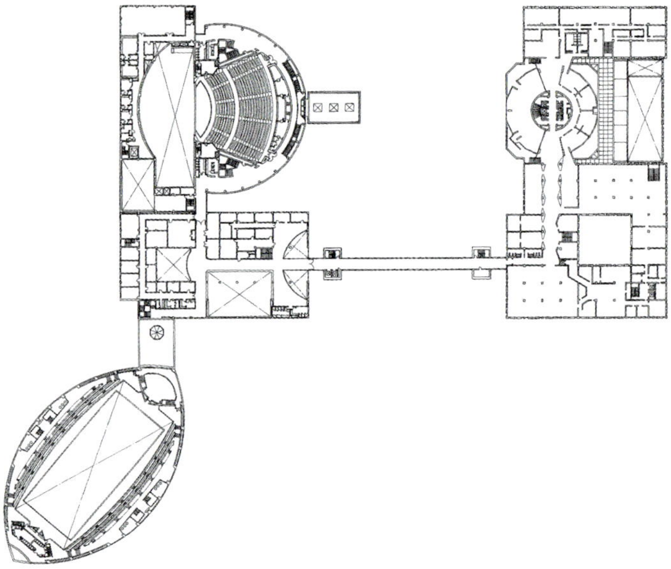

二层平面 Second floor

室内游泳池 Indoor swimming poor

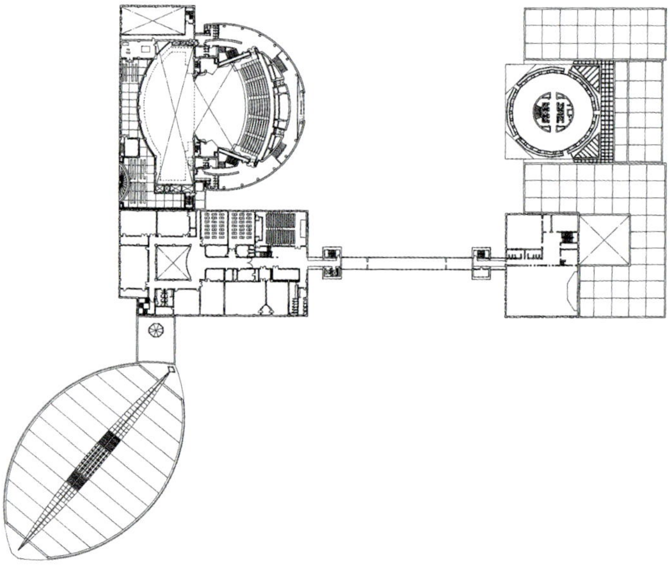

三层平面 Third floor

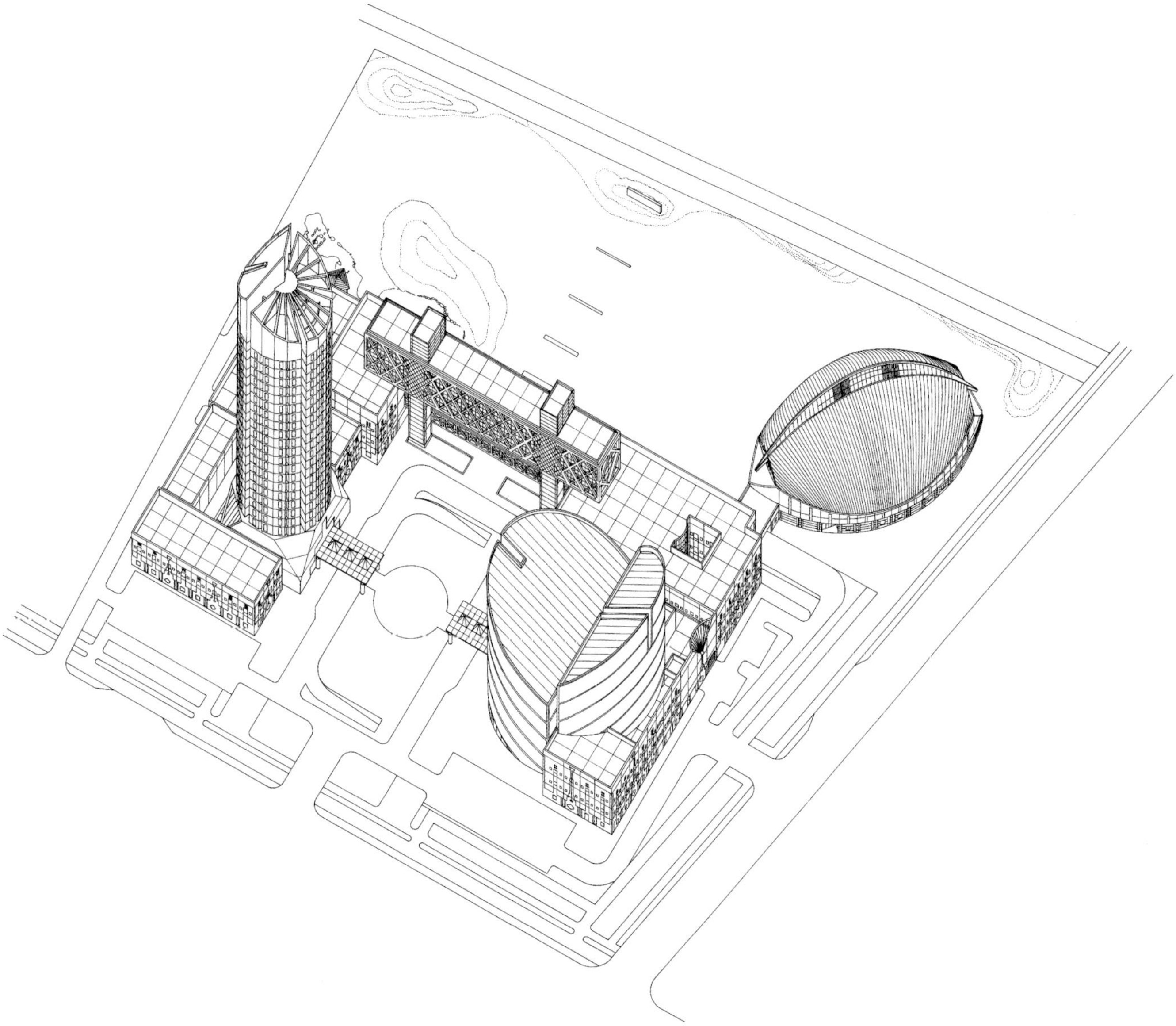

轴测 Axonometric

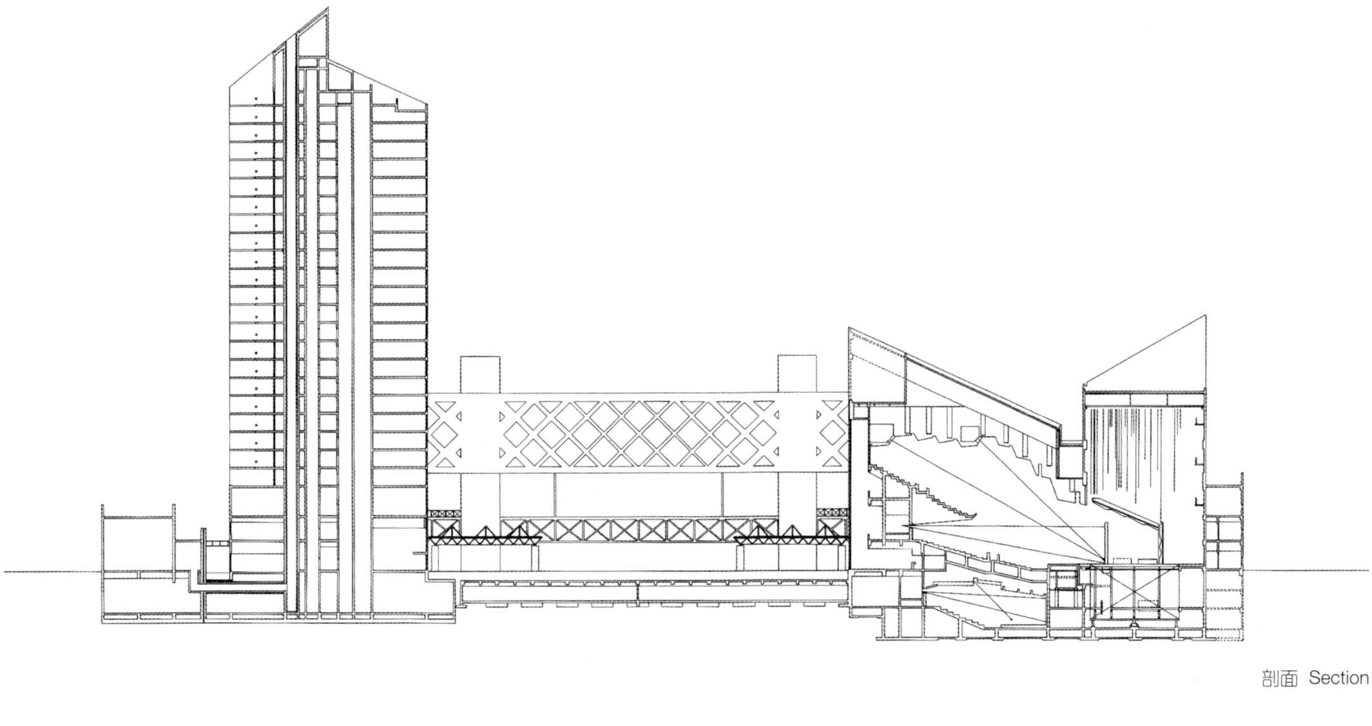

剖面 Section

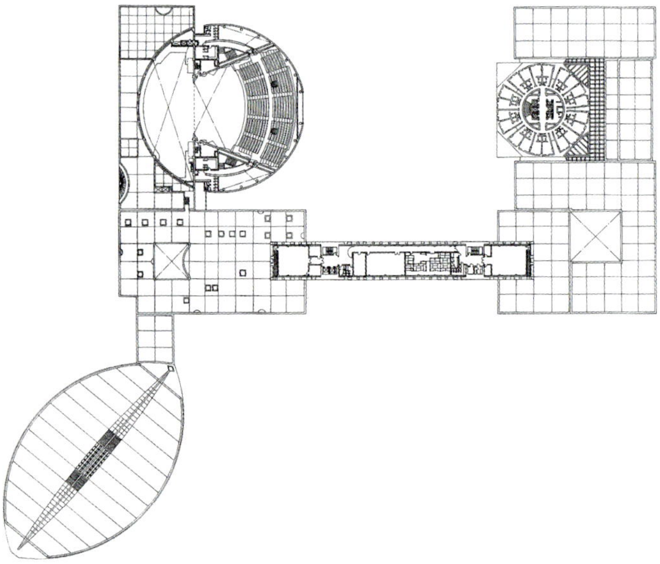

四层平面 Fouth floor

西侧外观 View from west side

西南外观 View from southwest

总体外观 Overall view from southwest

剧场三层门厅 Theater foyer on the third floor

剧场入口大厅 Entrance hall of the theater

剧场二楼过厅 Foyer of the theater on the 2nd floor

剧场室内 Interion of the theater

室内游泳池 Indoor swimming pool

三亚海滨旅游发展区

项目基地面积1170公顷，包括国际酒店、国内酒店、别墅、高尔夫俱乐部、小船坞、工匠村、渔民村、体育公园（主题公园、剧场、水族馆等）、宿营地、涉外学校等设施。位于海南岛南端，毗邻一个渔村，具有一种域外风情，是一处尚未开发的处女地。

方案的目标是将海南岛建成中国的夏威夷。它由海滩边的一大片国际度假酒店组成，在另一侧有为国内人士而设的度假酒店。在两组酒店的中间，是可为游客提供各样设施的中心区。围绕游客中心布置了山边别墅、海边别墅、高尔夫球场、小船坞、渔村、工匠村、酒店和公园等。

设计概念源于共生哲学。共生包括不同层面：中国传统和现代科技的共生，建筑和自然、民族形式及土地和大海的共生等。总而言之，规划的宗旨是自然风景和人工建筑共生共长。

Sanya Coast Tourist Development

Occupying an area of 1,170 hectares, this proposed development includes international hotels, domestic hotels, villas, golf club, marina, craftsmen's village, fisherman's village, sports park (theme park, theater, aquarium, etc.), camping area and outbound school facilities. Located in the southern end of Hainan Island, China's southern end island. This site is undeveloped, and it is near to a fisherman's town with exotic atmosphere.

The aim of this project was to make Hainan Island 'the Hawaii of China". It consists of a large number of international resort hotels facing the beach. In the opposite direction, there are resort hotels for the domestic people. Between the two hotel areas, there is a central area with all kinds of facilities such as hillside villa, seaside villa, golf course, marina, fisherman's village, craftsman's village, hotel, and park, etc. They are arranged around the tourist center.

The design concept drew from the philosophy of Symbiosis which comprises various dimensions such as the symbiosis of the Chinese tradition and the modern technology, the symbiosis of architecture and the nature, the symbiosis of nationalism, and the land and the sea. As a whole, it will be planned so that the natural landscape and the man-made architecture will be in symbiosis.

模型 Model view

深圳市中心中轴线上的公共空间规划。

本项目基于黑川纪章的生态－传媒工程计划。它位于深圳市中心，是一片长3公里、面积为174公顷的开敞空间，其中心为市政厅。公共设施总面积30万平方米，包括艺术中心、生态－传媒中心、电影中心、分配中心、购物中心、公园（屋顶花园、市政厅广场和生态公园）等。

方案在用地的两端，设计了两个充分利用自然环境的公园。在这两个公园的中间，则是建在人工填土层上的公园。许多设施如艺术中心将设于土层的下面，目标在于为每两年和每三年一次的艺术盛会提供一个新的艺术胜地。这个线形公园是一个多层次的结构，包括多种设施，其屋顶是一个人造园林环境。设计概念来自音乐作曲的方法，使用的城市音符如下:

1. 文化－政治－科学和技术－艺术－生态。
2. 传统中国园林－礼仪广场－旅游信息中心－生态－传媒中心－购物中心－艺术公园－生态公园。
3. 春－夏－秋－冬。
4. 典型的－正式的－中心的－复杂的－自由的。

不同层面的构思将进一步深入。

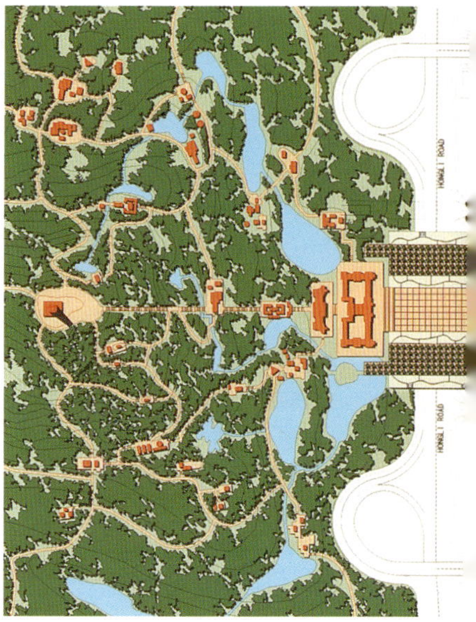

Public Space System along the Central Axis in Shenzhen City Center

This project is based on Kisho Kurokawa's Eco-media Project Plan. Located at the city center of Shenzhen SEZ (Special Economic Zone) adjacent to Hong Kong, an open space of 3 kilometers in length and 174 hectares in area is planned with the new city hall at its center. With a total floor area about 300,000 square meters, facilities such as an Art Center, an Eco-media Center, an Film Center, an Art Theater, a Distribution Center, Shopping Malls and Parks (roof gardens, city hall square and Eco-park) are deliberately introduced to the area.

At both ends of the site, parks making the best use of the natural environment will be provided, and in between them, a park will be built on manmade subsoil. Underneath the subsoil, many facilities such as an Art Center will be provided to create a new Mecca for artistic events. This linear park is multi-layered structure with an accumulation of facilities The roof will be a manmade park.

The design concept is taken from the method of music composition using urban score, as the following:

1. Culture-politics- Science & Technology-Art-Ecology
2. Traditional Chinese Garden-Ceremonial Plaza-Tourist Information Center-Eco-Media Center-Shopping Mall-Art Park-Eco-Park
3. Spring-Summer-Autumn-Winter
4. Typical-Formal-Central-Complex-Free

Concept stories at various levels will be developed.

模型 Model

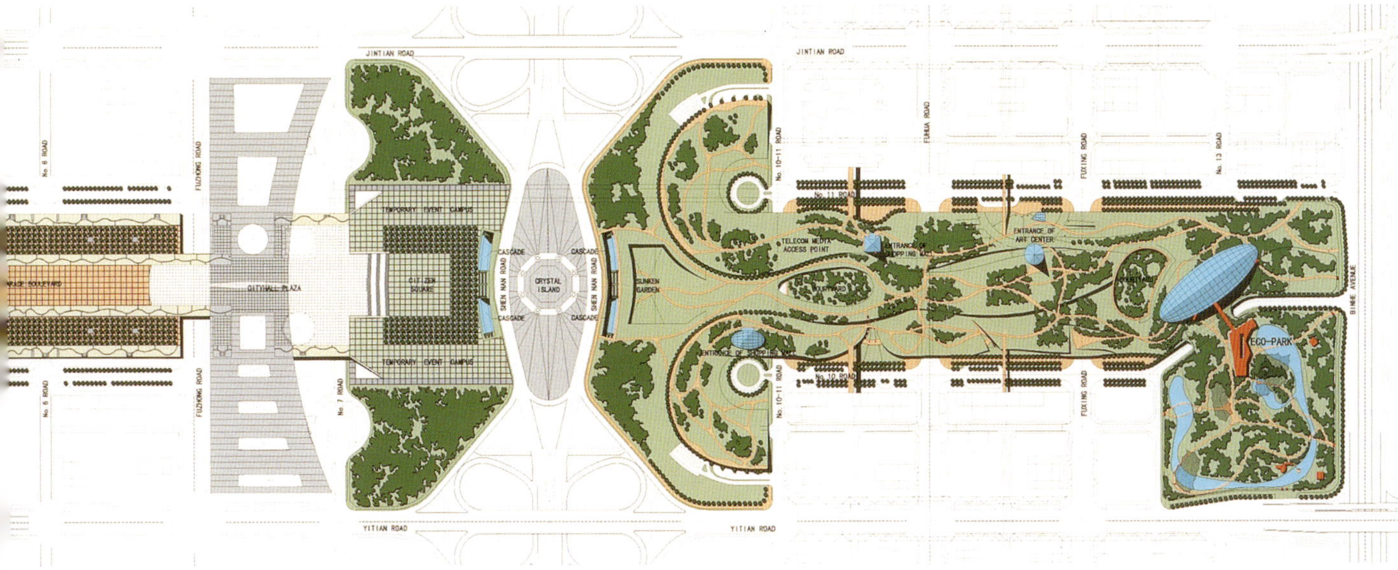

总平面 Site plan

模型总体 Overall view from south

Urban Score

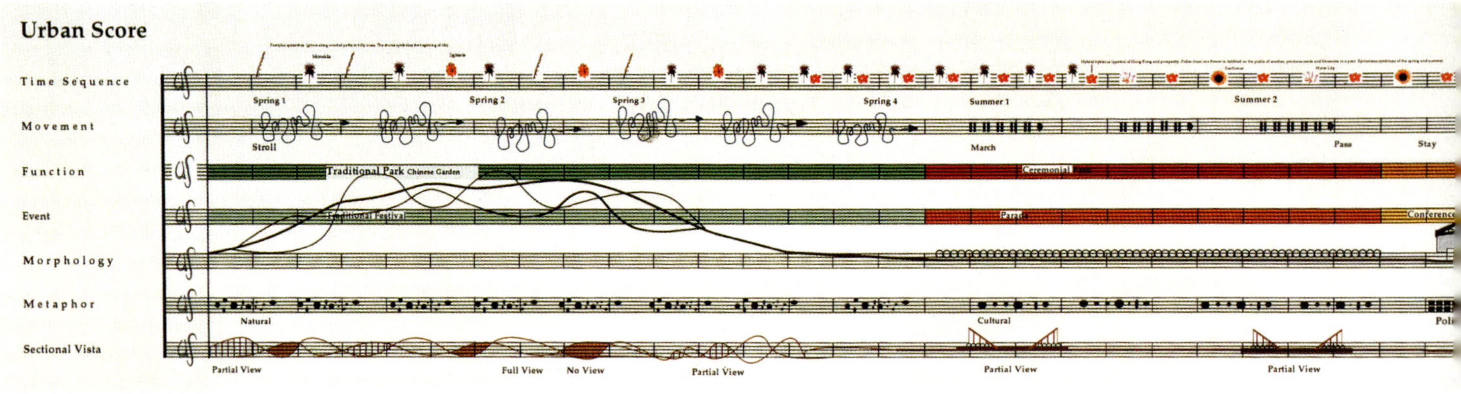

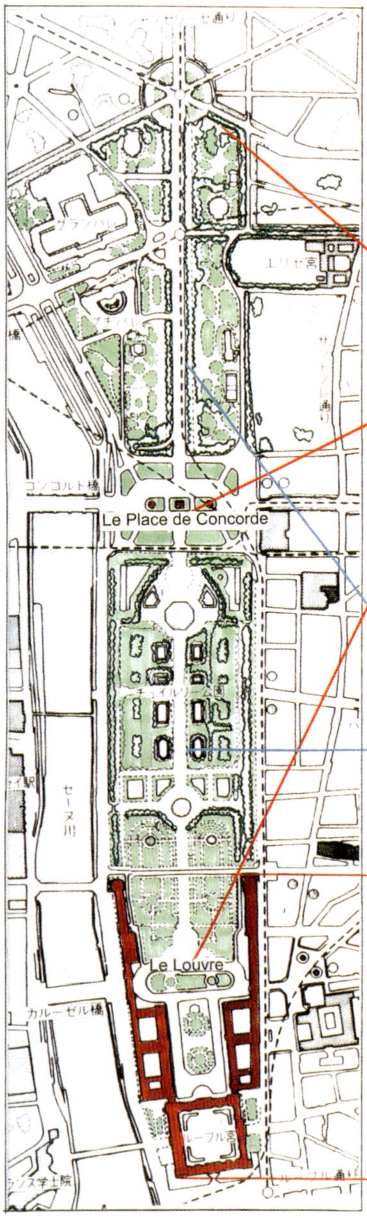

Urban Scale / Human Scale

The Shenzhen design provides an urban environment comparible in scale and variety to the great urban centres across the globe, such as the Champs Elysee in Paris. Shenzhen Multi-Complex is on a scale equivalent, if not larger than Le Louvre. However the scheme has been broken into a variety of Human Scale sections according to the urban score.

Nodal Point

Urban Promenade

Just as in Paris walking from Le Louvre to Le Place de Concorde, to l'Arc de Triumph, waking through the Shenzhen site from Lianhau Hill to the Eco-Park provides the pedestrian with a series of walks through a variety of spaces, connected by nodes and focal points, such as the art park, the shopping park, the city hall, ceremonial park.

Pedestrian Walk

Le Louvre

Shenzhen Multi-Complex

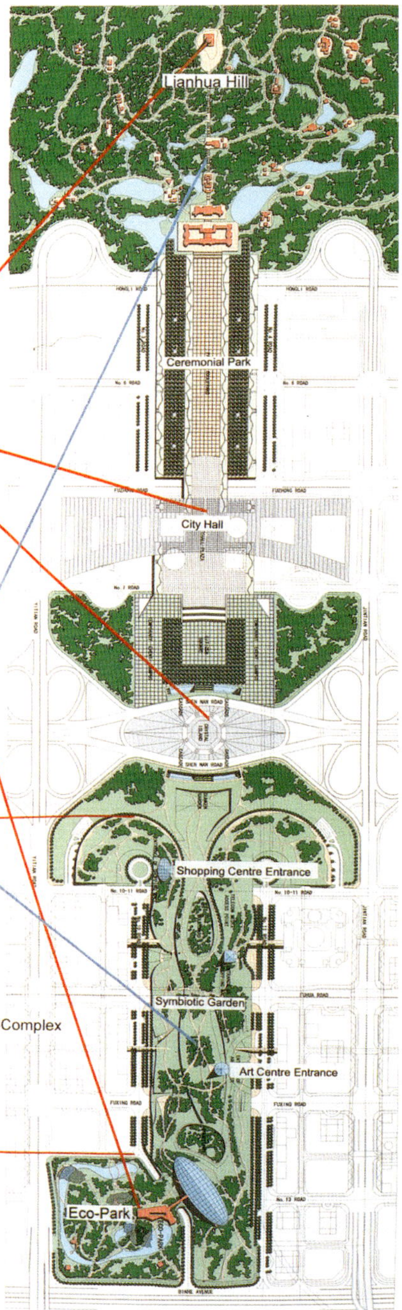

尺度比较 Scale comparison

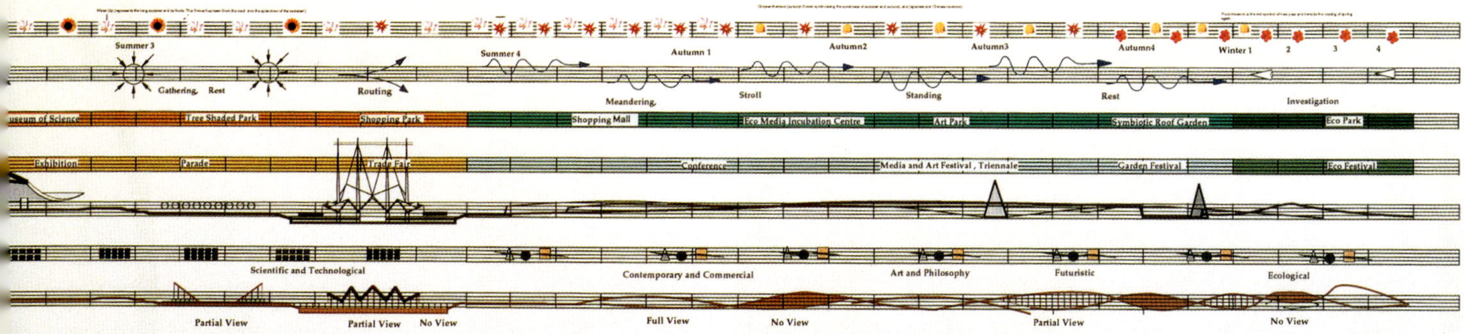

构思 Concept

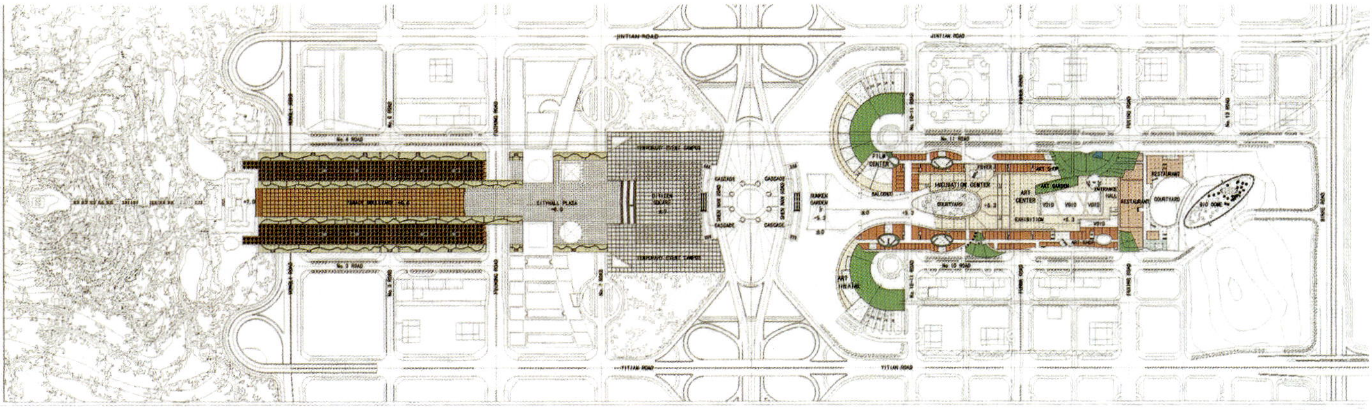

地下一层 Basement first floor

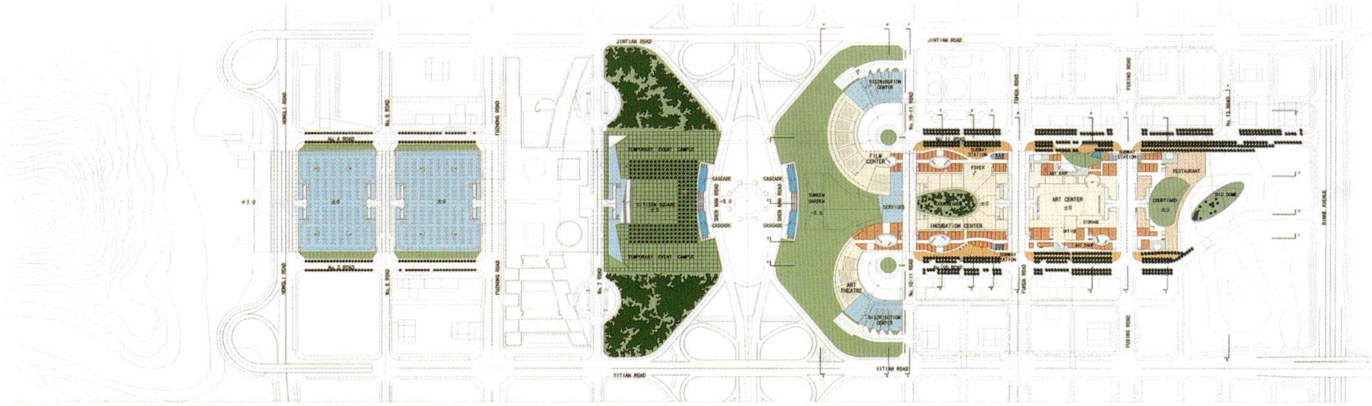

一层平面 First floor

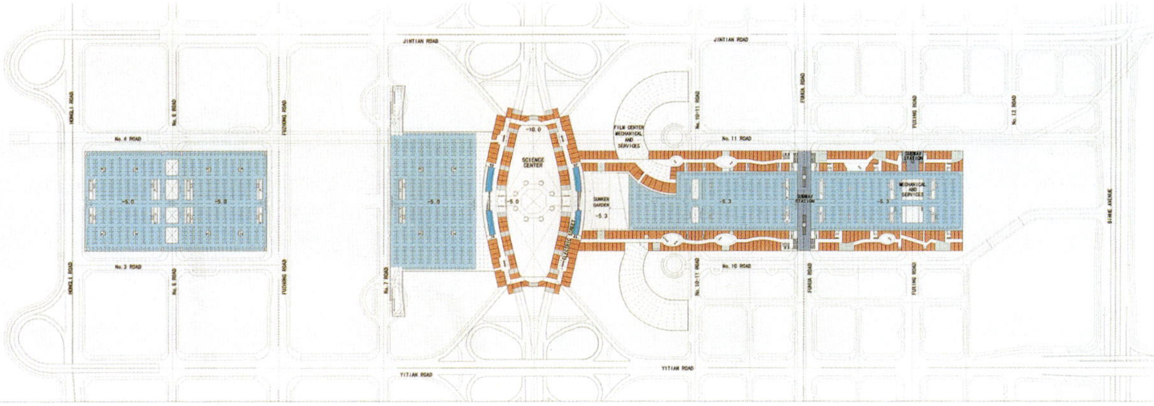

二层平面 Second floor

步行大道 Shopping Boulevard

艺术公园 Art Park

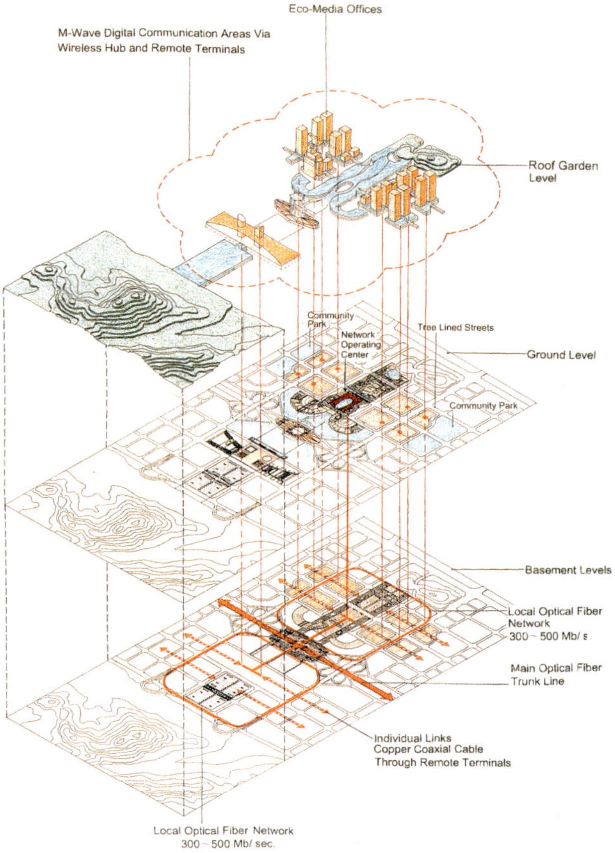

信息网络(生态－传媒设施) Information network

艺术公园入口 Entrance to the Art Park

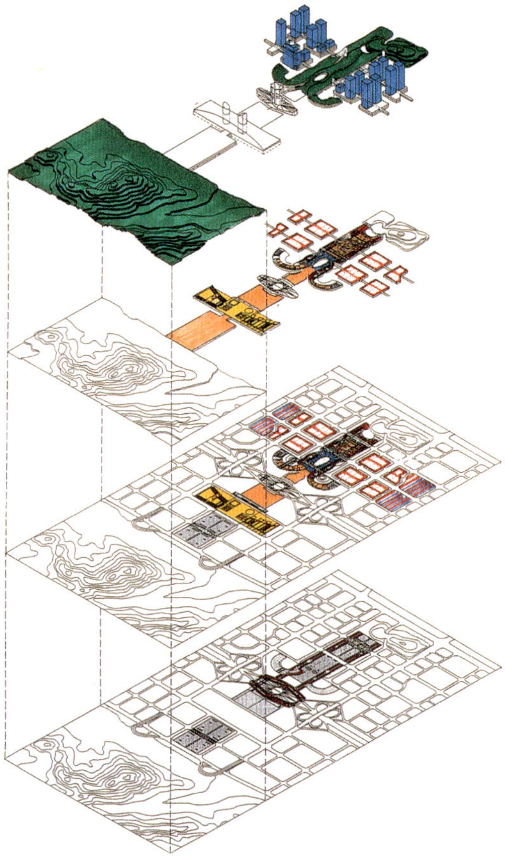

生态公园 Eco-Park

步行网络 Pedestrian network

Lighting Plan

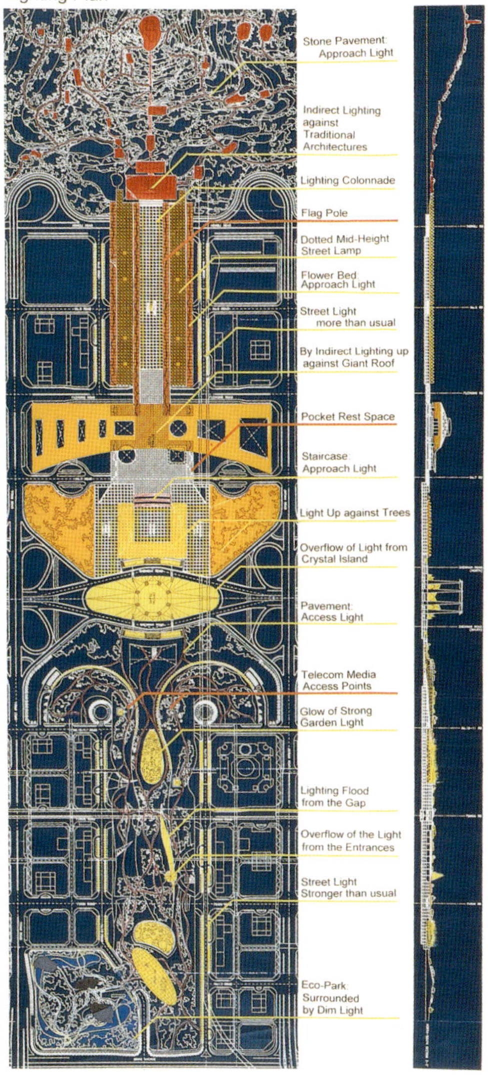

灯光规划 Light plan

广场 Plaza

模型 Model view from Shennan Road

艺术公园 Art Park view

外观 Model view from north

约翰·李名仪／迈克尔·廷丘勒建筑师事务所
JOHN M.Y.LEE / MICHAEL TIMCHULA ARCHITECTS

1993年，李名仪与迈克尔·廷丘勒继爱德华·L·巴恩斯/李名仪事务所后达成新的联盟，事务所在50多年的建筑设计专业实践中，完成了大量不同规模与不同类型的规划设计项目。客户包括大公司、机构、政府及私人和小的非盈利性机构。项目则由低层至高层，从小规模加建至大型的总体规划无所不包。

目前主要工作包括旧金山新法院、哥伦布斯的一所小学校及中国的高层办公楼等。1997年在深圳中心区城市设计中夺标。

事务所致力于拓展其项目的多元性，同时保持多年形成的优质的服务及设计整体性等优势。事务所对其专业队伍在管理不同项目方面的能力充满信心，面对当今复杂的建筑技术问题，其控制项目全过程的能力、经验及与各种技术人员和咨询公司的合作中游刃有如，最终使客户满意是事务所服务的明确目标。

事务所主要负责人李名仪先生在博物馆、学术、办公等建筑设计及总体规划方面经验丰富，其商业性项目包括IBM位于纽约麦迪逊大街590号的总部及莱西顿大街599号的波士顿物业公司大厦，堪萨斯城的皇冠中心及棕榈滩的Breakers Row公寓，并为纽约的亚洲社团及达拉斯艺术博物馆进行设计。而研究机构项目包括德州大学的西门子生物药品研究楼、达拉斯西南医药中心、犹它州立大学的科学技术博物馆及新加坡国立大学总体规划等。

在李先生的职业生涯中受到了大量的奖励，最近华盛顿联邦司法大楼得到1995联邦设计艺术成就奖。其中国项目在苏州的一个电子设备公司总部及工厂在建，深圳中国招商银行大厦及市政厅等正在设计之中。

In June of 1993, John Ming-Yee Lee and Michael Timchula formed a new partnership as a continuation of Edward Larrabee Barnes/ John M.Y. Lee Architects. With combined experience of over 50 years in the professional practice of architecture, their portfolio shows a diversity of project scale and type. They have planned and designed for major corporations, institutions, and governments as well as private individuals and small not – for – profit institutions. Their work has ranged from low-rise to high-rise, from small additions to master plans for large-scale projects.

Typical current work includes a new courthouse for the City of San Francisco, CA; an elementary school in Columbus, IN; and a high-rise office building in China. The firm was recently named winner of an international urban design competition for the center of the City of Shenzhen, China.

The partners are committed to expanding the diversity of their previous projects and maintaining the high level of design integrity and client service they have built up over the years. They are confident in the team's ability to manage projects at both large and small scales. Their experience has demonstrated ability to work within a multitude of team arrangements with a diver se group of engineers and consultants. Their clear goal is the ultimate satisfaction of their clients' design needs.

Mr. John M.Y. Lee was born in 1937 in Shanghai, China, got his Bachelor degree of Arts at Amherst Collage in 1959 and graduated from Yale University, obtaining a Bachelor degree of architecture in1963.

Prior to formation of the present firm, Mr. Lee was a partner at Edward Larrabee Barnes/John M.Y.Lee, Architects where he shared overall design responsibility with Edward Barnes form 1981 to 1987, an associate of the same firm from 1971 to 1981 and a designer from 1967 to 1970. During the years immediately after his studies at Yale Architecture School, he worked for Willian H.Metcalf in Washington D.C.

Mr.Lee's experience ranges from museums and academic buildings to office buildings and master planning. His commercial projects include IBM's 590 Madison Avenue headquarters and 599 Lexington Avenue for Boston Properties in New York, Crown Center in Kansas City and Breakers Row condominiums in Palm Beach. He has worked on the Asia Society in New York and the Dallas Museum of Art. His academic projects include the Simmons Biomedical Research Building for the University of Texas, Southwestern Medical Center in Dallas; the Science and Technology Library at Utah State University and the master plan for the National University of Singapore.

Throughout his career Mr. Lee has been the recipient of numerous prizes and awards for his work. Most recently the Thurgood Marshall Federal Judiciary building in Washington, D.C. was awarded a 1995 Federal Design Achievement of the Arts. His first project in China, the national headquarters and small factory for an electronic instrument company in the City of Suzhou, is under construction. A second project, a high-rise office building for China Merchant's Bank in Shenzhen is in the design phase.

世界贸易中心大厦

50层高的招商银行总部大厦分为三部分：裙楼、塔楼和塔顶。5层裙楼形状规则，5层高的中庭作为大厦的入口门厅。四周采用透明玻璃以及由两种灰色花岗岩形成的光滑表面。42层的塔楼平面由下部的正方形逐步向上收分成八角形。幕墙采用蓝绿色反光玻璃与金属框。当塔楼向上收分时，外立面形成三角形和梯形相间的格局。塔楼的顶部是一个空中花园，内设银行俱乐部。

基地位于深南路北，建筑占据地块的北部，覆盖率为39%。地块的南侧为20米宽的绿化带，西侧是一个带有大喷泉的庭院。遮荫的花架小径形成庭院的边界，庭院的西侧为拟建的酒店／公寓综合体，由东侧通道可达主入口及300车位地下车库。5层高入口中庭设于大厦的中间，它将东侧入口与西侧的庭院连为一体，中庭的南侧为银行营业大堂，其拱顶高3层。

World Trade Center Building

The World Trade Center Building, headquarters of the China Merchants Bank, will be fifty stories high. The structure is defined by three zones, the podium, the tower shaft and the crown. The five floors of the podium are rectangular, with a 5-story atrium serving as the entrance lobby to the complex. The podium is a simple volume with clear glass and two tones of gray granite detailed in sleek, flush planes. The 42-story tower shaft is a tapered form that begins as a square and ends as an octagon. The curtain wall is reflective blue green glass with metallic mullions. As the shaft form tapers upward, the vertical planes alternate between triangle and trapezoid. Above the shaft is a sky garden where refreshments are served at the Bankers Club in the crown above.

The building covers 39% of the lot north of Shennan Road. In the front southern portion of the site, a 20-meter green zone is planted with groves of trees, and to the west of the building is a garden courtyard with a large pool fountain. Heavily shaded trellis walks define the court garden. Further west of the courtyard, a hotel/apartment complex is planned for the future. Access to the main entrance and the 300-cars garage is from the access road to the east. At the middle of the building is a major 5-story high entrance atrium linking the eastern entrance to the western courtyard. South of the atrium is the grand banking hall, three stories high at the vaulted peak. (Co-designer: Shenzhen Second Architectural Design Institute)

透视图 View from Shenan Avenue

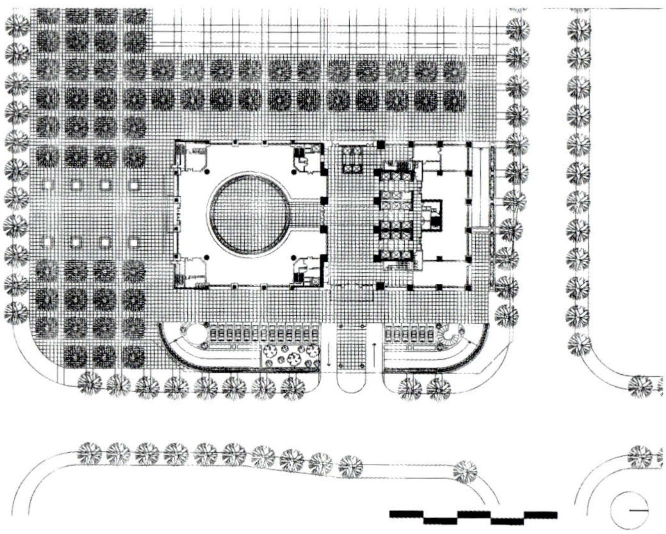

总平面图 Site plan

门厅透视 View of entrance lobby

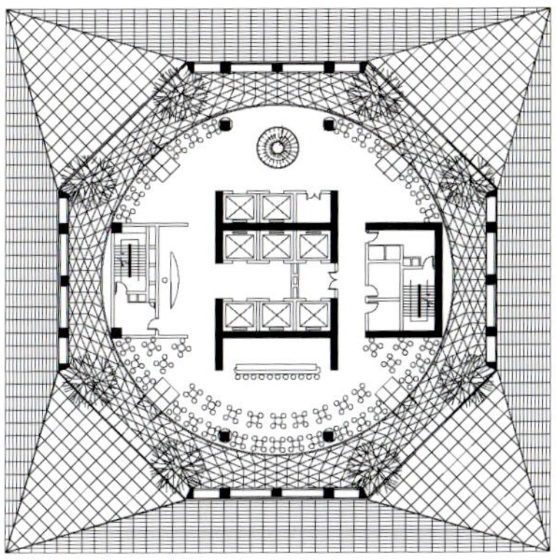

屋顶花园平面 Sky garden floor plan

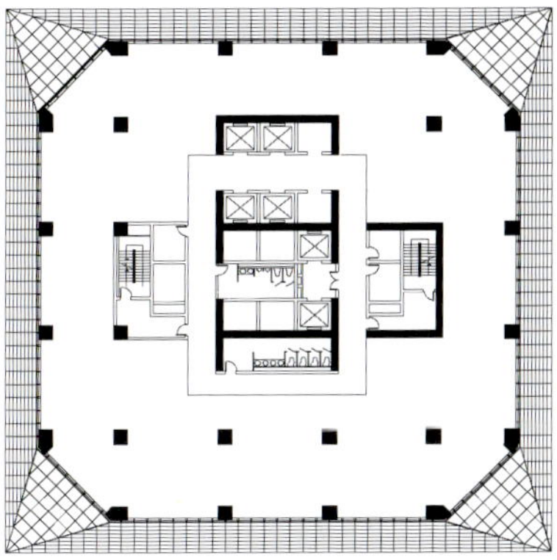

中段平面 Mid-rise floor plan

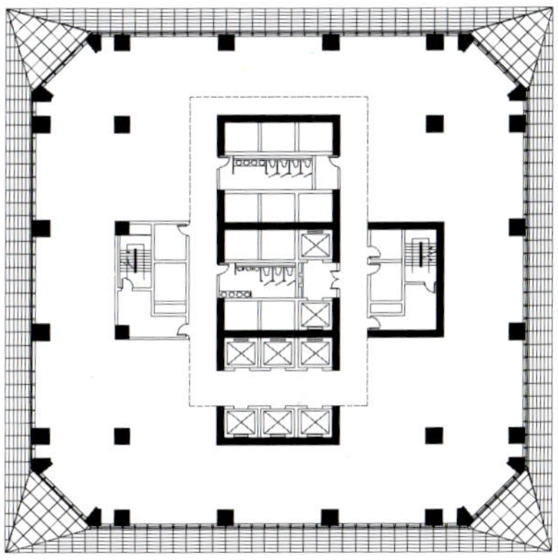

低段平面 Low-rise plan

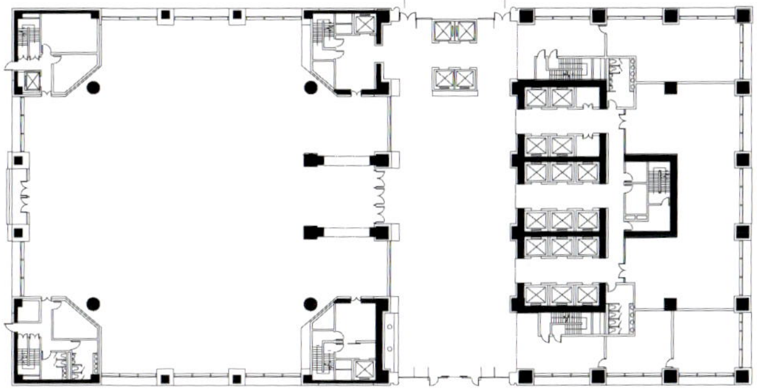

首层平面 Ground floor plan

深圳市中心

这是一个城市设计国际咨询获奖方案。中心位于福田新区，是沿一条南北方向长约3公里的轴线展开的中央公园绿化带，其北端为莲花山公园，南端为滨河路地铁枢纽。主要城市干道——深南路将中央公园分成南北两部分，北端为市政厅，南端则为中央绿化公园。为创造一个具有活力和吸引力的21世纪城市中心，设计强调人文环境与自然环境的和谐，城市能耗的更新与生产的平衡及环境的物质与精神方面双重满足等基本原则。

方案以广场将中央公园南北两部分连为一体。为强调中央公园的整体性，广场核心部位引入了水晶岛这一富有戏剧性而引人入胜的标志性建筑。其外形与市政厅相呼应，包括购物、视听、表演、大型会议、展示等功能。其造型是超时空的，晶莹、雕塑般的体形令人联想到百万年前大自然的演化及未来的神秘，日间晶莹、透剔，夜间遍体通明，显示了城市中心区的活力。它可以直接通向地铁、公交车站、停车场、中心广场与绿化带。南端的中央绿化带与中央广场贯通一致，两侧分布着附有庭园的餐馆、咖啡屋、茶坊、花房、精品商店等，而绿化带中央则引入宇宙太空园（九大行星为主题）、历史文化公园（中国古代四大发明为主题）及世界名人园三个花园系列。所有地下通道天窗伸出地面，成为三个花园雕塑的台座。同时方案在土地利用、交通系统、环境设计等诸方面均提出了进一步的建议。

Shenzhen City Center

This is winning scheme in an international design consultation. The new city center is located in the new district of Futian and is a central park green belt stretching along a three-kilometer-long north-south axis. At the north end of the axis is the Lian Hua Shan park and at the south the Bin He Road metro hub. A major expressway, Shennan Road, cuts through the park and divides it into a northern part and a southern one. To the north is the Civic Center, and the south the central park. In creating a dynamic and attractive 21st century city center, the design emphasizes such basic principles as harmony of the built and natural environment, balance between city's energy consumption and production, and satisfaction of both the physical and spiritual aspects of the environment.

The scheme connects the southern and northern sections with the central park. In order to emphasize the integrity of the central park, a dramatic and impressive crystal island is placed in the center of the plaza. Its exterior echoes that of the Civic Center and it houses functions like shopping, entertainment, conference etc. Its appearance is lucid, plastic and ultra-time-space, reminding one of the millions of years of natural evolution and the mystery of the future. It is transparent during the daytime and luminous in the night. It has direct access to the metro stations, bus stops, parking area, the Central Plaza and the green belt.

The southern end of the central green belt is connected to the Central Plaza, lined with gardened restaurants, coffee shops, tea houses, flower and souvenir shops. Three theme parks - cosmological space park, historical park and celebrate park - are introduced to the central green belt. All skylights for underground passages rise above the ground, forming bases for sculptures in the three theme parks.

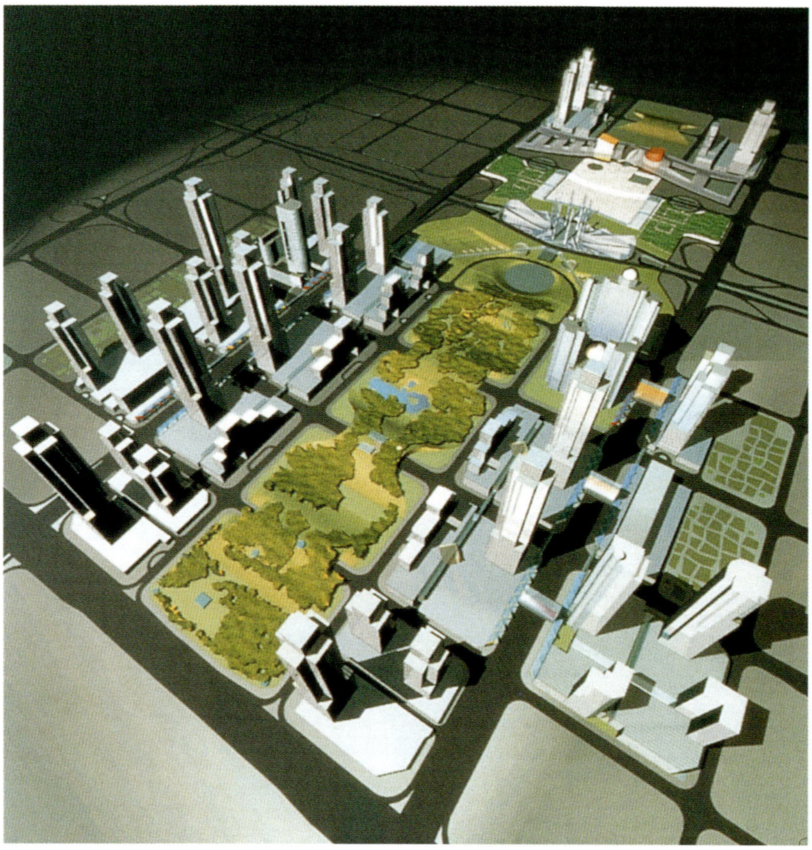

总体鸟瞰图 Aerial view towards city center

公共广场及水晶岛 Public square & crystal island

深圳市市政厅

市政厅位于深圳市新中心，其设计既是规则和纪念性的，同时又是低调而不张扬的。低调有以下几个好处：它可以促进市民和政府之间的交流，使大跨度空间以更快和更省的方式建造，将亲切的尺度同有力的屋顶形式联系起来，在无需电梯的条件下拥有更便捷的交通，以及创造安静的庭院空间和景色。

这座大厦形式上的重点是其曲面屋顶，像一只展翅的大鹏。它不仅是给深圳——鹏城的一个献礼，同时也呼应了传统中国南方的屋顶形式。屋顶除了美学上的价值以外，它亦有利于散热，并可以通过太阳能收集板收集和贮存能量。屋顶盖板的颜色和表面给人以中国传统琉璃瓦顶的联想。

建筑分成三部分，每一部分独立运作。中部为大礼堂、礼仪厅和市民活动空间。西翼包括向公众开放的办公室，而东翼为市长办公室和其他政府机构办公室。

Shenzhen City Hall Building Complex

Shenzhen has quickly become one of China's most important centers of commerce and industry. At the center of this explosive new expansion is the city hall building complex with total floor area about 100,000square meters. The city hall design is both monumental and formal, while at the same time maintaining a low profile. The low profile has several advantages. It facilitates interaction between people and the government, allows for quicker and more economical construction with greater potential for long span spaces, combines a human scale with a powerful roof form, provides easy circulation without the cost of elevators; and the potential for tranquil courtyard spaces and views.

The formal highlight of the building is its curving roof, soaring over the complex like an eagle in flight, a tribute to Shenzhen, "The Eagle City", as well as to traditional southern Chinese roof forms. In addition to its aesthetic value, the roof serves to dissipate heat gain and collects and stores energy by means of solar panels. The resulting power can be used to light the complex during the evenings. The panel's color and roof finish recall traditional Chinese glazed roof tiles.

The building components are separated into three sections, each of which will operate independently. The middle section houses large auditoriums, ceremonial halls and activity spaces for the citizens of Shenzhen. The west wing contains public access offices, while the east wing will hold the mayor's office and other municipal government offices.

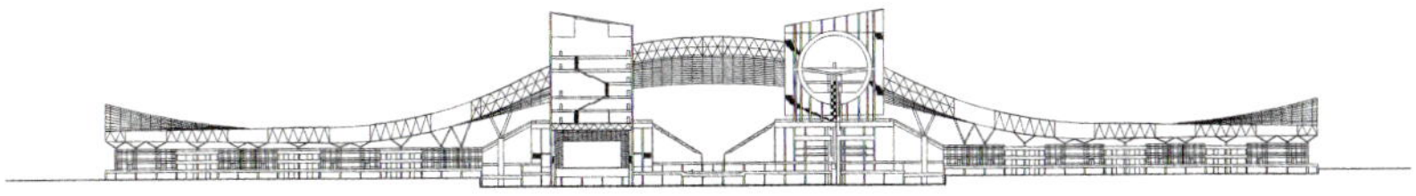

剖面 Section

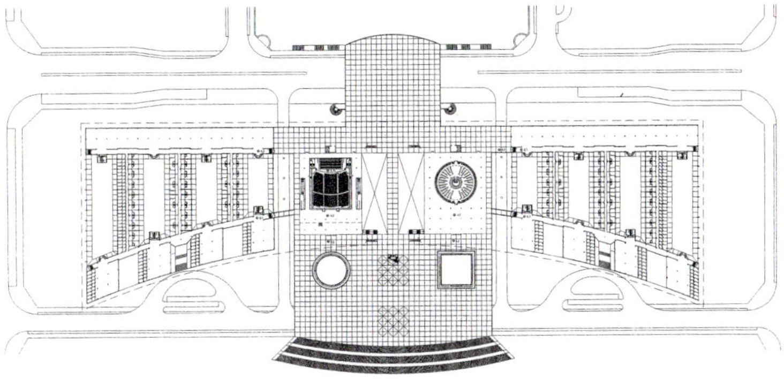

二层平面 Second floor plan

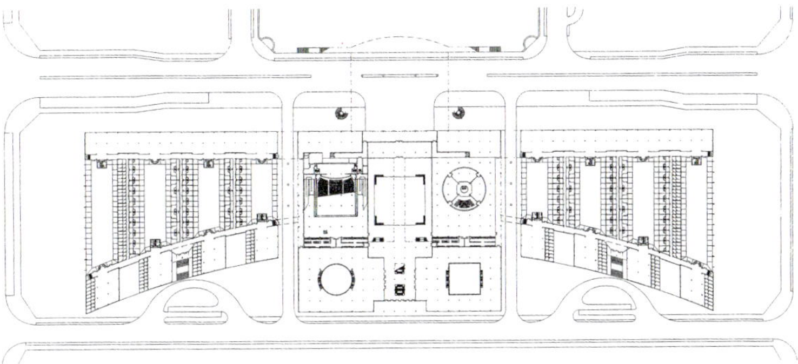

首层平面 First floor plan

市政厅中心鸟瞰 Overall view

市政中心屋顶 View of the roof

夜景 Night view

入口外景 Entrance

罗布·施拉士曼·哈克尔建筑师事务所
LOEBL SCHLOSSMAN & HACKL / HAGUE RICHARDS

罗布·施拉士曼·哈克尔建筑师事务所总部位于芝加哥，致力于大型综合设施设计，包括商业、高层办公楼、医疗设施、大学及机构建筑等。事务所坚持以良好的质量服务于遍布美国、欧洲、中东及亚洲的客户。

LSH/HR国际项目主要为高层综合性项目，这些项目以超越传统，勇于创新见长。最近6年，该事务所在中国完成总体规划及设计超过80万平方米。

由于良好服务，自1925年成立以来，LSH/HR事务所不断发展壮大，继续为许多以往的客户提供服务，约60%的新项目来自已有的客户。并且，为保证客户得到最优秀的服务，事务所有30多个项目与当地公司成功地合作。

为保证以优质的规划与设计服务于客户这一目标，事务所提供从总体规划、项目研究至建筑设计与项目管理、工程管理、现场监理等系列服务，并通过室内设计提供多样及整体的建筑设计服务。

LSH/HR由100位具有创新精神的专业人员组成多学科的专业队伍。事务所的设计遵循创新、现实可行及满足客户对项目的要求等原则。因而每一项目均有其独到的创新与合理性。其规划与设计方法试图超越当前面临的挑战而憧憬未来。

LSH/HR以高质量的设计，先进的技术与管理凝成一个经受时间考验的设计团体，该事务所共获得包括A1A及其它专业机构授予的85个主要奖项。总裁唐纳德·哈克先生1987年当选为美国建筑师协会主席，目前为国际建协（UIA）第三区副主席。

Loebl Schlossman & Hack/Hague Richards is a Chicago-based architecture, planning and interior design firm. It specializes in the design of large scaled mixed-use, retail, high rise, office, healthcare, university, institutional and hospitality projects. The firm has maintained a philosophy of design excellence through service to clients in the United States, Europe, the Middle East and Asia. LSH/HR is fully computerized and avails itself of various electronic media to facilitate practice worldwide.

LSH/HR brings to its international projects an extensive, award-winning background in high-rise and mixed-use design coupled with an ability to think beyond "conventional wisdom" and find new solutions to coupled problems. In the last six years, the firm has master planned and designed in excess of eight million square feet of mixed-use projects in china.

Since its founding in 1925, LSH/HR has successfully grown as a result of exceeding client expectations. The firm continues to serve many of its earliest clients, deriving more the 60% of new work from existing clients. And LSH/HR has successfully associated with local firms on more than 30 projects to ensure that clients receive the greatest value for their investment.

LSH/HR's mission is to achieve excellence in planning and design that faithfully serves its clients. To fulfill this mission, the firm provides a wide range of services from master planning and programming to architectural project management, construction administration, specifications writing, Shop drawing review, and field observation. Through its interior design practice, the firm offers diverse and expanded interior architectural services to create totally integrated design solutions.

LSH/HR 's 100-person staff of creative professionals is organized around multi-disciplinary teams that strive to achieve greater quality and success than individual efforts. The firm approaches design on both creative and practical levels, linking its client's mission and strategic vision with their project. Each project has its own innovative and rational solution. LSH/HR's planning and design methodologies look beyond the challenges of today, strategically repositioning it clients for the future.

LSH/HR'S quality of design, advanced technology and management skills encompass a body of work that has stood the test of time and has resulted in more than 85 major awards: from the American Institute of Architects and other professional organizations. The President of the firm, Donald Hackl, FAIA, was elected National President of the American Institute of Architects in 1987. Currently, he is Vice President, Region III, of the International Union of Architects (UIA)

深圳文化中心

中心由一座世界级音乐厅和一个中心图书馆组成。音乐厅内可容纳2000个座席，建筑面积20000平方米。中心图书馆藏书量超过400万册，约80%为开架图书，建筑面积35000平方米。它主要作为深圳市图书馆系统的中心，同时也包含为学术研究提供的专业参考书库。

作为深圳市文化中心区的关键性城市建筑群，文化中心的建筑形体不仅限定了公共绿地周围的空间，同时也通过自身强烈的视觉形象将环境统一起来。每个单体都根据各自内部使用功能而表现出相应建筑个性。在现代建筑材料和设计的基础上，二者都以自身独特的形象烘托市政厅。这两座纪念性公共建筑将形成一个举世无双的文化中心。

音乐厅设计以自然风景元素和乐器为基础。建筑表现各类元素在不同层次上的结合，象征性地将建筑与公园环境融为一体，反映出中国传统文化中"天人合一"的观念。音乐厅厅堂为一光洁的木质形体，圆滑的、带有纪念性的高科技元件从深色亚光花岗岩基座中展露而出，同时又"悬空"在由透明玻璃围合而成的、内有一簇簇象征着琴弦的细柱的人口大厅空间之上。顶部钛质伞形屋面如云一般，其反光的金属表面捕捉并反射自然光，将音乐厅与广场的水池连为一片，使其如同海市蜃楼，脱离地球引力而悬浮于空中。巨大帐篷屋顶轻盈流畅的轮廓犹如声学共鸣器，将其覆盖下的声能放大并辐射出来。

音乐厅厅堂凌驾于底层基座之上，由玻璃围合而成的壮观的人口大堂在迎接来访者的同时，又统领着周边环境。观众由一段富有纪念性的楼梯引至广场，然后穿过水池，到达礼拜堂般的大厅内。然后，分别由扶梯和坡道引导，来到安静而且空间适度的内厅。观众厅内饰面是由多种木料制成的光洁面板，先进的声学设计使人们能够在其中享受最美的音乐。

21世纪的新型图书馆将成为传统意义上的图书馆和现代全球电子信息网络系统之间的桥梁。通过最尖端的科技，新型图书馆将在使用、藏书和信息反馈等方面作出全

构思草图 Sketch

构思草图 Sketch

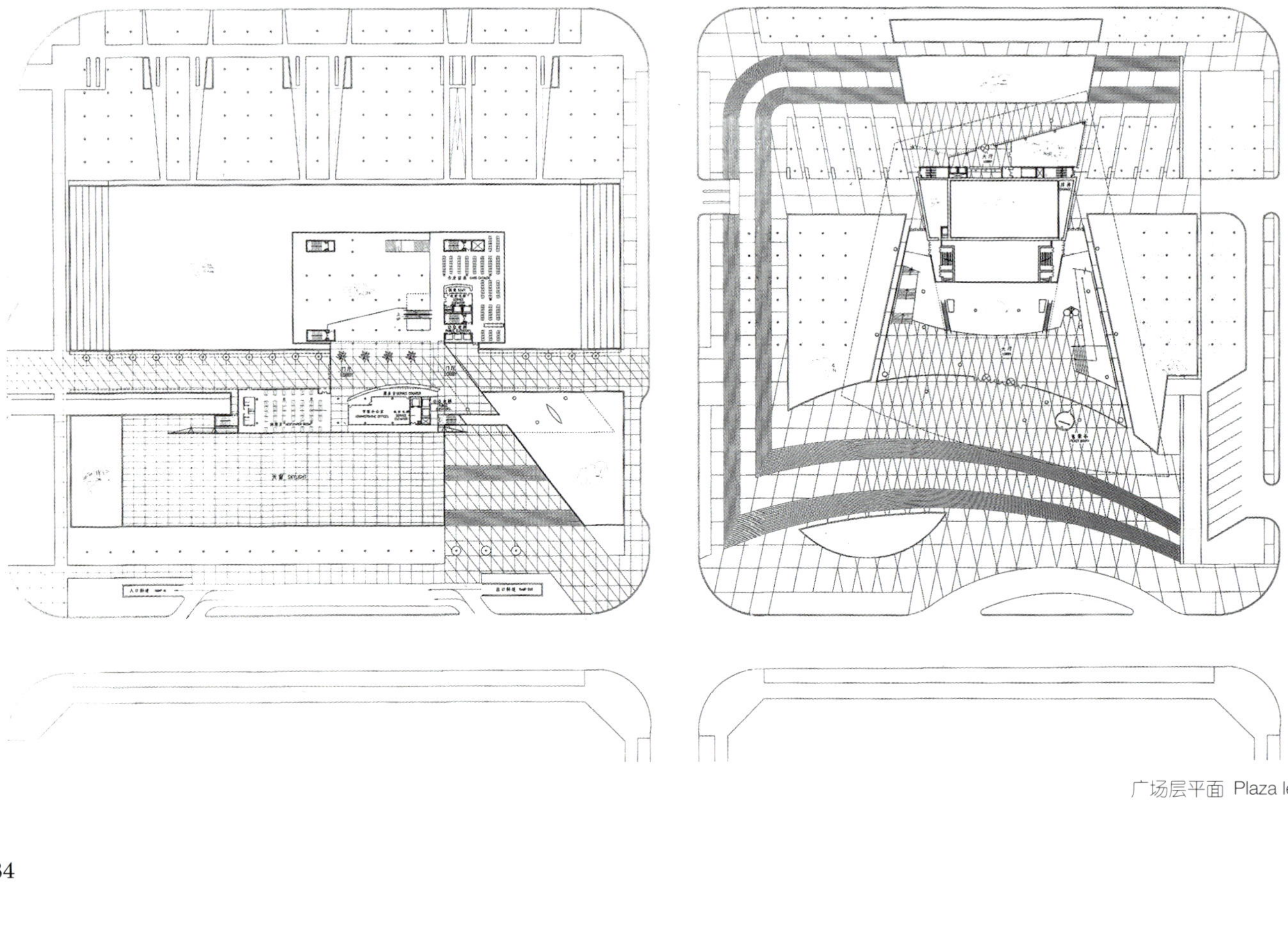

广场层平面 Plaza level plan

面的革新。数字/电脑化的数据处理方式给未来的图书馆提出新的要求，当今的图书馆已经成为多文化交流和学习的中心环境，孕育着文明和发达的社会。

书库塔楼外包半透明玻璃，内层使用木和石质材料，含蓄的半实体量以暗示内部较稳定的功能。相比之下，电子媒体大厦则是高度透明的信息构架外包透明玻璃。内部设有电脑和互连网平台、CD、DVD及数字化媒体阅读区，以及与之相应的管理功能。

Shenzhen Cultural Center

The Cultural Center consists of a world class Concert Hall and a 'state of the art' Central Library. The new Concert Hall contains 2,000 -seat performance hall with total floor area of 20,000 square meters. With a floor area of 35,000 square meters, the new Central Library houses over four million volumes with approximately 80% as open stacks. It principally functions as the center of Shenzhen's library network in addition to containing professional reference collections for academic research.

As key to the urban assemblage in the Shenzhen Cultural zone, the cultural Center buildings are massed to both define and provide a strong visual presence on the public green space that binds the surrounding together. Each building architecturally expresses it's own identity based upon the functions and uses contained within. While sharing a common language of

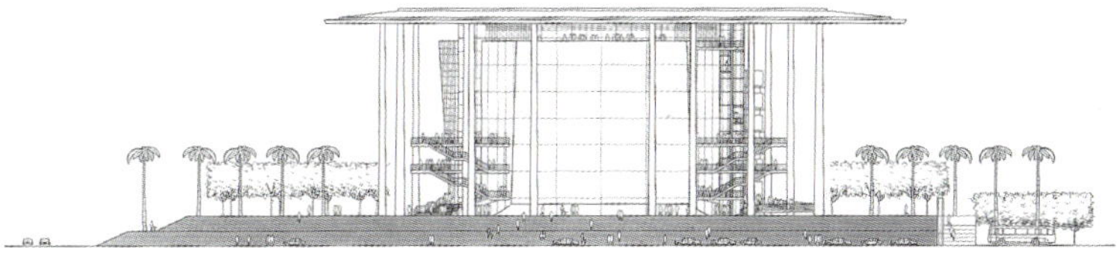

东立面 East elevation

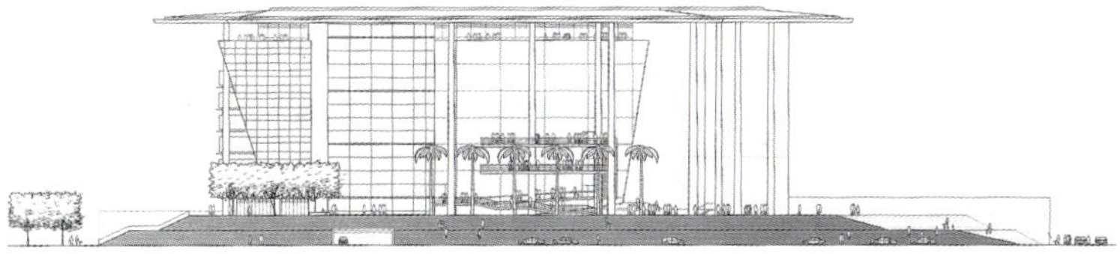

南立面 South elevation

模型鸟瞰 Model, aerial view

modern materials and design, each has a unique character which will complement the new City Hall. As envisioned, these monumental civic structures will create an urban Cultural Center like no other in the world.

The Concert Hall design is based upon allusions to natural landscape elements and to musical instrumentation. The building is composed of a layered ensemble of elements, which metaphorically integrate the building and its park setting, recalling the fundamental Chinese sensibility of man's harmonious relationship to nature and the cosmos.

The polished wood volume of the hall itself is expressed as a sleek, monumental high tech instrument emerging from its dark matte granite case, 'suspended' over a void in a clear glass lobby amongst a grove of thin columns reminiscent of the strings of an instrument.

Overhead, the titanium parasol roof 'floats like cloud, with its reflective metal surfaces catching and reflecting light, framing the hall between itself and the plaza's reflecting pools, dematerialized like a mirage, leaving the hall seeming to float free of gravity. The great canopy roof's thin sweeping profile suggests an acoustic resonator which amplifies and radiates the acoustic energy within its domain.

The Concert Hall is elevated onto a plinth where the great, glazed lobby embraces the visitor and commands its surroundings. A monumental flight of steps leads to a plaza and then through the 'stillness of the sun dappled reflecting pools. The cathedral-like lobby moves visitors by way of ramps or stairs into the confines of the inner hall, a quiet, appropriately scaled space, clad in rich varieties of polished wood, and acoustically designed for the enjoyment of the finest music of our time.

The new Library of the 21st century serves as a bridge between the traditional concept of library, to one of a global electronic information network. Utilizing cutting edge technologies, it will revolutionize the access, storage and retrieval of information. The digital/computerized methodology of handling data creates a new paradigm for the library of tomorrow, which now, more than ever, becomes the center of a cultural interactive meeting and learning environment through which intellectually advanced societies evolve.

The book stack tower volume, clad with etched, fritted, translucent glass, and containing wood and stone 'core' elements, is rendered as an ambiguously semi-solid mass whose translucence masks the interior functions-giving only a veiled shadowy impression of its inner solidity. The 'electronic' media building, in contrast, is a highly translucent information matrix clad with clear and computer and Internet access stations, CD, DVD and digital media access areas, along with administrative functions.

音乐厅室内 Concert hall interior

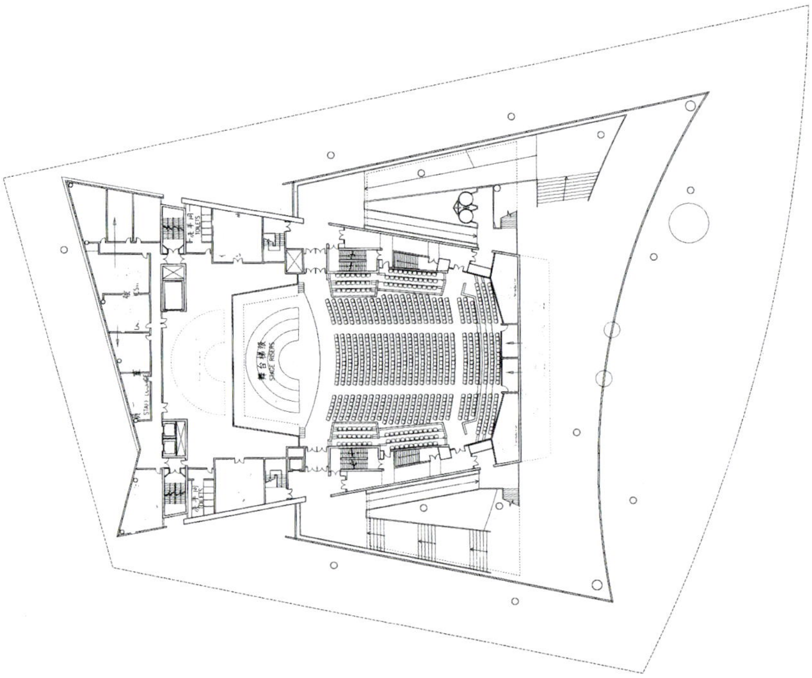

音乐厅平面 Concert hall floor plan

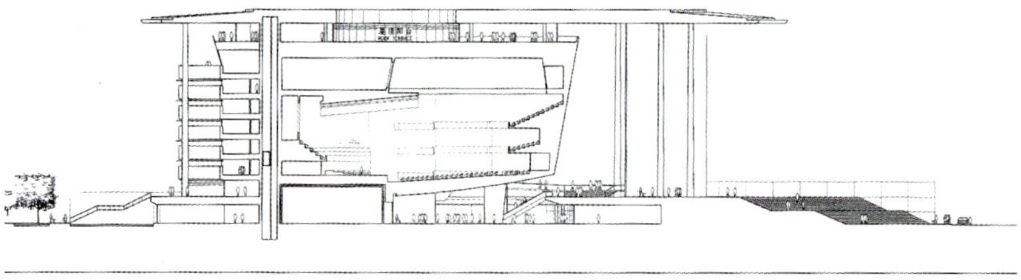

音乐厅剖面 Concert hall section

音乐厅西北外观 Concert hall view from northwest

中心图书馆西南外观 Central library view from southwest corner

深圳罗湖商业中心

中心是包括商业、旅馆、办公和停车设施在内的多功能综合体。建筑的8层裙房内设有零售空间、酒店服务、一个会议中心、一个娱乐中心和一个健身中心，3层地下室可停车260辆，塔楼包括一座五星级酒店、商住和办公空间，顶部的空中花园则容纳餐厅、夜总会和观景等功能。

塔楼在体量和形式上作了富有动感的层次处理，立面材料采用含色玻璃和不锈钢。通过对体量和玻璃色彩的处理使酒店同办公区分开来。这座深圳天际线中的标志性建筑的外表完全以钢和玻璃覆盖，空中花园给宽阔的内部空间以全方位的景观。白天，半透明的电梯、塔楼和蓝天浑然一体；夜晚，它是一束闪亮的光柱，象征商业的兴旺和个性的魅力。

Shenzhen Luohu Commercial Center

This mixed-use complex includes commercial, hotel, office, and parking facilities. The building's eight-story base encompasses retail space, hotel functions, a conference center, an entertainment center, and a health club. Three below-grade levels are devoted to parking for 260 cars. The tower features a five-star hotel, offices/apartments, and office space, culminating in the dramatic Sky Pavilion, which accommodates dining, nightclub and observatory functions.

The tower's dynamic layered massing and forms are clad in tinted, patterned frit glass and stainless steel. The hotel is differentiated form the office functions by its volumetric articulation and interplay of glass colors. The signature on Shenzhen's skyline clad entirely in glass and supported by monumental steel trusses, the Sky Pavilion provides a soaring interior space with panoramic views, accessed by an elevator platform which transits the building's antenna mast. By day, its surfaces by an elevator and translucent, visually merging tower and sky; by night, it becomes a luminous beacon of commerce and individual identity.

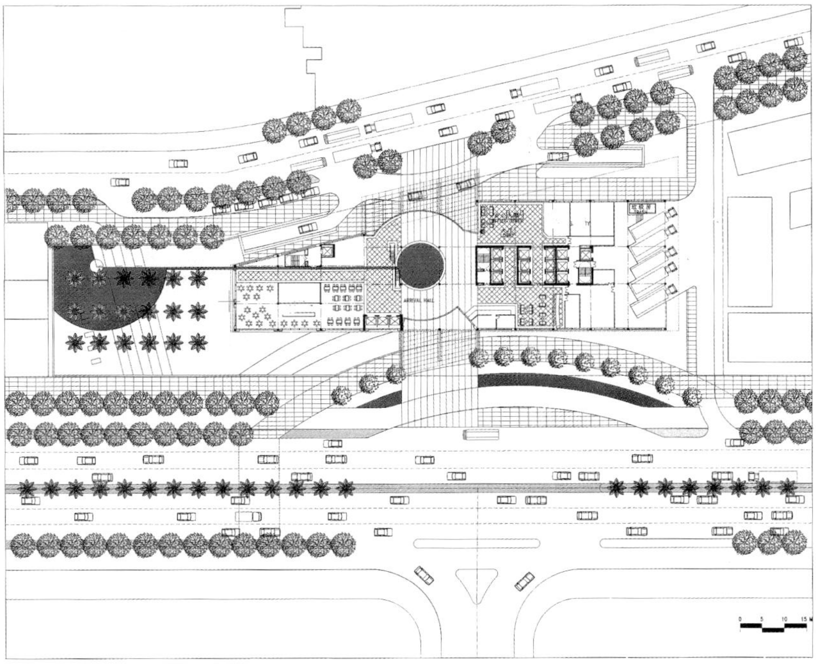

首层平面 Ground floor plan

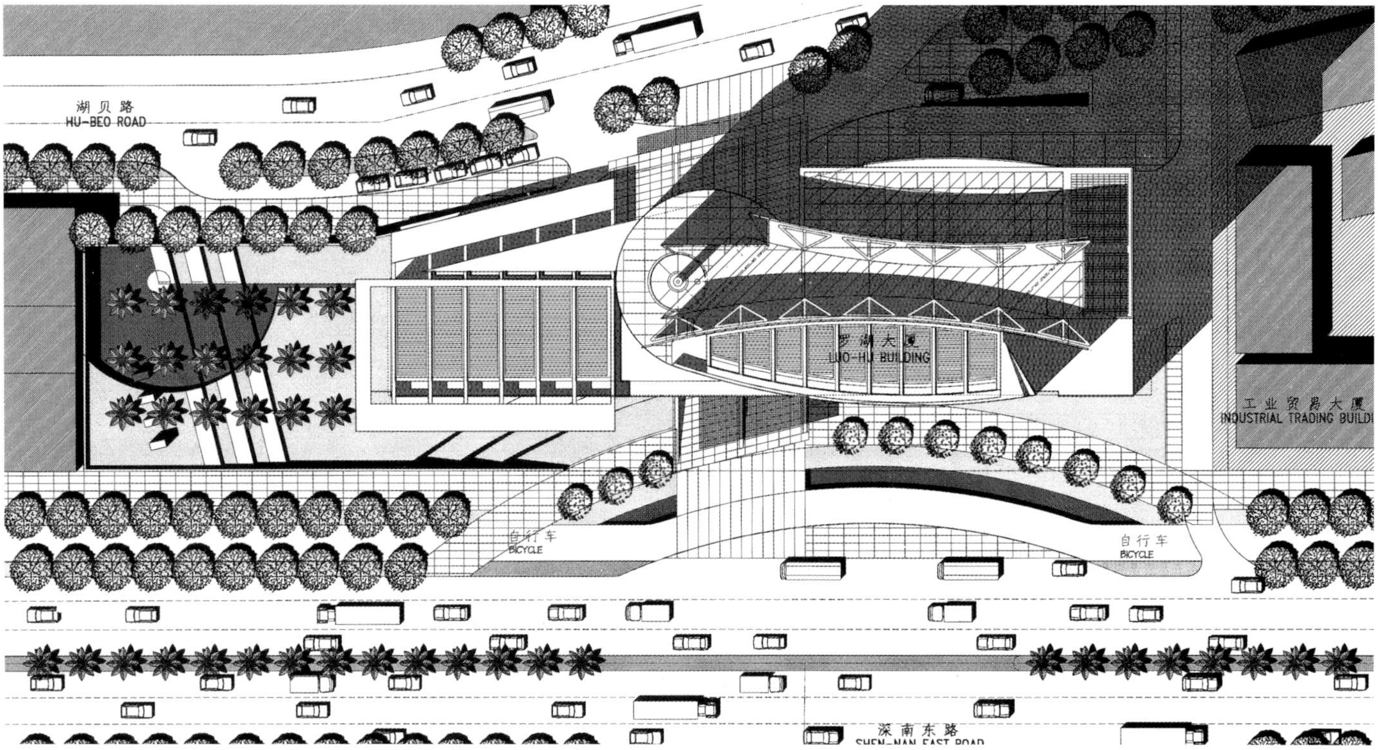

总平面图 Site plan

模型 Model

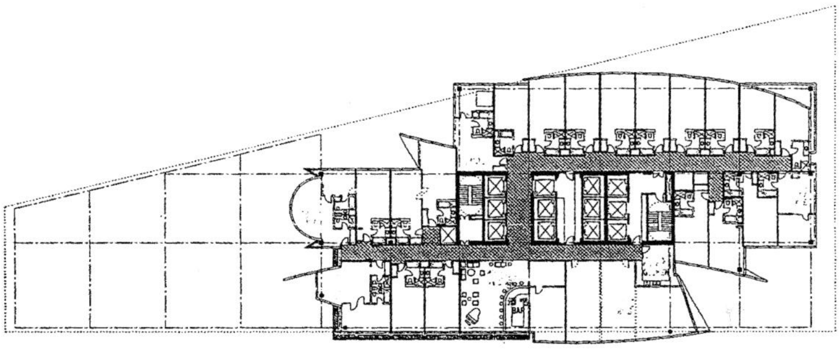

10层平面 10th floor plan

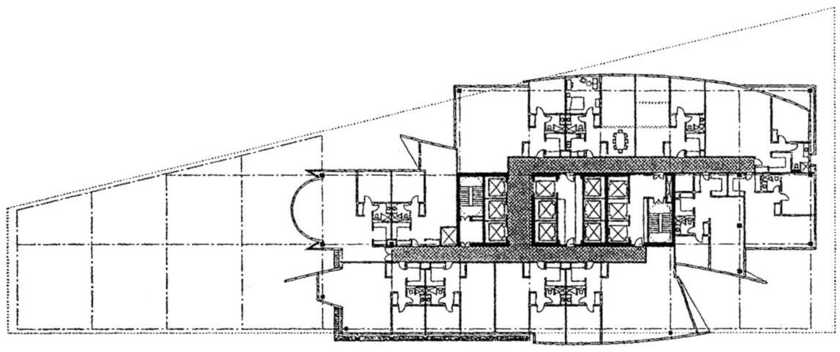

24层平面 24th floor plan

构思草图 Sketch

屋顶四季厅 Sky pavillion

模型 Model

长春太阳城

太阳城包括一座五星级酒店、两座办公建筑和一个零售中心，建筑围绕一个四季内庭布置。与长春的严冬鲜明对比的是其中的四季庭园，它作为一个宜人的气候调节中心，将整个建筑群结合在一起。冬天它将吸引购物者前来享受这里的娱乐设施和常年如一的热带花园。酒店共30层，557间客房，中庭自然采光，平面布置使每间客房都获得城市景观。两栋18层的办公塔楼内还包括市场、餐厅、零售、办公、健身、展览、会议和宴会等功能。

Sun Commercial City, Changchun

This proposed development is a mixed-use complex which consists of an enclosed winter garden surrounded by a five-star hotel, two office buildings, and a retail center. Unlike anything else in the frigid climate of Changchun, the interior winter garden will become the central thematic space unifying the project. During the winter, the space will attract shoppers and rejuvenate them in the entertainment facility and lavish, year-round tropical garden. The 30-story, 557-room hotel, with its natural light and foliage-filled atrium, has been positioned so guest rooms will be afforded views of the city. The two 18-story office towers contain a marketplace, restaurants, a health club, and retail, office, exhibit, meeting, and ballroom spaces.

中庭 Atrium

模型 Model

深圳蛇口港大厦

大厦位于伸入珠江口的蛇口半岛上，是深圳及华南地区重要的交通和商业枢纽。该工程将用于商业、办公、以及各类公共汽车、出租车、轻轨火车及其它交通方式的停靠站。总建筑面积79000平方米。

4层的交通和零售空间联系着该地区的轮渡与公共汽车系统，并与40层的办公楼相衔接。位于其中第二层的步行道可以到达码头及规划中的轻轨站。塔楼船形的平面和帆形的幕墙反映出中国历史上航海城市的现代风貌。塔楼外立面运用了三种类型的玻璃材料，其外形使人联想到传统中国帆船的风帆，夜间使用激光照明技术刻画出建筑的轮廓。建成之后，它将成为城市天际线中引人注目的一部分，并将是首先映入到达港湾的旅客眼帘的标志性建筑。（合作：深圳大学建筑设计院）

Shekou Harbor Building, Shenzhen

Set on a peninsula jutting into the Pearl River basin, the complex will be important transit and commercial hub for the city of Shenzhen and southern China. The project will be devoted to commercial, office, and parking, along with bus, taxi, light rail, and other vehicular arrival and departure facilities, with a total floor area of 79,000 square meters.

Connected to the 40-story office tower with its rooftop club/restaurant will be a four-level transit and retail structure linked to the area's system of ferries, buses, and cars. Second-level pedestrian walkways will provide access to the ferry and planned light-rail terminals. The tower's boat-shaped plan and sail-like curtain wall provide a modernist reflection of China's ancient seafaring history. Clad in three types of glass, the curtain wall of the tower will of be reminiscent of the sails of a Chinese junk, while night lighting using laser technology will define the building's shape, which will be a striking landmark on the city's skyline visible for miles from land and sea, day and night. The client believes that the "image" tower will be the first thing visitors see as they enter the harbor, making it a symbolic "second eye to China." (Co-designer: Shenzhen University Institute of Architectural Design)

模型 Model

深圳国际交易广场

这项综合性工程是一个国际证券交易中心，包括相互独立的有价证券、商品、资产和地产交易中心。另外还设有一座325间客房的酒店、高级公寓、一个大型的零售商场、娱乐中心及两座办公塔楼，总面积195100平方米。

方案在交易中心和商业区之间创造出一个独特的园林式城市空间。交易广场与城市公共绿地相平行，北接市政中心，南连各商业机构。以玻璃和钢结构建造的舒展的屋顶天幕结构创造出一个生动而富有活力的城市广场。

交易中心的设计运用了中国传统的风水原理，将建筑的形式、材料和朝向与环境和谐地联系起来。风水概念的中心是五行学说，要求结构服从环境规律。在该设计中，通过在"土"型的基地上建筑弧形的"金"状结构，以象征财富和巨大的商业成功，同时也暗示激烈的竞争。交易中心在完美地结合了风水元素的同时，还以内在的方式隐喻了中国的传统钱币。基地上的其它建筑运用了不对称曲面和玻璃面的流动线条以成"水"意，象征永久性的商业成功。

Shenzhen International Exchange Plaza

This 195,100 square meters mixed-use project incorporates a world class stock exchange facility that includes separate securities, commodities, assets, and real estate exchange centers. Other elements include a 325-room hotel, luxury residential apartments, a large scale retail and entertainment center, and two office towers.

The design creates a signature landscaped urban space between the Transaction Center and commercial areas that unifies the components of the project. Aligned parallel to the civic green space, the Exchange Plaza links the governmental complex to the north with the financial institutions to the south. A soaring roof canopy,

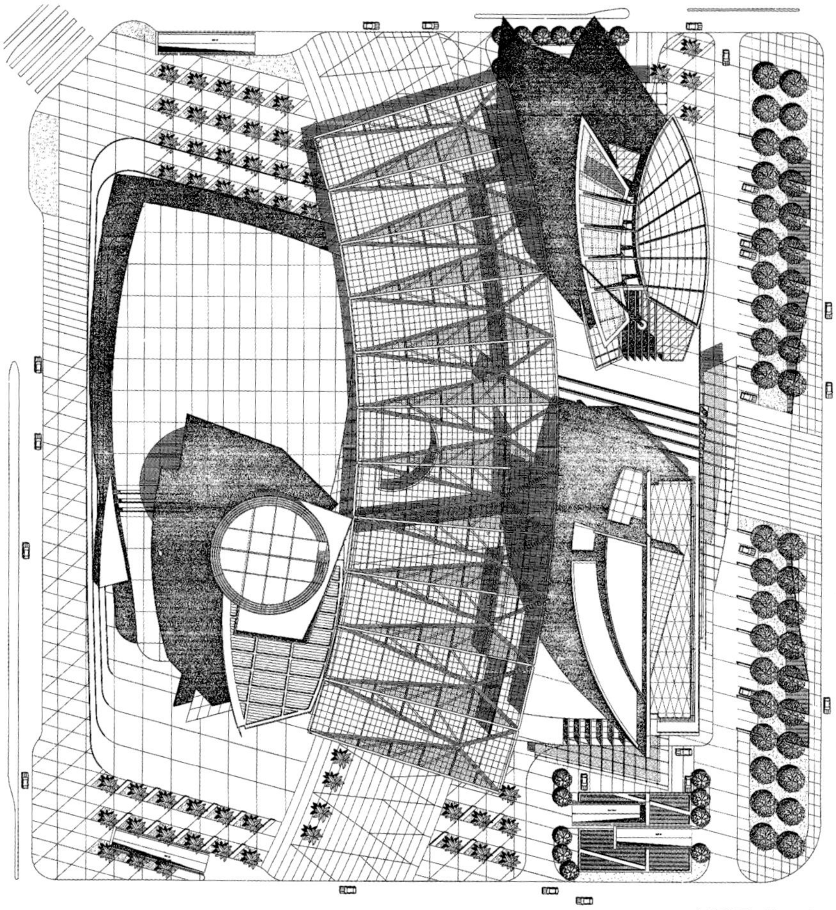

总平面 Site plan

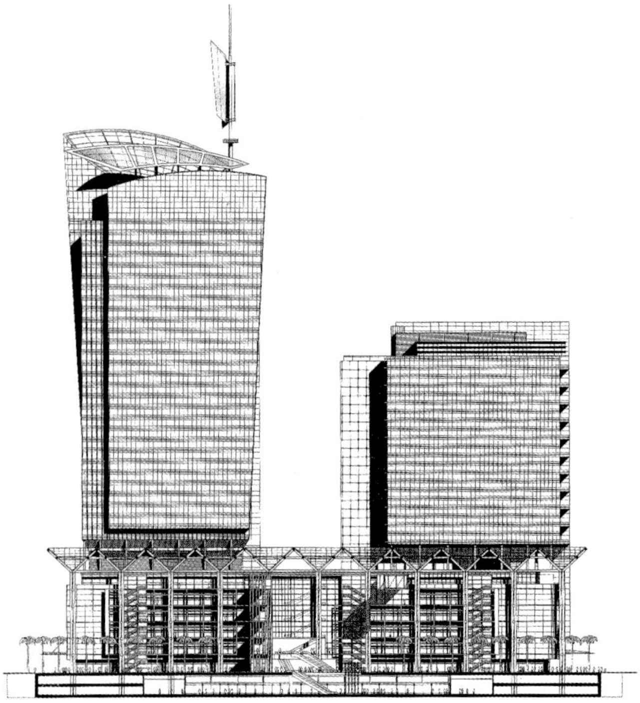

东向剖面 Section looking east

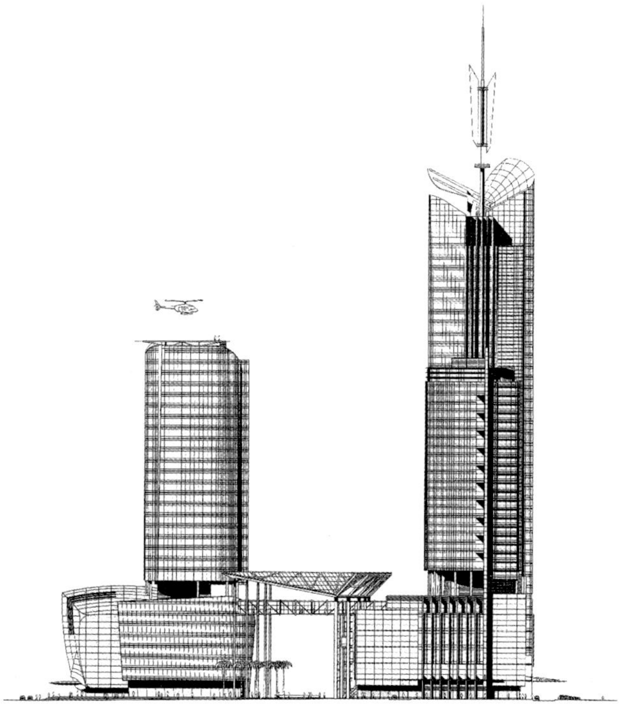

南立面 South elevation

in fritted glass and steel, shields the plaza and provides a lively public forum.

Design of the Transaction Center is based on the application geomancy in Chinese design, known as . feng shui, which relates building forms, materials and orientation to their environments in harmonious ways. Central to feng shui theory is the concept of the Five Elements which orders structures according to their environments. In this case, elements in a generative sequence are utilized- an "Earth" type of site produces a curved "Metal" shape structure - a situation representative of wealth and great financial success as well as connoting aggressive competition. The stock exchange is therefore ideally suited to this element as its attributes are also suggestive of traditional Chinese currency. The other buildings on the site use asymmetric curves and flowing lines rendered in glass. This places them as a "Water" element favorably located in sequence after "Metal", thus assuring their continued economic success.

广场街 Space between the Center and commercial areas

模型局部 Model view from south

模型 Model

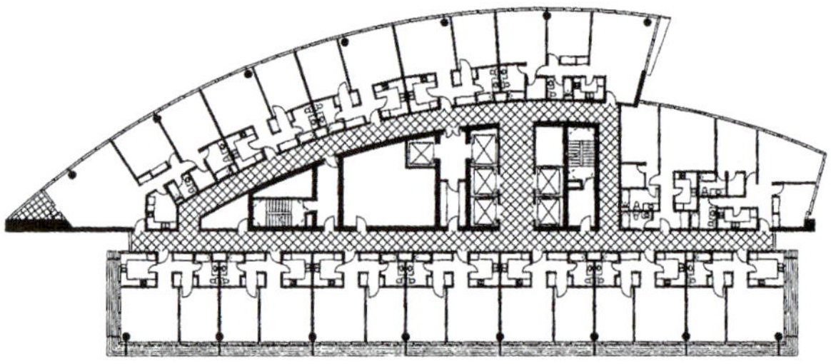

公寓层平面 Apartment floor plan

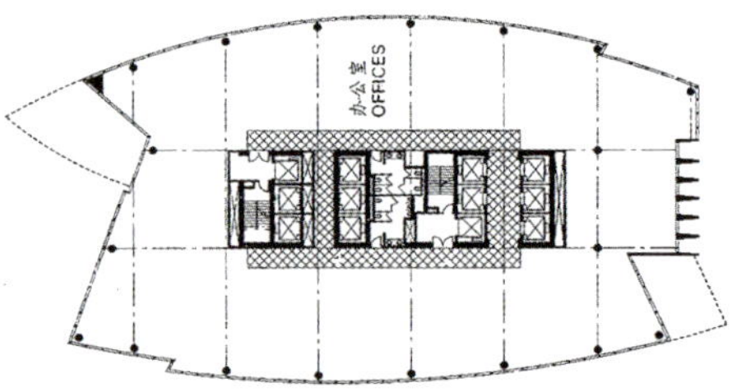

办公层平面 Office floor plan

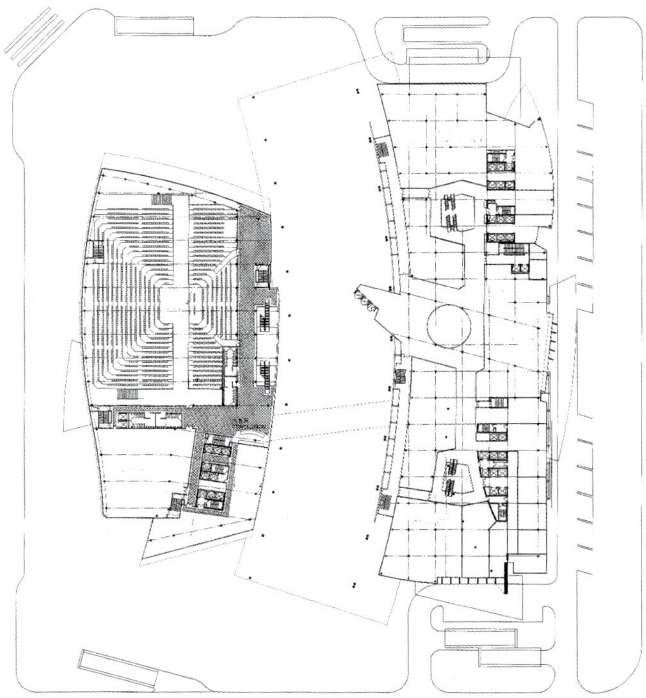

四层平面 Fourth floor plan

模型 Model

上海金辉广场

广场为一个111483平方米的综合性项目，包括金辉集团32层的办公楼和一座40层的金融大厦，大厦内还设有酒店和由观光电梯到达的屋顶餐厅。联系两座塔楼的裙房部分包括了零售及娱乐功能，另有健身俱乐部、泳池、银行营业厅、餐厅和停车场等设施。大厦内部采用一个30层高的曲形中庭，其顶部为玻璃面的观光平台和屋顶餐厅。巨大的中庭内将成为富有动感的公共空间，并以植物及喷泉装点。

金辉广场的设计结合了各具特征的两座塔楼。设计的构思来自古代中国的道家哲学原理，寻求将对立的双方组成运动的统一体。阴阳两极为道家学说的基本元素，两者缺一不可。金融大厦形体居高而棱角分明，是其中的"阳"者。金辉大厦光滑而富有曲线，是其中的"阴"者，其感性而不规则的线条与金融大厦的粗犷形成补充和对比。

Shanghai Jin Hui Plaze

This mixed-use development includes office, hotel, commercial and parking space, it combines a 32- story office building for the Jin Hui Corporation with a 40-story Finance Tower that includes hotel suites and a rooftop restaurant served by external glass elevators. Its total floor area is 111,483 square meters. The podium that links both towers contains retail and entertainment functions, a health club and pool, a banking hall, restaurants and parking. The Jin Hui building incorporates a dramatic 30-story, curved atrium in its design capped off by a glazed rooftop conservatory and restaurant. The grand atrium includes lively public spaces with plantings and fountains.

The design concept for Jin Hui Plaza integrates the two towers, each requiring an individual architectural identity, into a cohesive design. The concept is based upon the ancient Chinese philosophy of Tao, which seeks to unite opposing forces into a fluctuating harmony. The patterns of Tao are evident in the "yin" and the "yang" -a fusion of complementary opposites - light and dark, male and female -where one cannot exist without the other. The Finance Tower is thus given a taller, more angular and aggressive "yang" profile. The Jin Hui Building is treated as a sleek, curvilinear "yin" expression. Its irregular sensuous lines are an ideal complement to the edginess of the Finance Tower.

模型 Model

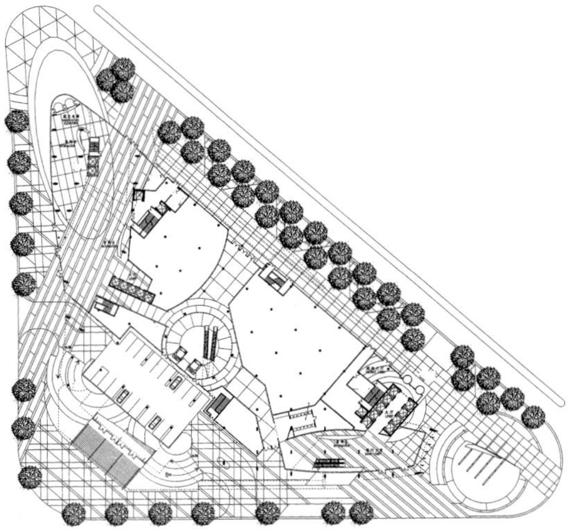

首层平面 Ground floor plan

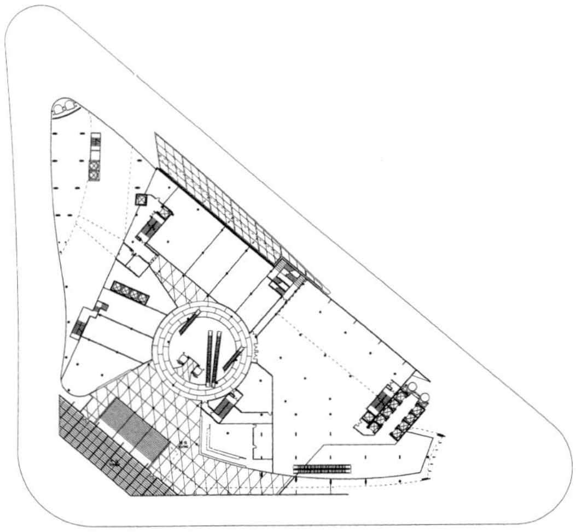

二层平面 Second floor plan

局部 Part view

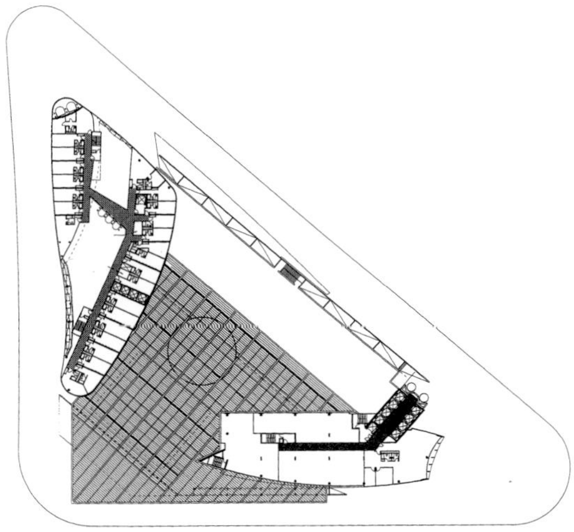

七层平面 Seventh floor plan

外观局部 Exterior wall detail

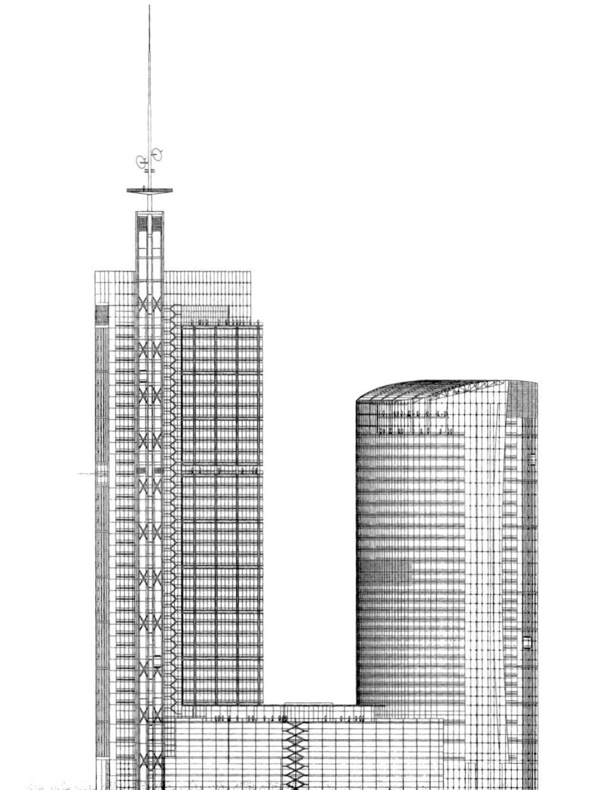
北立面 North elevation

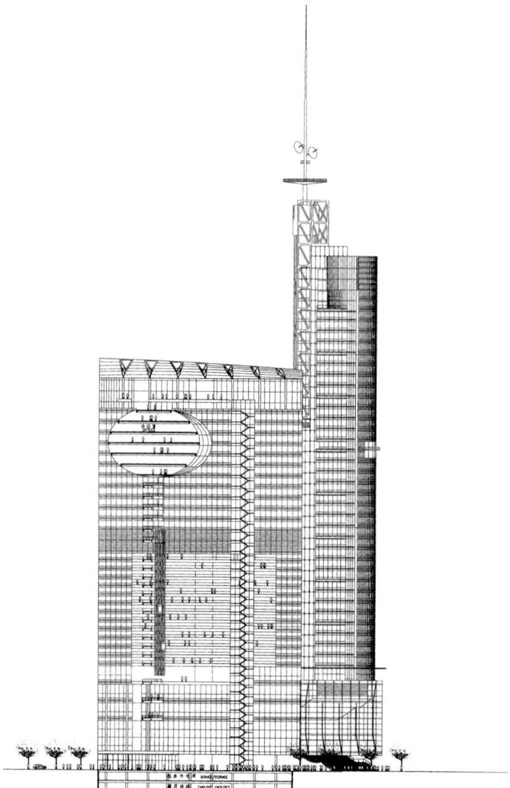
东向剖面 Section looking east

模型 Model

模型 Model, view from north

NBBJ 建筑设计公司
NBBJ ARCHITECTURE DESIGN PLANNING

成立于 1943 年的 NBBJ 建筑设计公司在全球建筑业中扮演着重要的角色，它已成为全球第五以及全美第二大建筑设计事务所，设计项目遍布北美、远东、欧洲及南美各地，涵盖了几乎所有的建筑类型。

NBBJ 正在成为突出的建筑艺术的形式创造者。像这样规模和范围的事务所，常常由于运作机制而牺牲了设计的优秀品质，而另外的一些事务所则以“标签”式风格而著称，总是实现单一建筑师的想法，每个项目都以类似的面目出现。

与此相反，NBBJ 倡导的是全体协同的设计，经源自并服务于人性文化的地方特点——以面向场所的设计表达文脉的复杂。没有单一的特点可以标示出NBBJ的设计，也没有单纯的学院理论作为驱动，地方主义的形式才是其设计基础。面对不同的业主和项目以及不同的场所和地点，甚至个性各异的公司职员，发现及创造地方主义形式的过程中，寻求共同基础的设计反而是 NBBJ 所面对最富挑战性的任务。

56 年来，NBBJ 共获得超过 300 项国际国内奖项。公司在美国洛杉矶、纽约、旧金山等 5 个城市设有国内公司，并在挪威奥斯陆、中国台北及日本东京设有国际业务公司。

NBBJ is a major player in the global business of architecture. Founded in 1943, NBBJ is today the fifth largest architecture firm in the world-the second largest in the US -with projects throughout North America, the Far East, Europe, and South America. There are few, if any, building types it has not designed.

It is also well on its way to being a significant shape giver to the art of architecture. In firms of NBBJ's size and reach, design excellence is often sacrificed to the care and feeding of the organizational machine. Others are known for a signature style, issuing in sketch form from the imagination of a single designer and identifiable in cvcry project.

NBBJ has instead embraced a firm-wide allegiance design that emerges from and is created for the people, culture, and ethos of a particular place-design for "context" in its greatest complexity and sophistication. No single, underlying design characteristic marks NBBJ's projects as the work one hand, nor are they driven solely by academic theory. Rather, the firm has adopted a form of regionalism as the common denominator. Given the variety of its projects and clients, of the locations in which it works, even of its own partners and staff, discovering and giving form to that concept presents NBBJ with its most challenging task: the design of common ground.

NBBJ is the recipient of more than 300 national and international design awards. The services they offered include architectural design, planning and urban design, interior design and space planning, graphic and environmental design, and economics and financial feasibility study.

上海复兴大厦

位于南外滩和豫园的交汇处，中山路和复兴路的交叉路口，大厦成为新旧城市中心的分水岭。两座塔楼采用单一的弧线构成，面对基地的主要角落，东塔楼面向黄浦江，外形规整，继承附近外滩中心的建筑传统。5至8层高的裙楼采用统一的建筑手法，使这一102000平方米的综合大厦与周围环境统一协调。塔楼通过步行天桥跨越中山路，将建筑与沿江环境连为整体。

Fuxing Mansion, Shanghai

Standing at the important intersection of Zhongshan and Fuxing roads, the connecting point between the developing South Bund District and Yuyuan Gardens, this mixed-use complex serves as a defining architectural nexus between the old and new centers of the city.

The two towers collaborate in a single curving composition addressing the main corner of the site. The eastern tower presents to the Huangpu River a formalized frontal posture honoring the architectural traditions of the adjacent historic Central Bund. A podium moving from five to eight levels provides the 102,000 square meters office and retail complex with its unifying element, and anchors it at street level to the neighborhood, while the towers rise to pedestrian bridges linking public open spaces and crossing Zhongshan Road to Huangpu River.

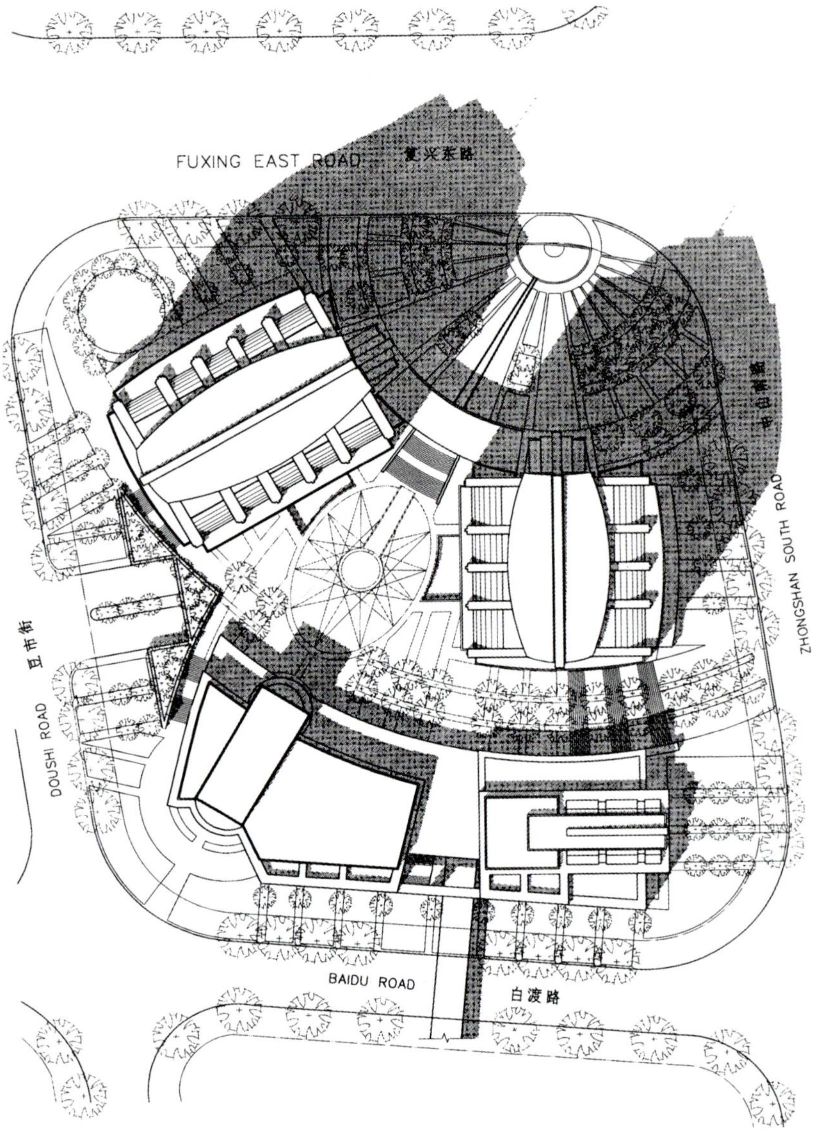

总平面 Site plan

模型鸟瞰 Overall view

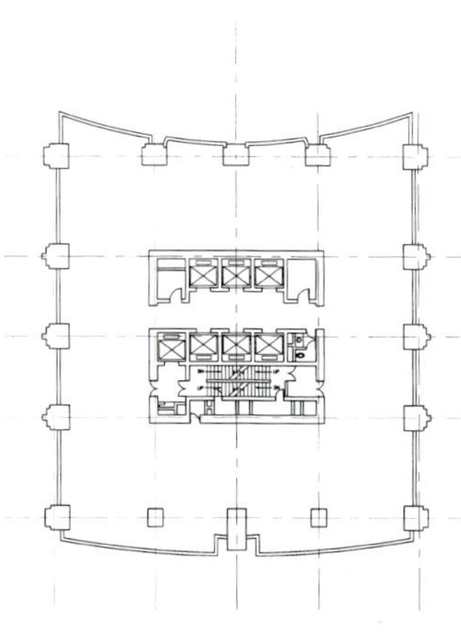
一号主楼平面 Tower 1 floor plans

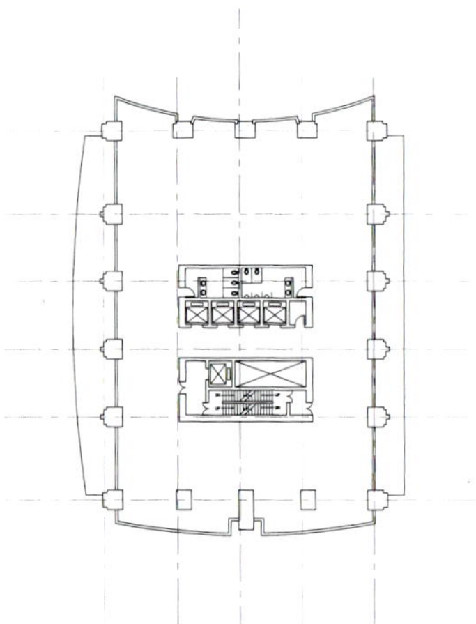
二号主楼平面 Tower 2 floor plans

模型 General view

上海美国学校

学校提供西方认可的幼儿园至中学的教育，以英语或其它语言为主要语言进行教学。方案试图创造一个外国学生满意的受教育与成长的场所，同时又具有的中国特色。

设计采用适合中国和校园教育特点的现代表达方式，而不是因袭传统的中国建筑形式，从中国传统园林设计原则和观念中吸取灵感。使学生的学习从教室延伸至整个校园，在每一步学习过程中，通过一种柔和的方式让学生学习和了解其周围的世界。为了兼具学者、诗人及画家的气质，校园设计试图追求儒家对秩序的钟情及道家对自然的热爱之间的平衡。

Shanghai American School

The Shanghai American School offers western accredited education from kindergarten through high school to students with English as either primary or secondary language. The desire for a campus that conforms to western students of education and construction while capturing the unique qualities of China deeply influenced the design.

Rather than copying traditional Chinese architectural forms, the design establishes a modern expression appropriate to China and the educational nature of the campus. Inspired by the principles and philosophy of Chinese garden design, the Shanghai American School extends learning beyond the classroom to encompass the entire physical setting of the campus. At each step, one is invited in a gentle way to learn something about the world around them. Embracing the qualities of scholar, poet, and painter, the campus balances the Confucian love of order with the Taoist love of nature in a descriptive comparison of virtues.

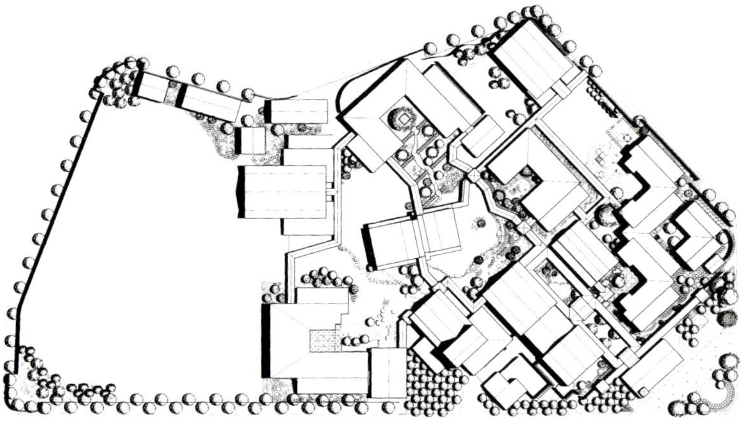

总平面 Site plan

鸟瞰 Aerial view

庭院局部 Courtyard view from corrider

庭院局部 Courtyard view

庭院局部 Courtyard view

北京中国远洋运输公司新总部大楼

将传统的中国建筑体量同远洋货轮的蜿蜒曲线相结合，本设计为1994年远洋公司新总部大楼的国际竞赛中的获奖方案。作为国际运输业中的一个主要竞争者，中国远洋运输公司要求它的新总部大楼既要反映其地处首都的特殊性，又要反映公司的全球业务所要求的现代性和对未来发展的抱负。设计既尊崇中国的传统又反映海洋贸易的特征，以一种明显现代的方式表达了中国远洋运输公司对未来的远大理想。

China Ocean Shipping Company, Beijing

Combining historical Chinese massing with the sinuous lines of ocean freighters, This design won an international competition in 1994 for Cosco's new headquarters. As a major competitor in international shipping, Cosco asked that its new facility reflect the sensibilities of its central Beijing location yet announce its global vision and role with a building embodying both modernity and aspiration for the future.
The result is a headquarters building that honors Chinese precedents and recalls maritime commerce, incorporating these influences in a distinctly modern statement that expresses Cosco's bold vision of its future.

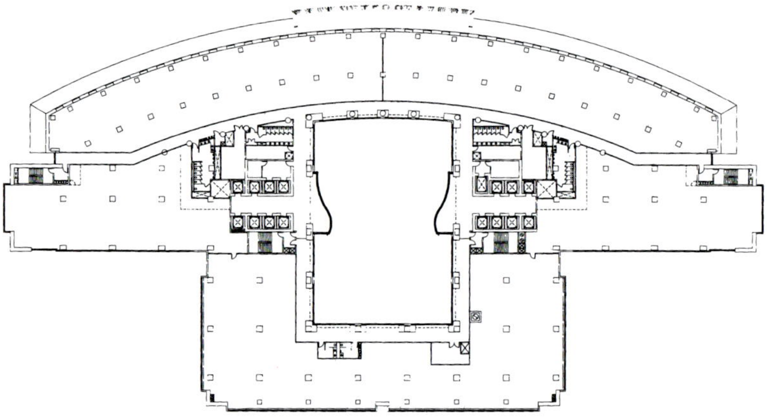

标准层平面 Typical floor plan

透视图 Perspective view

日建设计
NIKKEN SEKKEI

日建设计目前是日本最大、最资深的建筑、结构和规划设计事务所。其前身是1900年创立的日本最大的商业集团之一，其中的建筑设计与营建分部经过一个世纪发展到目前的规模。目前的组织框架形成于1950年，从此，事务所不断地扩大规模、获得经验、赢得业内声望，除国内项目外，日建在全世界近50个国家有设计项目。以其创新的设计思想、前所未有的建筑新技术研究和土木工程技术以及城市设计方法获得无数个设计与工程技术奖。与其科研与发展策略相一致的是，日建集团还积极地投人未来预测及实用研究的开发，其研究领域广至城市文化，细至环境工程，成就走在专业同行的最前列。

公司以位于东京、大阪和名古屋三地的事务所为主要基地展开业务。其附属公司包容了一系列设计、规划和土建工程领域，其多样化的发展还表现在日建集团众多科研机构，其中包括日建城市文化研究院与日建地质技术研究院等。除国内工程外，日建还在海外包括新加坡，中国上海、台北，以及汉城、吉隆坡等地设有事务所。在本土以外的工程当中，日建一贯积极寻求与当地机构与事务的合作，形成遍布世界的业务网络，以提高服务质量。为保持相对于外部机构或实业的绝对独立地位，集团的资产属本集团内永久性员工所有。因此日建作为顾问机构只对自己的业主负责，而不会受任何外来承包商与制造商的压力影响。

日建作为综合性多专业的设计机构闻名于世。绝大部分工程的全部各项设计都可以在事务所内完成，高质高效并极为细致。在日建超过1600名永久性专业人士与职员当中，规划师、建筑师、工程师及其它专家如文本专家、概预算专家、电脑专家、环境评估专家与建筑承包经理等占1300名。室内设计人员归属于日建空间设计有限公司，是日建集团子公司之一，必要时他们与日建集团密切合作。多专业技术人员保证了负责工程不同设计阶段的人员之间的交流与合作，实现高效而开明的设计实践。

Nikken Sekkei has evolved into the largest and most prestigious practice of consulting architects, engineers, and planners in Japan from their modest origin in 1900 as the building design and construction supervision section of one of the nation's largest historic business conglomerates, to the present day. Since being organized into its current corporate structure in 1950, the firm has grown in size, in experience, and in professional reputation. In addition to its domestic work, Nikken Sekkei has carried out projects in nearly 50 countries. It has won numerous design and engineering awards for its innovative ideas and often ground-breaking research into new architectural techniques, civil engineering solutions, and urban design methods. Consistent with its interest in research and development, the Nikken Sekkei business group is enthusiastically engaged in futures forecasting and applied research in fields as broad as urban culture and as specialized as environmental engineering - of which it is a pioneer among its professional peers.

Operating from three principal Japan-based offices - Tokyo, Osaka, and Nagoya - Nikken Sekkei's developed diversification is evidenced by an array of affiliate companies encompassing a wide variety of design, planning, and engineering disciplines, and technical institutes such as the Nikken Sekkei Urbicultural Institute (NUI) and the Nikken Sekkei Nakase Geotechnical Institute (NNGI). In addition to its domestic operations, Nikken Sekkei currently maintains an overseas subsidiary in Singapore and offices in Shanghai, Taipei, Seoul, Kuala Lumpur. In each of its ventures outside of Japan, Nikken Sekkei has actively sought collaboration with local firms, and woven a network of consultants around the globe to increase its responsiveness to its clients. In order to maintain absolute independence from any outside organization or industrial entity, all capital shares of Nikken Sekkei are owned by its permanent staff. Therefore as a consultant, it pays loyalty to its clients only, and is free from any outside influence or pressure of contractors and manufacturers.

Nikken Sekkei is best known as an integrated, multi-disciplinary organization capable of undertaking most projects in-house, efficiently and effectively, and with considerable attention to detail. Of Nikken Sekkei's over 1,600 permanent professional and support personnel, 1,300 are planners, architects, engineers, and other experts such as specification writers, cost controllers, computer experts, environmental impact assessors, and construction contract administrators. Interior planners and designers who belong to Nikken Space Design Ltd., one of their affiliate companies, work together with the staff of Nikken Sekkei as necessary. Inclusion of a variety of specialists ensures close communication among people in charge of various phases of a project and contributes immeasurably to an efficient and enlightened design process.

敦煌石窟文物研究保护展览中心

中心是日本政府无偿援助的项目，是为防止举世文明的世界文化遗产——敦煌莫高窟千佛洞日趋严重的龟裂、崩坏、壁画及雕像的退色、磨损与剥落等自然性破坏的进一步加剧而建设的。它既是一个对石窟及壁画等文物进行摄像保存、记录研究、资产分类等活动的科研设施，同时又是一个以展示8个具有历史代表意义的石窟实物模型、出土文物、临摹壁画，使一般游客能直观地理解敦煌艺术的展览中心。

建筑利用其基地的丘陵这一特殊地形，把大部分的展览中心设于地下，从而保存了莫高窟1700多年的历史环境和自然景观。建筑中采用了敦煌黄土烧成的粘土砖外墙，展示空间采用自然采光、气化潜热辅冷、楼板供暖等空调系统，敦煌的地域特征有机地融入了现代建筑空间。

The Dunhuang Caves Relics Research and Protection Exhibition Center

This center, donated by the Japanese Government, is built for the purpose of preventing the well known world cultural heritage - the Mo Kao Grotto at Dunhuang - against the more and more serious natural destruction like cracking, collapsing, and fading, wearing and peeling off of the frescoes and sculptures. The primary function of the project is a kind of scientific research facility including photographing to preserve, recording to research and studying the materials to sort the relics. It is also an exhibition center, displaying eight representative historic cave models, copies of frescoes as well as the unearthed relics, which makes visitors directly perceive the art of Dunhuang.

The designer makes full use of the site of a chain of undulating hills, laying the main part of the exhibition center under the ground level so as to keep the more than 1700-year old historical environment and natural landscape of the Mo Kao Grotto. The local brick exterior walls were applied. The exhibition area uses a natural lighting and traditional air-conditioning system, dissolving these Dunhuang regional features into the modern space of architecture.

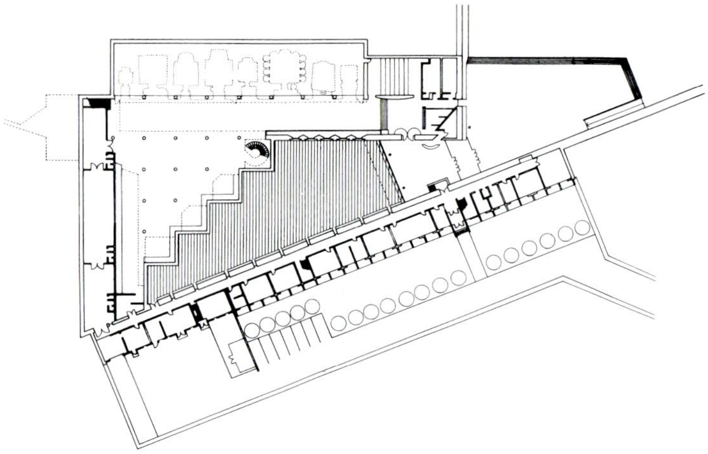

首层平面 First floor plan

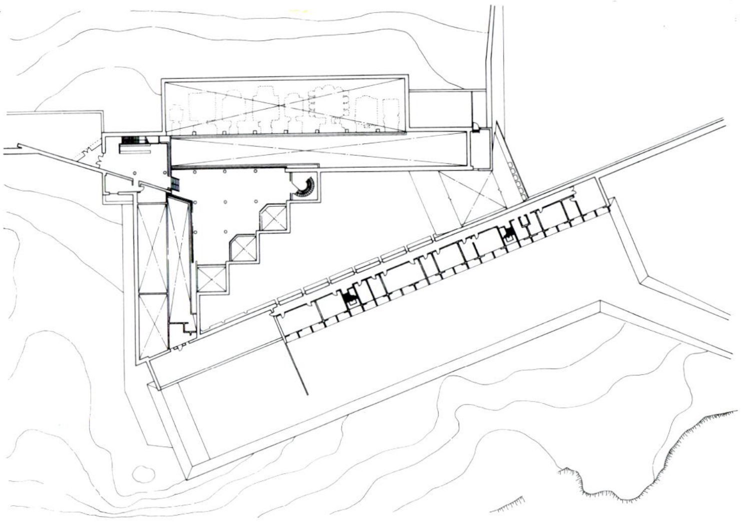

二层平面 Second floor plan

效果图 Perspective view

外观 Exterior view

入口 Entrance

上海信息枢纽大楼

大楼作为信息港工程的标志，被上海市政府指定为重大工程之一，是一座集展示、通信、智能办公、卫星通讯等多项功能的综合体。建筑沿百米宽的主要城市干道，位于陆家嘴金融开发区的东侧入口处。因此如何考虑大楼的特殊功能要求，并反映其形象特征，是本设计的一个重要课题。

设计根据基本功能要求，采用双向筒体的构成形式。中央的空间保持了与各项功能相适应的自由灵活特性，同时把功能、结构、空间特性直接反映于建筑的外部形象，形成建筑主要的视觉特征。大构架的空间结构的利用、使建筑的接地部分缩小至最小限度、从而实现了建筑底部宽43米高32米的大型空透无柱的共享空间。这不仅突出了建筑空间的超时空的象征意义、更为超高层林立的都市地面环境提供了一个宽敞开放的公共空间。

Shanghai Information Center

Construction started in 1996, the information center building was designated as one of the most important projects by the municipal government. As a prominent project for the future information port, the center consists of exhibition, telecommunication, and intellectualized office space and satellite communication facilities. The location is at the east gate of the Lujiazuo financial development zone along the 100-meter wide boulevard---the central axis of the district, which makes it an important issue for the designers to endow the building with a proper image.

Based on the functional requirement, the building applied a two-way cylindrical form. This formal composition make it possible for the central space to keep its flexibility and adaptability to various uses, and at the same time, its functional, structural, and special characteristics was represented directly through the external figure. The use of a large span space-structure minimized the building's ground coverage, thus a 43 by 32 meters transparent atrium space was created in the podium with absolutely no column inside. This universal space not only creates a timeless image to the building, but also provides a generous open space to the public on ground level among the downtown high-rise jungle.

模型 Model

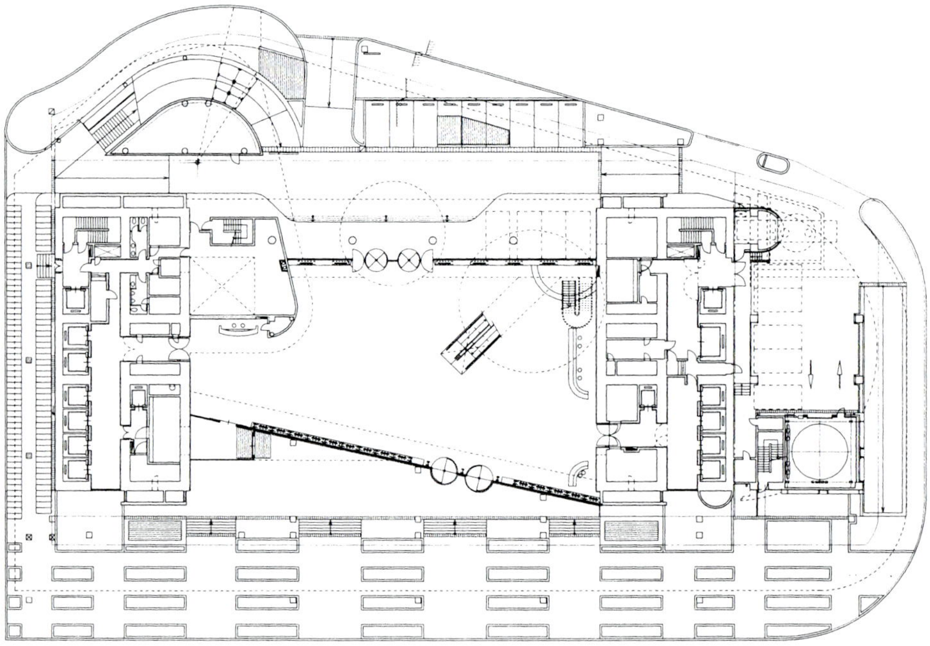

首层平面 First floor plan

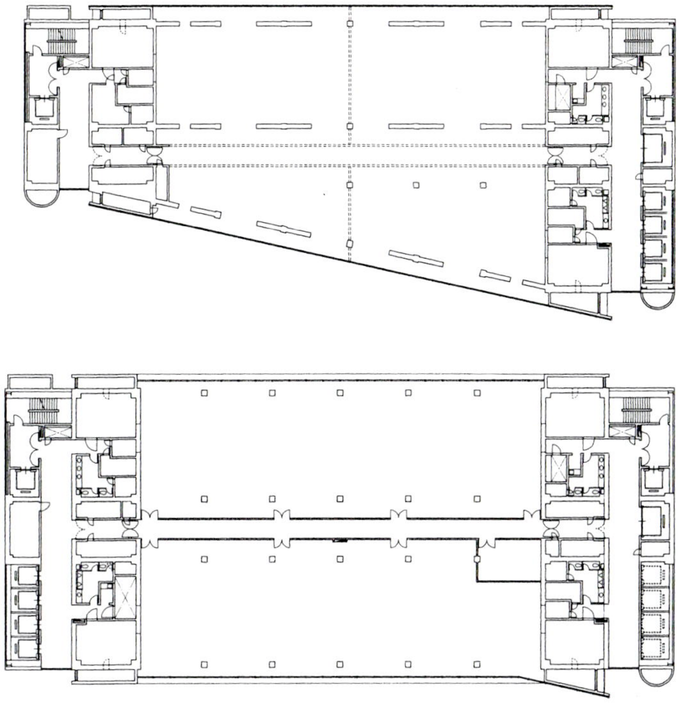

标准层平面 Typical floor plan

模型 Model

上海浦东国际金融大厦

大厦是以中国银行为主体的投资集团出资建造在上海浦东陆家嘴地区的综合性办公楼，总面积 110000 平方米，53 层。方案由国际设计竞赛选定的。

浦东陆家嘴地区是在创建亚洲国际金融中心为目标的方针指引下，作为上海发展的象征性地域，超高层大楼相继建设，使区域面貌日新月异。为使大厦成为该地区中最具有象征意义的建筑，设计在注重形态符合功能要求的基础上，体现了跨世纪的风貌。根据“天圆地方”——以正方体和圆形、直线和曲线相融汇的独特的形态创意，采用矩形办公楼和椭圆形宾馆（在实施阶段改为单元式办公室）共享同一主楼的方案。方案不仅新颖和美观，建筑形态更具有合理性和独创性。建筑师的想像力与结构、设备等工程技术取得完美的融和与统一。

Shanghai International Finance Center

With total floor are a of 110,000 square meters and 53 stories in height, international Finance Center is an office complex developed by an investment group led by Bank of China. The Scheme is an international competition-winning project located in the central business district of Lu Jia Zhui. The design endeavors to make this building a landmark of the city. Based on careful considerations of the building's functional requirements, the design adopted "the heaven and the earth" concept, using contrasting elements such as square and circular forms, straight and curved surfaces to create a building that combines rectangular offices with elliptical hotels in an unified volume. The project itself is an elegant unification of architectural creativity, functional efficiency and technological excellence.

模型 Model

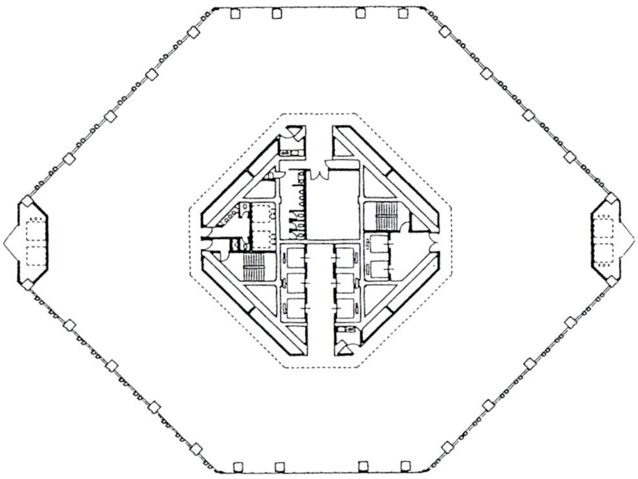

办公层平面 Office floor plan

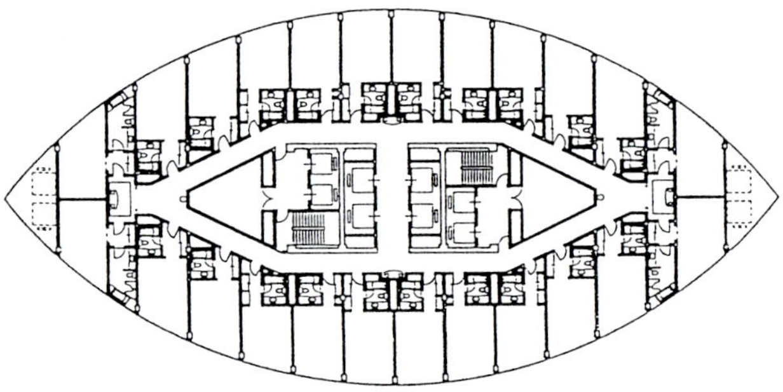

客房层平面 Hotel floor plan

浙江省国际金融大厦

大厦位于风景秀丽的杭州西湖东岸，无论在环湖风景线还是西湖东岸的城市轮廓中，都具有举足轻重的地位。在建筑的整体布局、形体和立面设计上结合杭州的历史、文化、环境进行了充分的斟酌。利用高层主楼底部的无柱骑楼空间，将外部广场空间和周围城市空间有机地衔接和统一起来。使各种流线明确、合理。在形体和立面设计上，利用横向带形窗和顶部檐口的处理减轻建筑的体量感，并与西湖亭台楼阁的建筑形式相呼应。

为使建筑成为具备国际金融业务所需的高度信息处理功能的智能大厦，在结构和设备设计中采取了适应将来发展的超前设计。方案力图因地制宜，利用中国当地的技术和材料体现现代建筑的精神，使其成为西子湖畔孕育出的标志之一。

Zhejiang International Finance Building

With a total area of 40,000 square meters, the building is situated at the east bank of the beautifully scenic West Lake. It plays an important part either in the scenery around the Lake or in the skyline along the east bank of the Lake. To get a better understanding of the project and its context, the designers fully examined the history, culture and environment of Hangzhou. The sotto portico without columns at the first floor of the main building is adopted to link the outer square areas with the surrounding urban space. The circulation is also carefully arranged. To balance the volume and match the architectural form of pavilions, terraces and towers in the area, transverse windows and a overhead protruding loft is used.

The current advanced methods are applied in designing its structure and equipment in order to meet the needs of the future development. In designing the building, the designer tries to follow and match the local environment, make use of the local techniques and materials to embody the contemporary designing spirit of architecture, making it a symbol emerging from the bank of the West Lake. The building is 95 meters in height with 20 stories above the ground level and 2 stories underground.

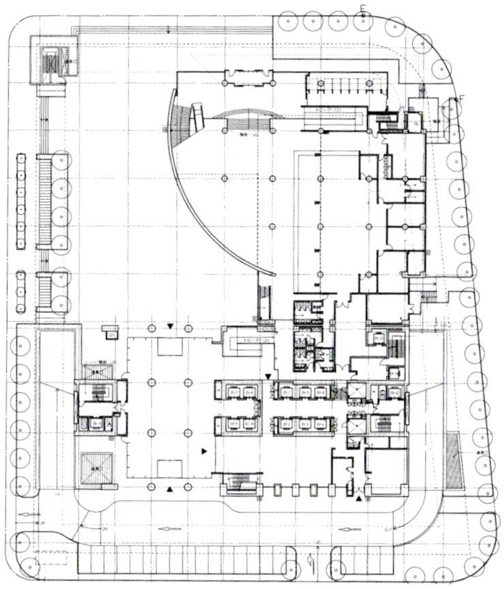

首层平面 First floor plan

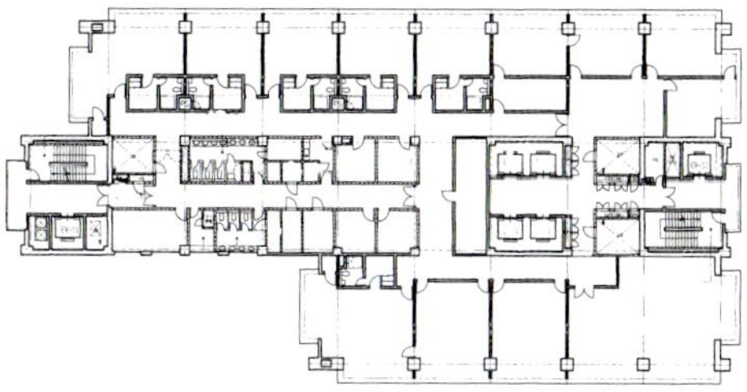

标准层平面 Typical floor plan

模型 Model

大连电视塔

世界著名的大型港口工业城市——大连以美丽的林荫街景及海洋风景而闻名。电视塔位于可纵览眺望大连市与海洋景色的山丘之上，总高190.5米。

设计在考虑作为传播信息媒体设施的电视塔这一重要功能的同时，着重反映、体现了其作为城市标志的特征，使其成为一处可一览大连景色的观光娱乐的名胜之地。

塔身平面为外径25米的12边形，塔体外周采用空间网架及纤细交错的结构形式，表现出轻快明确的外形特征。空间网架结构的采用，使建筑结构构件达到少类多量的工业化生产目的。简化了工程作业上的烦琐，并提高了工程效率和作业安全性，从而成功地创造出均一高质的塔体结构。

Dalian Television Tower

Dalian is a world famous coastal industrial city known for its beautiful tree-lined boulevards and fantastic sea-view. The site is on top of a hill overlooking the sea and downtown Dalian.

Except for the major considerations of the 190-meter high construction's function as the media-broadcasting center, the design also acknowledges its landmark quality in the city. Thus it is designed in a way that it can serve as a tourist attraction from where people can get panoramic views of the city.

Plan of the tower measures 25 meters by 12 meters. The exterior was supported by an interlacing slender skeletal structure to give the tower a light and elegant character. The use of space skeletal structure also reduced the number of a the types of constructional units, simplified the producing process, and thus secured efficiency and safety of the project.

远景 General view

近景 Detail

夜景 Night view

约翰·波特曼建筑师事务所
JOHN PORTMAN & ASSOCIATES

约翰·波特曼建筑师事务所是一家国际知名的建筑和结构设计公司，总部在美国乔治亚州的亚特兰大市。另外在中国上海和印度Mumbai设有分所。事务所共有65位专业人员，以其富有创意同时又切合业主和使用者需要的设计成就而获得国际声誉。

事务所于1953年成立，在酒店、办公、商业广场和多功能城市综合体的设计方面具有突出成就，他们的设计在世界范围内为振兴各地的城市作出了贡献。1967年事务所设计第一座酒店，其22层高的中庭为当代的酒店设计带来了全新的概念，这种独创性空间形式的推广，为室内设计带来了彻底的改革。建筑内部的开放空间一直是设计成功的关键因素，这些设计的宗旨就是面向建筑的使用者，将功能需要和美学要素紧密结合，创造出实用而激动人心的工程作品。

20多年以前，波特曼事务所开始国际工程设计业务，一开始是在欧洲，以后扩大到东南亚。在东南亚的第一个项目是1978年新加坡的摄政酒店（原名新加坡洲际酒店），此后不断在香港、马来西亚和印尼设计项目。波特曼在上海的工程从1980年上海中心的设计开始，这项工程的成功为其带来在马来西亚、印尼、越南和印度的一系列工程。波特曼事务所在国内和国际工程中寻求与当地的事务所合作，解决设计规范、条例和政府管理等方面的问题。同时对环境问题以及不同的文化对建筑的影响等都加以特别的关注。

通过与客户之间的密切合作，他们认识到为满足经营赢利的需要，造价与功能要求极为重要，波特曼事务所在无数工程中都实现了设计、节能和城市振兴等多方面的成功。

所获奖项包括：FIABCI杰出成就奖，美国建筑学会乔治亚分会亚特兰大最佳地产奖——办公建筑类，亚特兰大城市设计委员会城市设计优秀奖，美国建筑师学会创新设计银奖，美国建筑师学会创新酒店设计奖等等。

John Portman & Associates is an internationally recognized architectural and engineering firm headquartered in Atlanta, Georgia. Additional Portman offices are located in Shanghai, China and Mumbai, India. With a staff of more than 65 professionals, John Portman & Associates is recognized internationally for innovative, responsive design solutions that are effective for the client and the user.

Established in 1953, John Portman & Associates is best known for its expertise in designing hotels, offices, trade marts, and multi-purpose urban complexes that have revitalized cities around the world. Their first hotel, with its 22-story atrium, revolutionized contemporary hotel design in 1967. The popularity of this innovative use of space radically changed the design of interior spaces. Opening space within the built environment continues to be an important element in the success of the projects that are strongly oriented to the people who use them. Our design approach fully integrates practical requirements with the aesthetic qualities that create attractive, functional projects.

The international work of John Portman & Associates began over twenty years ago in Europe and expanded to Southeast Asia in 1978, first in Singapore with the design of The Regent Singapore (formerly the Pavilion intercontinental Singapore), then Hong Kong, Malaysia and Indonesia.

John Portman & Associates began work in Shanghai in 1980, leading to the design and development of Shanghai Centre. The success of that project led to a number of other design projects in Malaysia, Indonesia, Vietnam and India. John Portman & Associates is experienced in working with local architects, domestically and internationally, on projects with a wide range of codes, regulations and governing agencies. They are sensitive to environmental issues and the importance of local culture on the context of the architecture.

Through their close working relationship with companies that own, manage and develop the buildings designed by them, they recognize the importance of the life cycle costs and the functional requirements that must be met for profitable operations. John Portman & Associates has been recognized on numerous occasions for excellence in design, energy efficiency and urban revitalization. These awards include: FIAB Award of Distinction (1997); Best in Atlanta Real Estate Award-Office Category (1995); Award for Excellence in Design by the AIA Georgia (1994); Award for Excellence in Urban Design by Atlanta Urban Design Commission (1993); Building of the Year by Atlanta Building Owners & Managers Association (1991); Award of Excellence by Urban Land Institute (1985); AIA Silver Medal for Innovation Design (1981); AIA Medal for Innovative Hotel Design (1978) and etc.

上海中心

中心位于市中心的南京路一侧，是上海第一个最大的建筑综合体。三座塔楼戏剧般地兀立于8层裙房之上，包括一系列空前的豪华设施：472套豪华公寓、25000平方米一流的办公场所、3层商业广场、上海中心剧场、900平方米的商业品牌展示中庭及600套客房的豪华国际旅馆。

豪华公寓集中于两栋30层的塔楼内。每套公寓内设进口设备的西式厨房，独立控制的中央供热及空调系统，由美国南贝尔公司提供的电话系统。另外设有单独的水处理系统，水质标准超过世界卫生组织标准。为满足不同类型和规模使用者需求，25000平方米的办公空间划分成不同的规模和不同的类型，如独立走廊、独立阳台及多层办公空间。办公中心内所有区域均十分便捷、直达，6部电梯服务于每5层办公室，所有楼层直接采光且具有中庭或花园景观。围绕中庭组织空间，为公司提供了面对商业及文化中心的可能性。3层商业广场面对著名商业街——南京路，世界顶级零售商在由绿化、水景、小桥构成的明亮而优雅的商业氛围中展示其产品。另外，上海中心亦包括在中国唯一由外国人拥有和经营的剧场，丰富多样的娱乐形式使这一错层设置的1000座剧场成为上海最繁忙与优雅的艺术殿堂。

Shanghai Center

Located in the heart of the city on famous Nanjing Road, Shanghai Center is the first and largest multi-use complex in Shanghai. The building is comprised of three towers which rise dramatically from an 8-story podium. This vast complex offers superior standards with an unprecedented range of facilities-472 luxury apartments, 25,000 square meters of prime office space, an upscale tri-level retail plaza, the Shanghai Center Theater, a spectacular 900 square meter trademark exhibition atrium, and a 600-room deluxe international hotel.

The Center offers 472 luxury apartments in twin 30-story towers. Every apartment includes a western-style kitchen with imported appliances. Individually controlled central heating and air-conditioning, and state of the art phone service provided by BellSouth of the United States. The Center has its own on-site water treatment plant which cleanses local water beyond World Health Organization standards.

With over 25,000 square meters of prime office space in the heart of Shanghai's business community, Shanghai Center provides offices of various sizes which may be customized to accommodate all types and sizes of tenants. The Center's central location makes office space easily accessible to customers, clients, and staff. Architectural features include private balconies, private corridors, and connected floors.

All areas within the office center are easily accessible. There are six elevators serving five office floors. All floors are exposed to natural light and have either an outside, atrium, or garden view.

入口 Entrance view

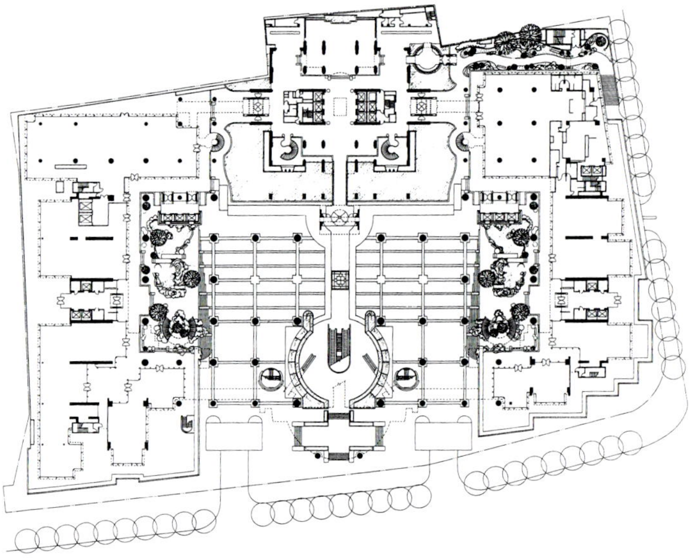

底层平面 Ground floor

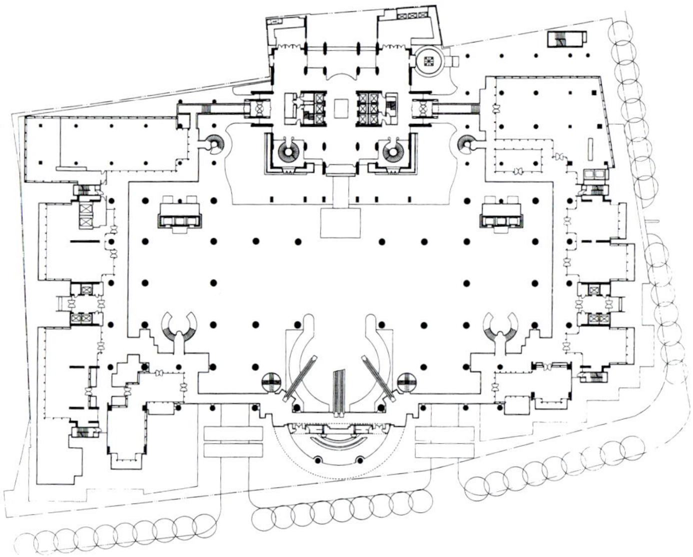

商业层平面 Retail floor

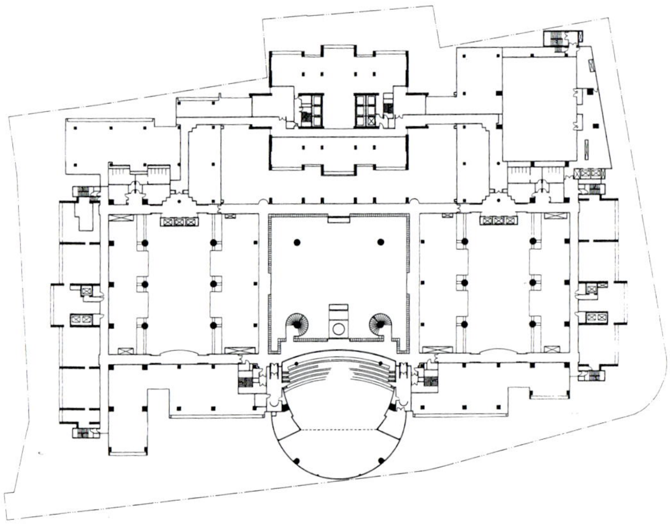

办公层平面 Office floor

Space surrounding the central atrium provides those companies needing exposure with frontage into the business and cultural center of the city.

The Plaza at Shanghai Center contains three levels of exclusive shops and services. Located on Nanjing Road, China's most famous shopping street, world-class retailers exhibit their products in a bright, elegant shopping environment graced with trees, waterfalls and bridges.

The Center also includes the only Western owned and managed theater in China. This split-level, 1000-seat theater has become Shanghai's busiest and most prestigious arts venue by hosting a variety of entertainments from off-Broadway shows and Grammy winning musical artists to the best in Chinese performing arts.

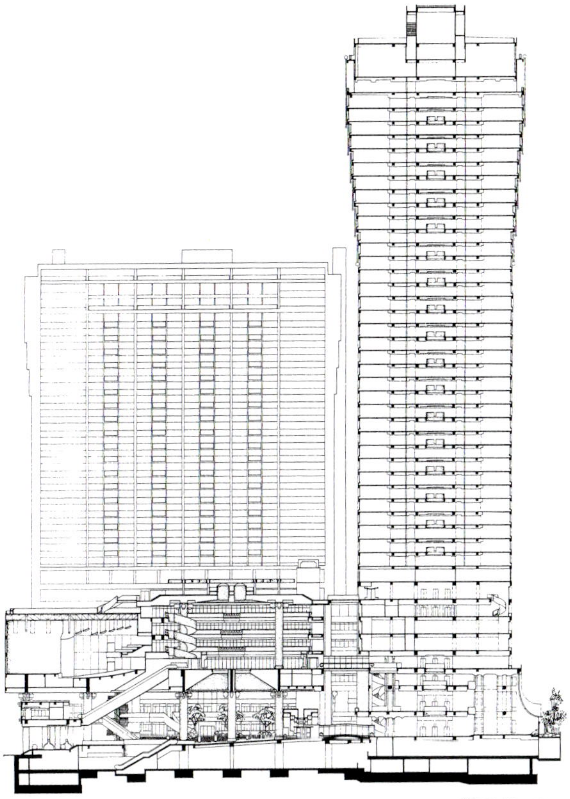

剖面 Section

外观 Overall view

上海大宇商务中心

中心位于上海西南的徐汇区，基地面积为35343平方米。基地的前方是新建成的徐镇路，西侧是一栋6层的公寓楼，北侧隔一条规划道路与一栋6层的公寓楼相望，而东侧则为正在兴建的发展中心的主入口。

420米高、92层的办公/宾馆塔楼是项目的主体结构，它赋予中心强烈的视觉效果。其便利的地理位置，独特惊人的外观以及智能大楼的先进技术将向商业人士展现出无穷的魅力。金属和玻璃墙面的建筑形体直截了当地按几何形式向空中伸展，线条的变化标志着建筑内部功能的划分。1～61层为办公部分，62层为一公共观光层把宾馆分隔开来，63～92层为宾馆。宾馆上方是一座引人注目的针塔，其顶端为一个从城市的任何一角落都能看到的锥形针塔尖。

塔楼平面为正方形。当建筑功能于观光层从办公楼转换成宾馆时，正方形的平面在此处减小，并作45度旋转，四角向内凹嵌成巨大的三角形。在92层再次进行类似变化，塔楼大幅度内缩形成针塔。针塔顶部，一块块磨光搪瓷玻璃形成四个大钻石的形状，围绕着41米高的塔尖。夜晚放射出璀灿光芒的钻石将使塔楼独树一帜地矗立于城市的上空。

塔楼东侧的大宇百货商场和塔楼西侧的一座34层高的公寓楼使塔楼与周围建筑之间尺度上的过渡显得柔和。设有餐厅和专卖店的7层商廊成为购物中心主体——百货大楼的补充。百货大楼独特新颖的正面朝向徐镇路，吸引着当地商业区和住宅区的购物者。商廊与百货商场相连并沿基地的北侧伸展，透明玻璃外墙的设计向周围和广场上的人们展示了商廊内的各种活动。大型步行广场在街面层贯穿整个商廊，花草树木、水池、和独特的干/湿喷泉使广场充满生机与活力，并为旅游者和居民提供了一个诱人的聚集场所。

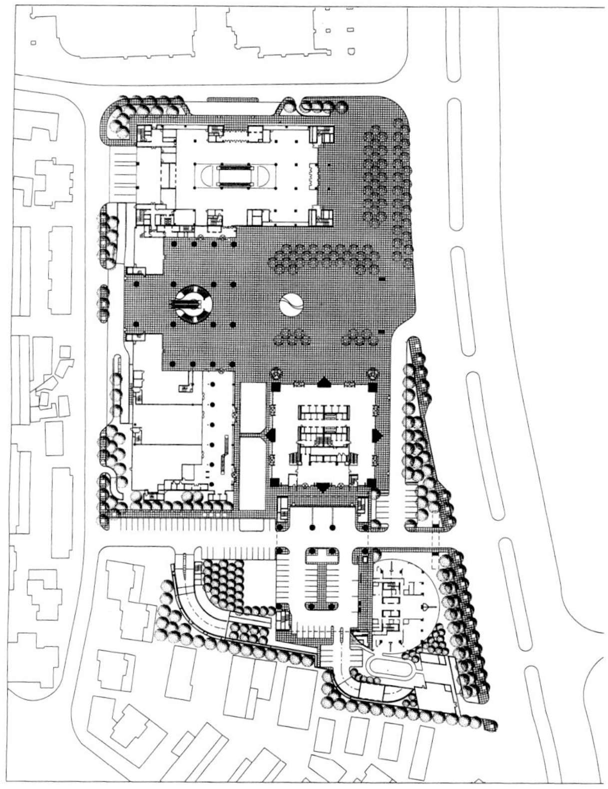

总平面 Site plan

Shanghai Daewoo Business Center

With a total floor area of 275,500 square meters, the proposed project is located on a 35,340 square meters' site in Xuhui District, a southwest district of Shanghai. It includes four inter-related structures: high-rise office/hotel tower, high-rise luxury apartment tower, major department store, and low-rise special retail galleria.

The 420-meter, 92-story office/hotel tower is the dominant structure and gives the Center unmatched opportunity to create a powerful visual impact that will identify the Xuhui Commercial District. The form of the building reaches skyward with metal and glass facades rising upward in a straightforward geometric progression that makes the functions within. The offices are on the first 61 levels, separated from the hotel by a public observation level on the 62nd level with the hotel located on levels 63 through 92. Above the hotel a distinctive pinnacle terminates in a spire that can be seen throughout the city. The plan of the tower is a square. When the function changes at the observation level from office to hotel, the square plan is reduced in size and rotated 45 degrees and the corners slope inward to form large glass triangles. The rotation repeats again at the 92nd level where the tower steps inward to form the pinnacle. At the top, plans of fritted glass form four large diamond shapes that encircle a 41-meter spire. The diamonds glow dramatically at night, distinctively locating the Shanghai Daewoo Business Center on the city's skyline.

The tower is flanked on the east by the Daewoo Department Store and a 34-story apartment tower on the west to make the transition in scale to the neighboring buildings. A seven-level galleria of restaurants and special shops in the special function building complements the department store which is the anchor of the shopping complex. The department store has a prominent presence on Xuzhen Road to attract shoppers from local business and residential communities. The retail galleria connects

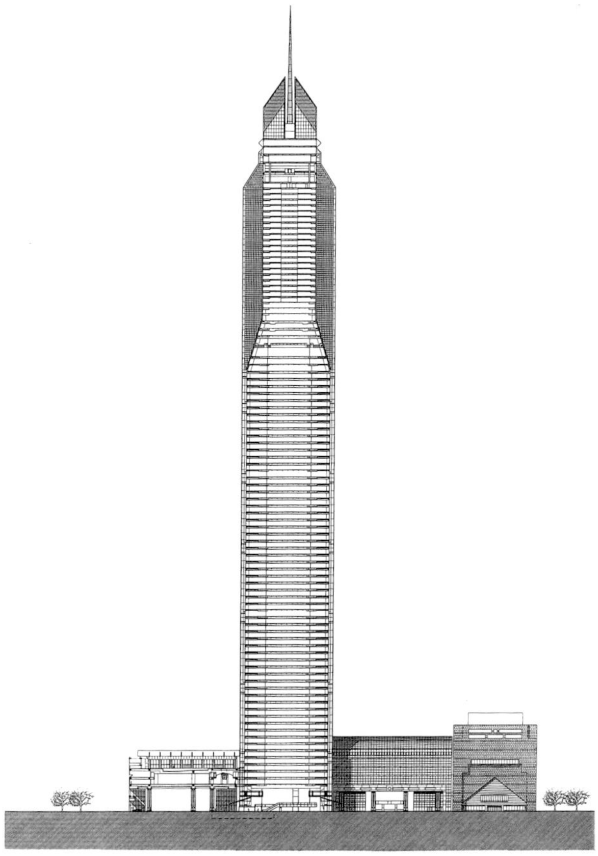

剖面 Section

to the department store and extends along the north side of the site. The transparent glass facades of the galleria open the view of the activity within to the surrounding streets and plazas. A major portion of the site is dedicated to a large pedestrian plaza which extends through the retail galleria at the street level. The plaza features landscaping, pools and a unique wet/dry fountain that animates the plaza and creates an inviting gathering place for visitors and residents. Together the buildings and plaza are a well-orchestrated complex that is a progressive new urban center symbolic of Shanghai's dynamic future.

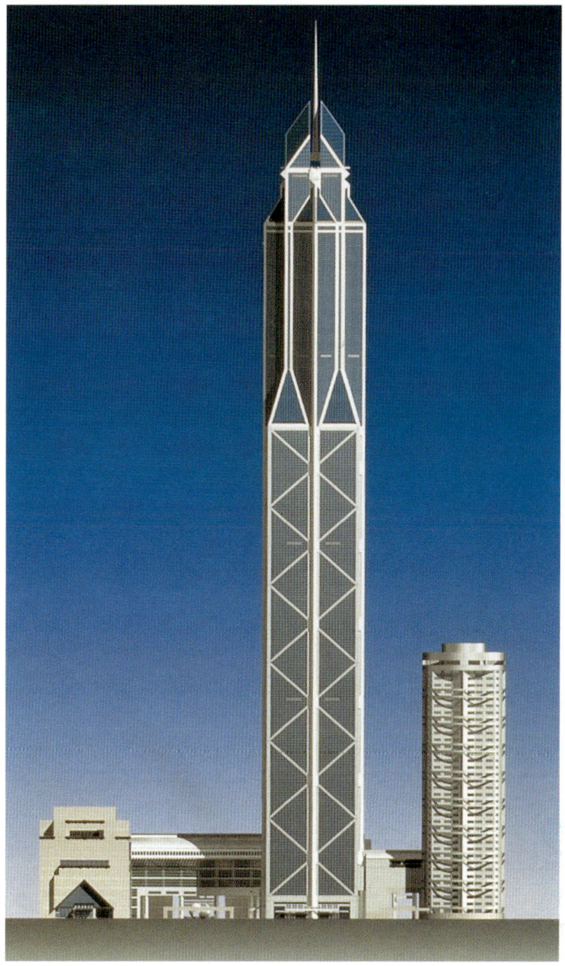
立面 Facade

入口广场 Entrance plaza

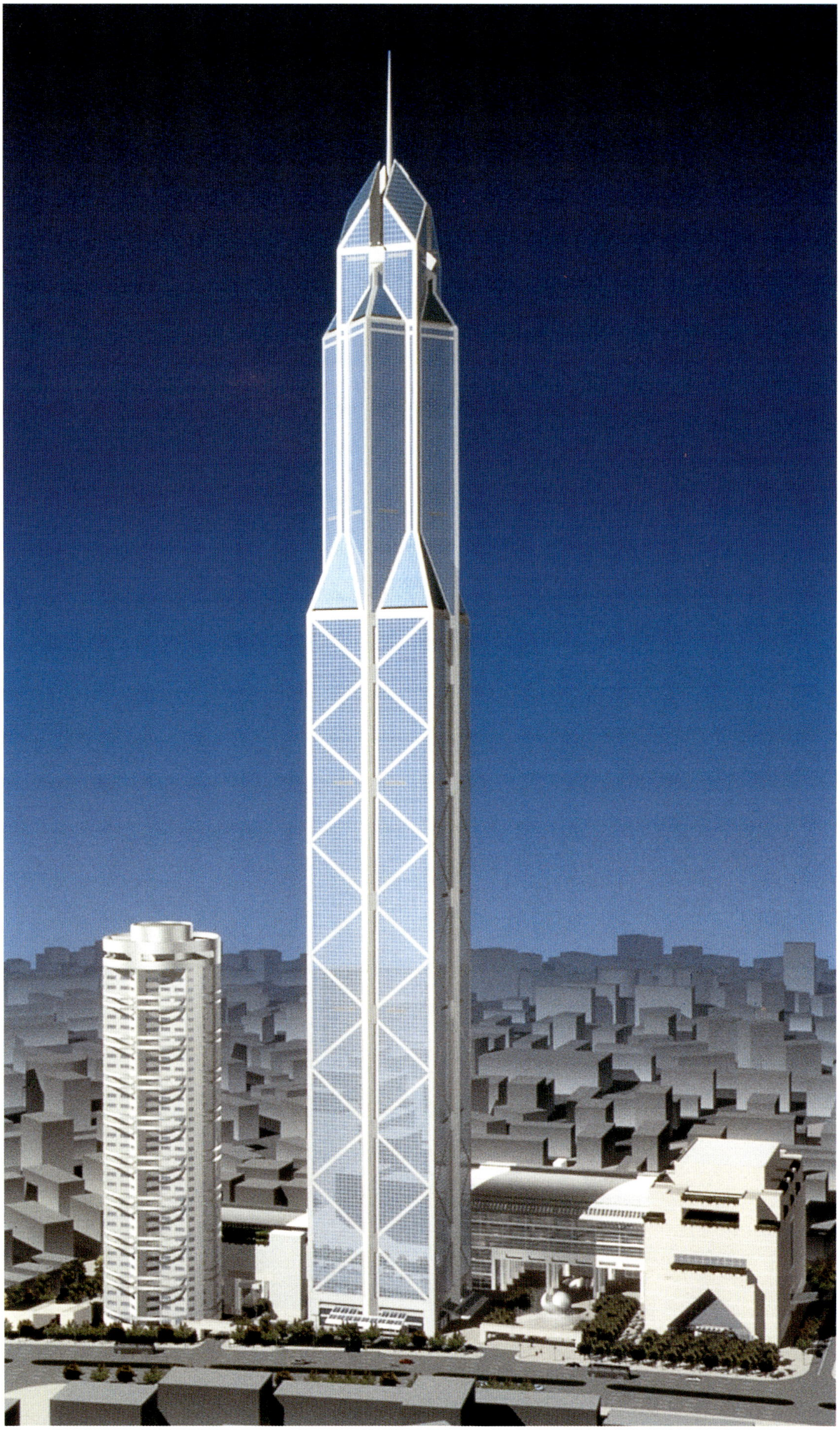

鸟瞰 Aerial view

杭州凯悦酒店

酒店位于西湖风景区的东岸，西临湖滨路，北傍学士路，东靠东坡路，南依平海路。总建筑面积83522平方米。

本项目由392间客房的酒店、公寓套房及购物中心三部分组成。其中酒店为该幢建筑物的中心，以其新月形的平面形式张开臂膀拥抱西湖，从而极大限度地使游客饱览西湖的秀色。酒店后面是公寓楼，公寓楼通过一个购物和餐饮的综合性多层购物中心与酒店相连接。设计不仅满足杭州城市规划要求，同时又具有诱人的魅力与风采。地方文化的表现贯穿于设计之中，自然景致如山石流水、花草树木精心地安排在建筑之中，加强了环境改造和场地自然美在心理上的联系。建筑物华丽的石材贴面则体现了建筑的高质量和永恒性。

Hyatt Regency Hangzhou Hotel

With a total floor area of 83,522 square meters, this project is located on the eastern shore of the scenic West Lake on a 21,000-square-meter site that is bound by Hubin Road to the west, Xueshi Road to the north, Dongpuo Road to the east, and Pinghai Road to the south. It consists of a 392-room hotel, an apartment building and a retail complex. The hotel is the centerpiece of the complex. Its crescent-shaped plan embraces the lake with open arms and maximizes the magnificent views for the hotel guests. Beyond the hotel, apartments span the length of the site nearest the city Itself and are linked the hotel by a dynamic, multi-level retail complex that provides shopping and food service.

The complex is designed for maximum efficiency to comply with the City's planning criteria without sacrificing the charm and elegance that draw people to this region. A rich cultural and environmental heritage makes Hangzhou a exceedingly popular tourist destination. The tradition of the region is planned to be an integral part of the luxurious hotel. Elements of nature such as water features and landscaping are also carefully integrated into the project to reinforce the Psychological link between the built environment and the natural beauty of the site. The stone facades of the buildings reflect the enduring quality that is vested in this project and speak to the timeless contribution it will make to the life of the community for years to come.

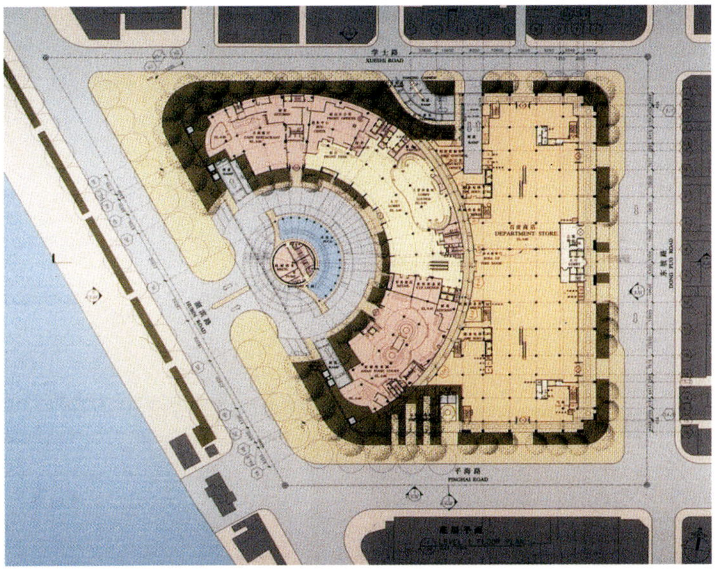

总平面 Site plan

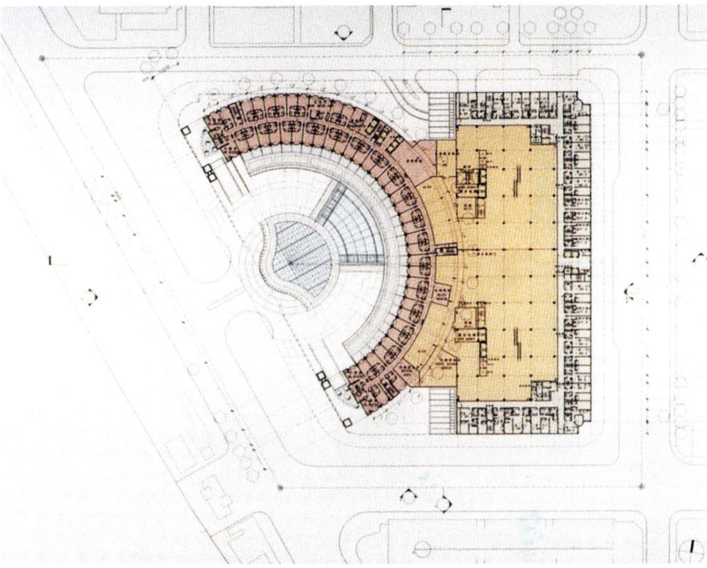

三层平面 Third floor

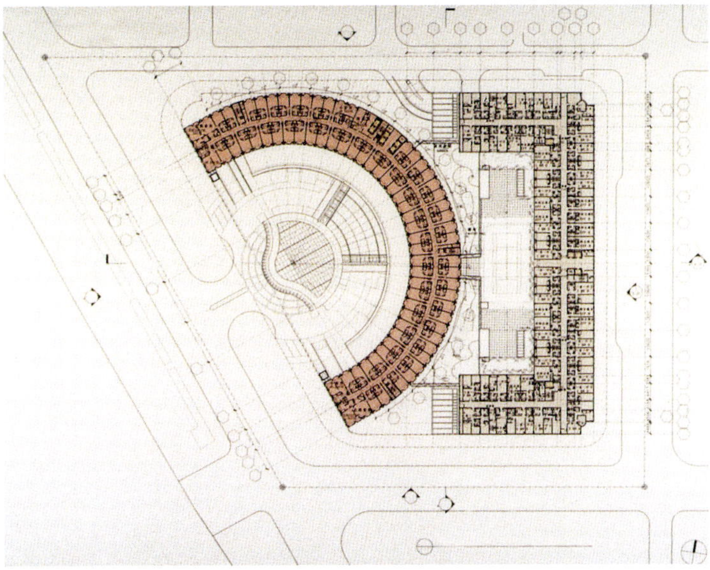

七层平面 Seventh floor

室内大堂 Interior lobby view

全景 Overall view

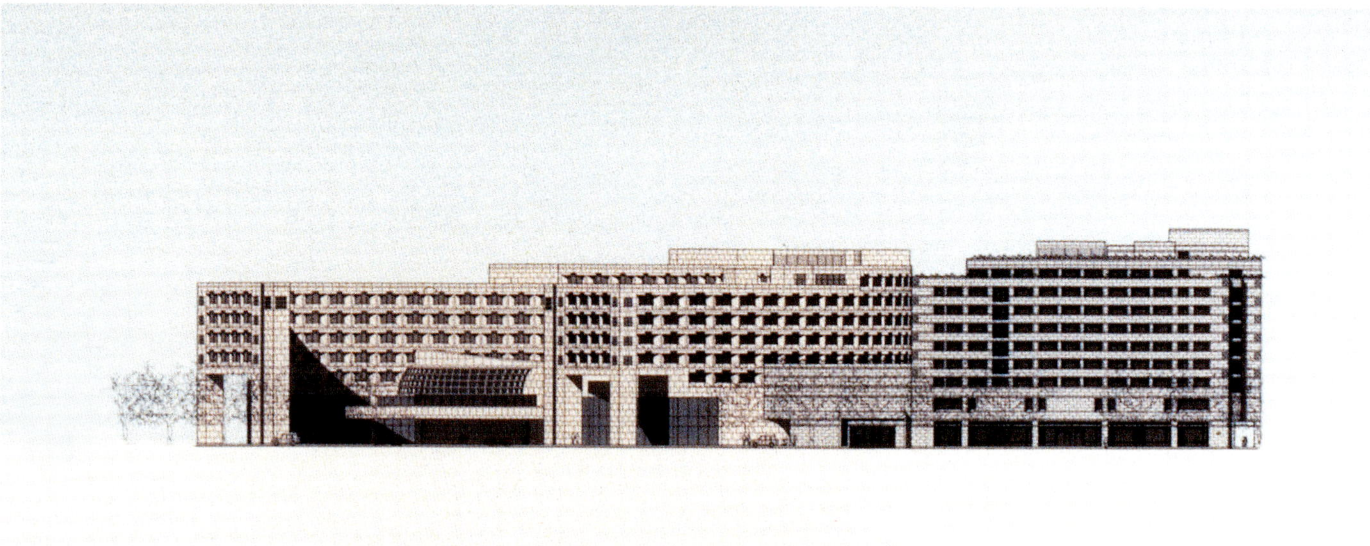

立面 Elevation

立面 Elevation

山东大厦

大厦位于济南南郊宾馆的东北角。东北两侧分别为马鞍山路与舜耕路，西侧与原有南郊宾馆的地界相连，它东看千佛山，西眺英雄山，南与泰山相望，北面有大明湖与豹突泉。所有这些都是济南市举世闻名的风景点。

方案有两个主要的侧重：在主体建筑与济南南郊宾馆之间创造一个和谐的共享环境空间，同时提供一个带有辅助会议厅、会议室及一个四星或五星级园林式宾馆的大会堂设施。方案根据传统中国建筑的精神，将主体建筑、室外景观与水体融合在一起，为周围环境作了理想的补充和完善，使其成为济南市的主要风景点。

建筑设计力图反映新科技在施工方法与材料上的应用，并运用具有地方特色的设计语言，突出方案本身的特殊功能。独特的形式及共享环境空间不仅为使用者服务，更显现出一种代表山东省的形象与精神。

2500座的大会堂座落在一条宽阔且景色宜人的林荫大道尽端，与马鞍山及庄重的"公共广场"相连。它庞大的体量在广场中显示了它的重要意义。比例匀称的室内空间可以容纳大量听众。精心雕琢的室外立面与周围环境水乳交融。

具有独特形式的带有690间客房的四星或五星级园林式宾馆是接待大型团体的理想场所。引人注目的中庭空间与精心设计的小桥流水流动于宾馆的公共场所内外，宾馆入口明显地设置在与南郊宾馆相对的中轴线上，它的位置与曲线形式，给城市提供了良好的景观效果。

有机布置的会议厅是项目中两大建筑主体的连接体，共同享有主要的公共广场，为了使用便利，主要入口设置在临近大会堂的位置。同时对公共环境进行良好的处理，将绿化景点设置在轴线两旁，利用园林空间的设计，给行人提供一个宁静、典雅的环境，给人们以丰富的感受。会议厅独特的造型，作为一个设计元素，有效地衬托和完善了包括宾馆和大会堂的群体设计。

Shandong Building

Consisting of a 2,500-seat convention hall, a 690-room 5-star atrium hotel and a conference center, the project is to be situated at the northeast corner of Jinan South-suburb Guesthouse with a total floor area of 90,400 square meters. Ma-An-Shan Road is along the north side and Shun-Gen Road is to the east. The existing Nan Jiao Hotel and grounds borders the western side of the site. Thousand Buddhist Hill is to the far east and Hero Hill is on the far west. Tai-Shan Mountains are to the south Da Ming Lake and Bao-Tu Spring are to the north. All of which are Jinan's world-renowned scenic spots.

The primary objective of the design concept is two-fold: to create a harmony within the setting shared with the Jinan South Suburb Guesthouse, and to provide a grand convention hall facility with supporting halls and meeting rooms and a 5-star atrium hotel. Respectful of traditional Chinese architecture and planning, the masterplan strategically locates the main buildings and integrates landscaping and waters throughout the project. This recognizes and complements the immediately surrounding site and scenic highlights of Jinan. The design strives to reflect new technologies in building systems and materials and acknowledges indigenous design vernacular symbolizing the significance of its function. The powerful forms and public spaces will prove to not only serve its users but enhance the prestige and spirit of Shangdong Province.

酒店中庭 Hotel atrium view

酒店中庭 Hotel atrium view

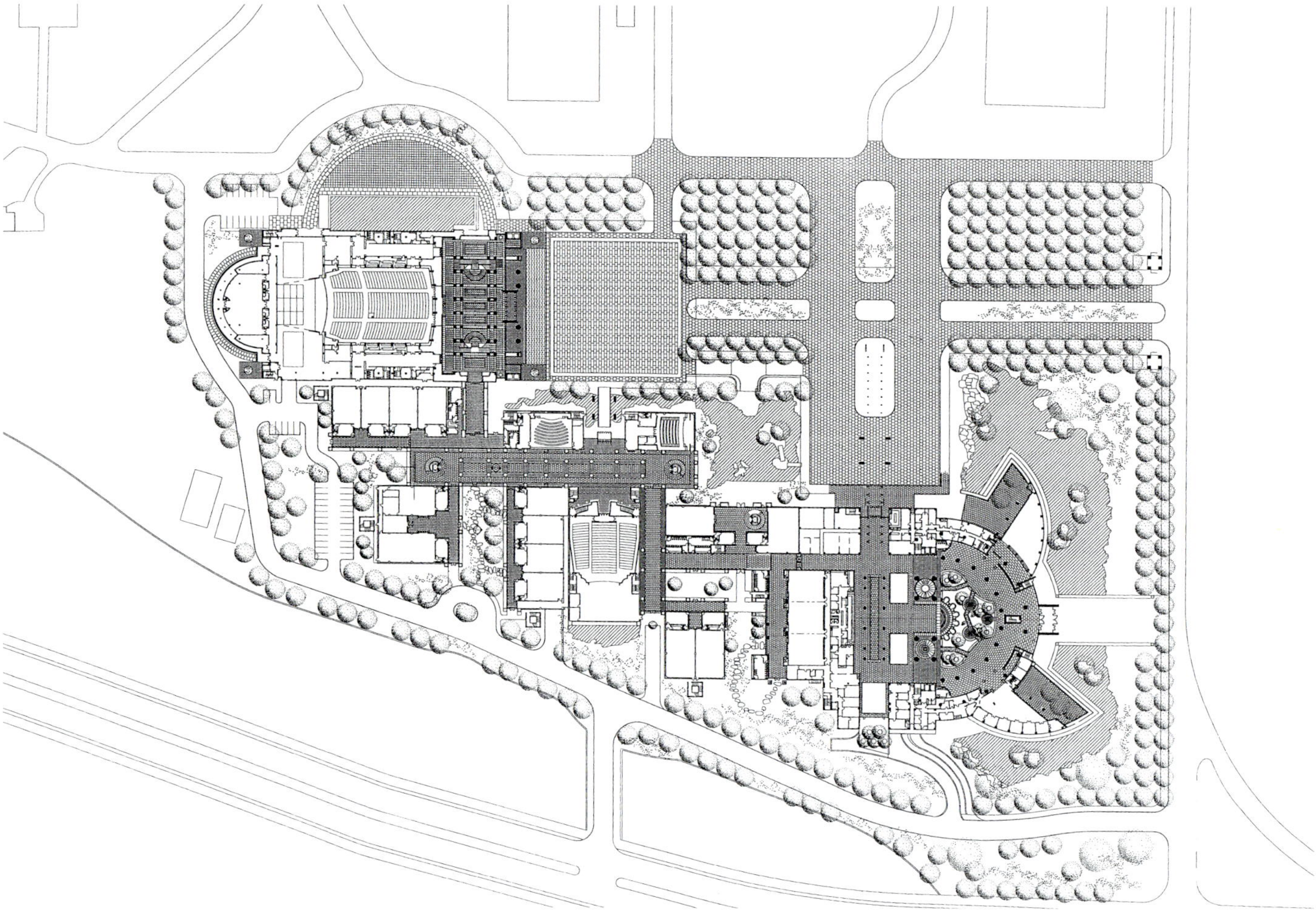

一层平面 First floor

鸟瞰 Aerial view

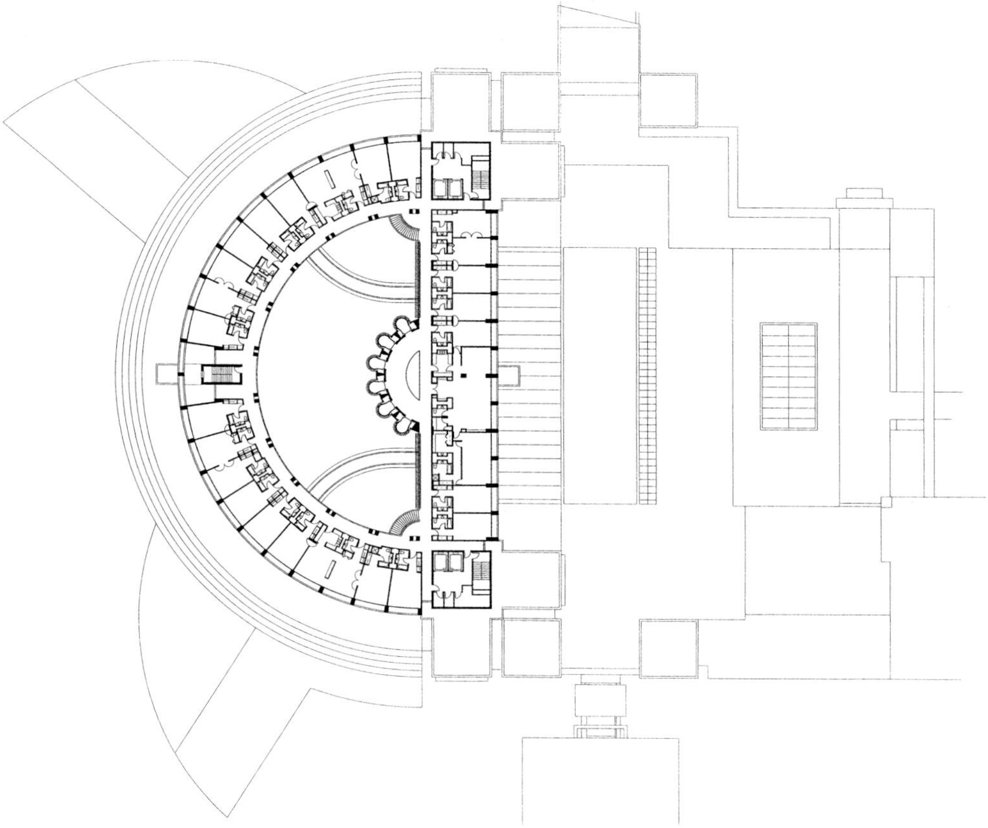

酒店标准屋平面 Typical hotel floor plan

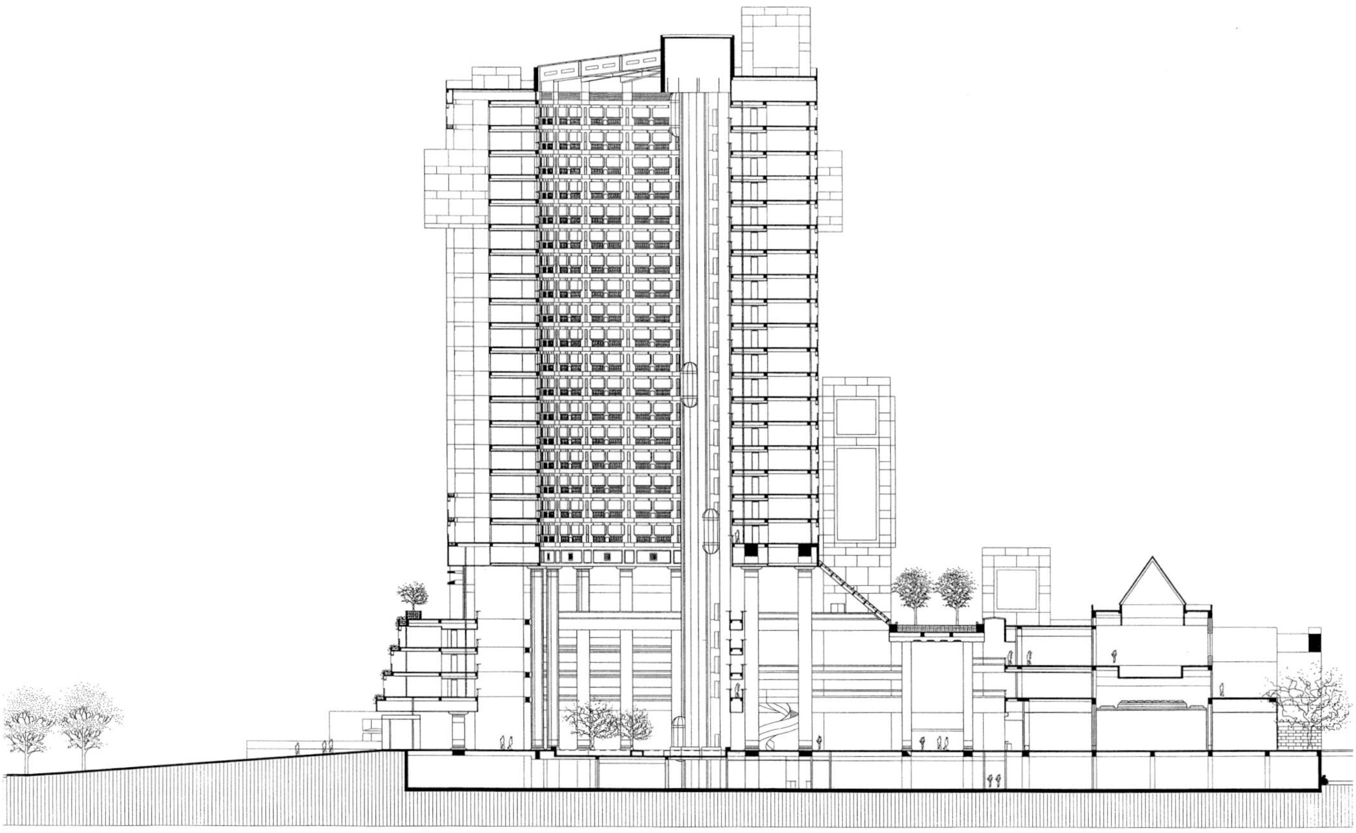

剖面 Section

会议中心侧厅 Side lobby of conference center

中庭 Atrium view

交通银行十六铺大厦

大厦位于上海南外滩的北部。基地与四条干道相邻，北接会馆弄，南邻老太平路，东西侧分别为外马路及中山南路，与黄浦江隔街相邻，地段北部有良良饭店和连连餐厅。总建筑面积29000平方米。

由于大厦处于老外滩和南外滩的显要地段，因此设计上不仅强调与老外滩30年代的建筑相协调，又将以其与众不同的建筑形式成为南外滩的焦点，并喻示交通银行的身份和雄厚实力，反映出国际银行的气派。大厦的几何形体反映了地块及周围的几何形象，这一几何体使其最大程度地展现在中山南路及外马路两侧。

地下设双层停车场，从停车场到外马路设汽车和自行车的出入口，银行的金库位于地下一层，并由特别入口与银行大厅相连。底层有两个不同的人行道入口，从中山南路和外马路可直接通过主入口进入醒目的银行大堂。主要银行大厅及办公大厅都有各自的客运电梯，底层的主要功能为银行大厅，包括人民币部、外汇部、财会部、黄金交易部及其它公共服务设施。

3～6层为银行的其它附属功能区，如会议中心、贵宾餐厅和健身房等，这些是交通银行作为国际金融集团所必备的。而第7～17层为办公区。

Bank of Communication Shiliupu Building, Shanghai

Prominently located at the conjunction of the Bund and South Bund, the project is designed to harmonize with the quality and architectural context of the 1930's buildings of the Bund. Also, because of its distinct architectural form it will be a focal point marking the entrance into the south Bund. The structure will project the bank's status and permanence and reflect its international banking image.

The geometry of the building reflects the geometry of the site and adjacent buildings. The geometry allows the building to have the maximum presence on Zhong Shan South Road and Wai Ma Road. The two parking levels are designed for perpendicular parking. There is vehicular and bicycle entrances exits from the parking off Wai Ma Road. The treasury room is located on 1st basement level with special access to the Banking Hall.

The ground level features two distinct pedestrian entrances. Grand entrances from Zhong Shan South Road and Wai Ma Road lead into the impressive Banking Hall Lobby. The main Bank Lobby and Office Lobby contains their own separate passenger elevators. The main function of this level is the Banking Hall which includes the Department of RMB, Foreign currency, accounting, gold transactions, and other public services.The 3rd through the 6th levels contain the remainder of the banking support functions required by an international financial institution, for example, conference center, VIP offices, restaurants, health club, etc. Levels 7 through 17 contain office tenant space.

模型 Model view

室内 Interior view

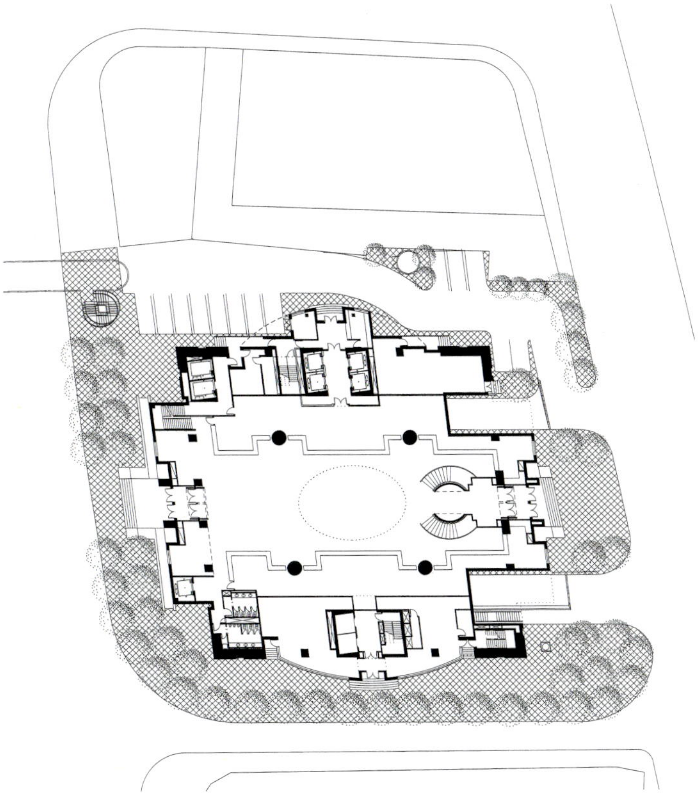

一层平面 First floor

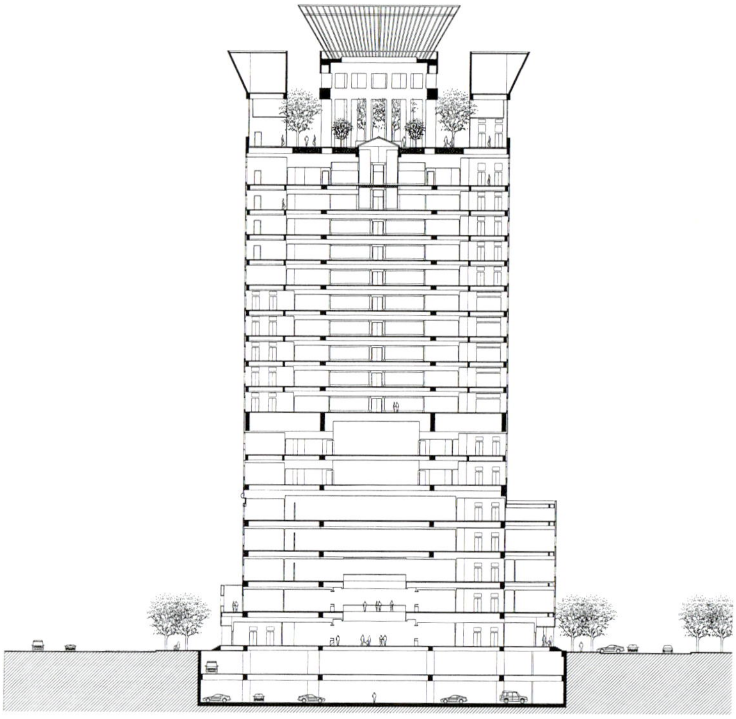

剖面 Section

模型 Model view

外观 Exterior view

上海明天广场

广场位于黄浦区第27号街区，由北面的南京路，东面的黄陂路，南面的江阴路和西面的住宅区所环绕。除去南京西路和黄陂北路拐角处的小公园，此街坊呈L形。

基地由构成上海主要商业区的两个地块组成。当人们从人民公园接近基地，南京路的拐弯处将呈现一幅奇异的街景，高层塔楼与低层裙房的相互衬托构成强烈的视觉效果。塔楼从绿化广场拔地而起，俯瞰环绕基地的两条主要街道。铝框玻璃外表的建筑物以几何造型垂直向上伸展，简洁明快的线条体现出现代对未来的展望。建筑物顶部和底部显著的三角形体加强了建筑垂直上升的动感。

塔楼平面为正方形，座落于环形中庭内。7～35层为办公室和商务公寓；36层为机械和避难层；37～55层为宾馆。从37层的宾馆层起，平面旋转45度，这种设计保持了建筑物简练的线条。两个交错的正方体之间的过渡形成若干长三角形，长三角形在结构上支撑上部楼层悬臂部分的重力。其上方的若干较小三角形标志着宾馆大厅的位置，休息厅层有带天篷的外部阳台。塔楼的最高点为一个开放式针塔，针塔的明亮耀眼的球体仿佛是一座醒目的上海之空里程碑。塔尖内设有远距离通讯设施。

公园的新设计将与明天广场的风景规划相结合，广场现有的自动扶梯和电梯将增设亭子。顾客可从亭子到达现有的地下餐厅和商店。绿化广场、屋顶花园和水池将为城市提供公园式的环境，也为拥挤嘈杂的城市增添了一个雅致幽静的世外桃源。包括商廊和会议中心的裙房横跨西侧基地。正门设在南京西路，江阴路上的办公楼入口可使行人进入塔楼和裙房之间的大型中庭。

Shanghai Tomorrow Square

The project has a golden commercial geographic advantage. It is located on the #27 block in Huangpu District, situated on the block bound by Nanjing Xi Road to the north, Huangpi Bei Road to the east, Jiangyin Road to the south, and some residents to the west. The block is L-shaped excluding the small park at the corner of Nanjing Xi Road and Huangpi Bei Road.

The two plots that comprise the site in the #27 block make one of the city's prime commercial locations. As one approaches the site, the curve in Nanjing Road around People's Park affords an extraordinary vista from the street level. The proposed plan maximizes the visual impact of this site by dividing the project components into a high-rise Tower and a low-rise Podium. To increase its visual impact, the Tower rises directly from a landscaped plaza at the street level, facing two of the major street that border the site. To reinforce its strong vertical form, the Tower and Podium are visually separate though functionally linked via a skylight atrium.

The sleek 55-story Tower symbolizes Shanghai's dynamic future. The aluminum and glass facade of the building reaches upward in a straightforward, geometric manner. The lines are clean and uncluttered with a contemporary look of the future. The vertical movement is reinforced by the dominant triangular shapes at both the top and base of the building. The plan of the Tower is a square which is situated in the circular atrium that encompasses the building. Levels 7 through 35 of the building are designated for offices and office/apartments. Level 36 is a mechanical and refuge level. Level 37 through 55 are for the hotel. At the 37th level, where the hotel begins, the square plan is rotated 45 degrees, maintaining the clean, simple lines below. The transition between the two rotated squares creates long triangular forms that structurally support the projected flow of gravity between the cantilevered corners. The smaller triangular forms above, which mark the hotel's lobby and lounge levels, are canopies for exterior balconies. The tower culminates in an open pinnacle in which a dramatically lit sphere serves as a distinctive landmark to Shanghai's skyline. The spires will contain telecommunications

鸟瞰 Aerial view

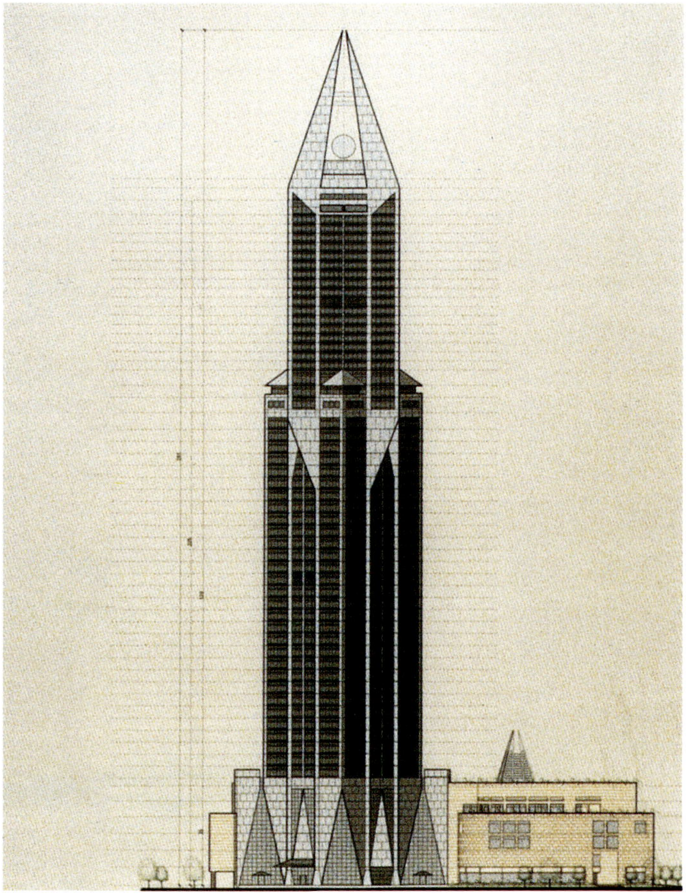

立面 Elevation

functions.

The landscaped plaza is an important aspect of the project. Its park-like setting enables the people of Shanghai to enjoy the beauty of nature with proximity to shopping and transportation. Additionally, the landscaped plaza places the Tower in a position of prime importance and gives the project unmatched visual strength. A new design for the park will be incorporated into the Tomorrow Square Landscape Plan and will feature new pavilions for the existing escalators and elevator in the plaza. Patrons will access the existing underground restaurants and shops through the pavilions. The Podium which contains the Retail Galleria and Conference Center spans the western portion of the site. The main entrance is from Nanjing Road. The office entrance on Jiangyin Road provides pedestrian access to the large atrium between the Tower and the Podium.

室内一角 Interior view

中庭 Atrium view

外观 Exterior view

RSP 建筑规划及工程设计公司

RSP ARCHITECTS PLANNERS & ENGINEERS (PTE) LTD

RSP 建筑规划及工程设计公司 1956 年成立于新加坡，以 Raglan Squire & Partners 命名。1980 年 12 月公司更名为 RSP 建筑规划及工程设计公司，人员由 1956 年的 14 人发展至今超过 300 人，现已成为新加坡及东南亚最大和实力最雄厚的建筑规划及工程设计公司之一。该公司 1992 年在上海成立分公司。

RSP 在印度、迪拜、吉隆坡、雅加达、伦敦及巴林岛的下属公司、分公司及联合公司除完成相应地区任务之外，亦与新加坡总部进行联合项目设计。公司并设有机电及工程分部(Squire Mech Pte Ltd)。

公司注重设计质量及项目管理，并赢得了许多设计奖项。以高质量的专业标准及管理控制，以保证高质量地按投资与时限完成任务，公司在当地是第一批通过ISO9000建筑设计与咨询质量管理认证的公司之一。服务范围包括建筑规划、设计、工程监理、城市规划、市政工程、室内设计等。

RSP Architects Planners & Engineers (Pte) Ltd. was incorporated in Singapore in February 1992. Its history dates back to 1956 when the practice was established in Singapore under the name of Raglan Squire & Partners. In December 1980, It was renamed RSP Architects Planners & Engineers. The practice, which grew from a staff of 14 in 1956 to more than 300 today, has become one of the largest and most established architectural, planning and engineering practices in Singapore and South East Asia.

ESP's subsidiaries, branch offices and associate firms in India, Dubai, Kuala Lumpur, Jakarta, London and Bahrain besides undertaking their own work in their respective areas also pool resources to carry out some projects jointly with the Singapore office. The combined experience of the staff has made it possible for the practice to produce work of a consistently high standard. To complement its services, the practice also works closely with its own M&E Division, Squire Mech Pte Ltd.

The practice places strong emphasis on design quality and project management, it has earned recognition for high levels of creative design and management skill, a fact supported by the number of projects which have been awarded design excellence awards. The practice aims to maintain high levels of professional standards and management control to ensure consistent quality and project completion within budget and time constraints. The practice is also one of the first in the region to achieve the ISO 9000 Quality Management System certification for Architectural for Architectural Design and Consultant Services.

The firm provides architectural planning, design, supervision and administration of building contracts, urban and regional planning, civil and engineering, interior design and construction management service.

上海船厂改造和开发工程

船厂位于浦东陆家嘴开发区边缘，是一个大型的城市改造项目，占地57公顷，完成后将容纳3600个高级住宅单元及440000平方米办公和商业空间。

两对标志性双塔将成为进入该片区的门户。其中较高的一对为50层，另一对的高度约是前者的二分之一，其作用是与高塔的造型取得平衡，同时使西面的人口在高度上获得渐进的感觉。区内的主要道路和带状公园都以南北向布局，以保证江景不受阻挡。为了扩大沿江景观面，江边主要布置点式住宅。对于后部的板式住宅来说，这些点式住宅还起到取景框的作用。

为获得协调统一的街景，每一个街区的建筑都沿街道布置。这样不但有助于清晰地限定各街道空间，同时又在每个住宅单元的内部创造出各自的公共绿地。在整体统一的城市环境中，通过建筑形式和高度上变化的获得多样性，创造出优美的城市天际线。区内主要大街的设计考虑到行人和汽车两方面的要求，成为小区具有感染力的环境特点之一。街道以特殊的树种美化。两边的建筑将遵循具有节奏和韵律感的模式，使街道的个性完整而独特。

小区内有多种娱乐设施，其中之一是以旧船厂的轮船下水坡道为中心的大型广场，成为各种节日和庆典活动的主场地。由于广场面向水体，将吸引步行者沿林荫大道来到水边。小区中还有其它各类公园，其中有一些是带状绿地，还有一个校园广场兼公共公园。

Shanghai Shipyard Redevelopment

Located at the fringe Pudong Lujiazhui, Shanghai Shipyard is a massive urban renewal project. Measuring 57 hectares, Shanghai Shipyard Redevelopment comprises 3,600 units of high-class residence and 440,000 square meters' office and commercial spaces.

Two pairs of landmark twin towers will serve as gateway to the district. The taller pair, which is 50 stories in height, is immediately visible from neighboring districts. The shorter pair is about half the height of the taller tower. The shorter towers therefore anchor the taller towers and graduate the ascent as one approaches the district from the west. The roads and linear parks which are oriented north- south safeguard "view corridors" towards the river. People from further inland can be drawn to the riverfront through them.

Additional "windows" or "openings" are also created by having only point blocks by the riverfront. There are point block frame views of the river for those slab blocks behind them. The district will have its buildings aligned with the edges of every street as unifying and cohesive urban design elements.. Not only does this help to define the edges of each street block more clearly, it also creates private internal common spaces within each residential parcel. Variety within the larger unified urban structure and framework is achieved by introducing buildings of varied building forms and heights. These are carefully adjusted throughout the entire district so that an elegant overall skyline is achieved.

The main boulevard will be an important and potentially impressionable thoroughfare for the district. It should be distinguished in character for both pedestrians and motorists. The boulevard can be lined and beautified with special trees. The boulevard can be further enhanced by the rhythmic pattern of the buildings beside it. Simple modules of alternating building heights may be repeated for the entire length of the boulevard.

The district will have a variety of public spaces for the community's enjoyment: A large plaza, focusing on the shipyard's launching ramp, can be a hub of excitement and festive activity. It opens out to the waterfront and invites pedestrians to have a closer experience with the river along an attractive promenade. Various types of parks will be distributed within the district. There will be linear parks, and even a shared school field-cum-public park.

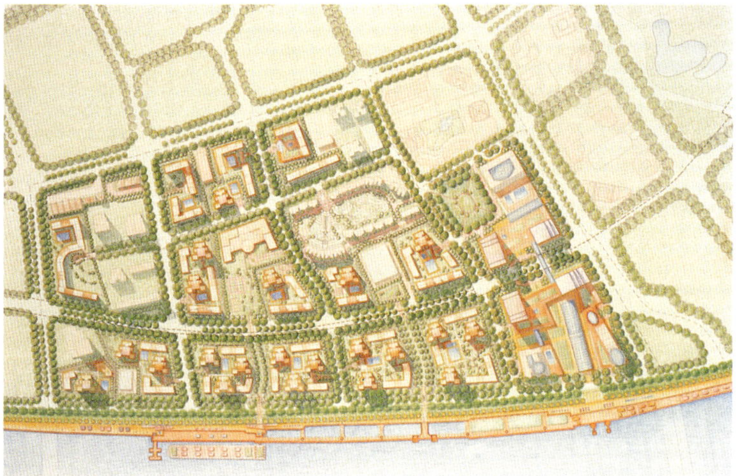

总平面 Master plan

鸟瞰 Aerial view

模型 Model overall view

福州长乐国际机场

福州长乐国际机场是中国最先进的国际机场之一。第一期工程将容纳每年650万客流量，其中70%为国内旅客，30%为国外旅客。总建筑面积118500平方米。

虽然设计的起点是650万年客运量和一条跑道的建设为基础，但根据设计要求，长远的分阶段实现的发展规划必须考虑扩大到1500万以至最大3000万的年客运量及两套候机楼和联结桥系统。这样的配置最终决定候机楼必须设在跑道系统的几何中心，以缩短机场内各功能设施间的交通联系。旅客的所有登机手续，包括登记、行李托运、安检及海关都设在候机楼内。旅客的过往交通则设在联结桥内。

一期工程规划到2005年，由一个集中型的候机楼、联结桥和一条跑道组成。根据客流量的发展，二期工程可以将营运能力提高到每年1500万。当年客流量达到3000万时，才开始第三期工程，建设第二跑道，达到每小时100架飞机的起降数量。

Fuzhou Changle Interational Airport

This 118,500 square meters' airport is one of the best-equipped international airports in China. The Phase1 development is designed to accommodate 6.5 million passengers a year. 70% of the flights is domestic and 30% is international.

The design is based on the capacity requirement of 6.5 million passengers per year with one runway to start with. The development plan for the long term in the stages as required in the brief illustrates the possibilities of the concept for an expansion to 15 million passengers per year to a maximum of 30 million passengers per year with two separate unit terminals with linear concourses. This configuration would be the ultimate development of the passenger Terminal Complex located at the geometric center of the runway system to achieve short distances for all types of transport and short lines of communication between all airport functions and facilities. All passenger processing

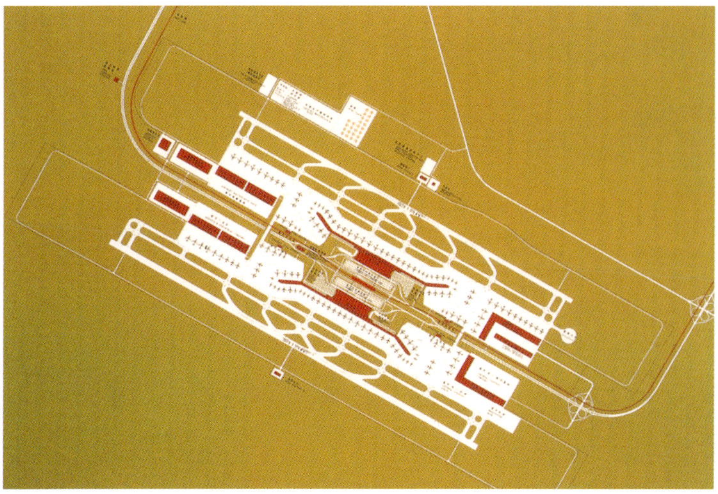

总平面 Site plan

functions, including check-in, baggage handling, security screening, immigration and customs are located in the processing terminals. Passenger circulation to, from and between aircraft occurs in the concourses.

Phase1, which is planned to accommodate the projected 2005 demand of 6.5 million passengers a year, consists of a centralized processing terminal and connected concourses with one runway. When additional capacity becomes necessary, Phase II can be constructed to bring the passenger terminal capacity up to 15 million passengers a year. Phase II consists of an extended centralized passenger processing terminal and concourse. Phase III will only be required when the passenger demand reaches 30 million a year and the second runway will also be needed to accommodate the expected aircraft movement of 100 per hour.

室内 Interior view

模型 Model overall view

T.R.汉沙及杨建筑师事务所

T.R. HAMZAH & YEANG SDN. BHD.

T. R. 汉沙及杨建筑师事务所由T. R. 汉沙及杨经文博士于1976年发起成立。公司总部位于吉隆坡，以设计为主，并致力于高层生态建筑及大型项目的设计。

公司聘请世界各地雇员90余人，项目遍布全球。主要进行项目前卫性研究、设计，创造新的建筑类型及探索绿色高层设计。致力于对气候、生态在高层设计中的运用，创造节能的建筑形式与技术，以此提高生活的质量。

公司追求整体设计的哲学，与各领域的专家对建筑进行系统的研究与探索；对每一设计采用理想与现实相结合的态度，充分反映客户对项目及投资要求。

公司实际项目获得大量奖项，包括1996年建筑阿卡·汗奖，作品在欧洲、亚洲及美国广泛发表与展览。

T.R. Hamzah & Yeang Sdn.Bhd. was formed in 1976 by Tengku Robert Hamzah and Dr ken Yeang, following their graduation from the AA (Architectural Association) School in London. With its headquarters in Kuala Lumpur, Hamzah & Yeang is regarded as a design-emphasis firm, whose expertise is in ecologically responsive high-rise buildings and large-scale projects.

The firm employs over 90 personnel of international nature with projects worldwide. Underlying the buildings and projects, is a program of cutting-edge research, design and development, focusing on a new building type, the green skyscraper. They believe that tall building design is "d" derives from the systemic understanding of the role climate and ecology can play in finding new forms and technologies that are energy efficient and which can enhance the quality of life for occupants and are ecologically-responsive.

The firm insists a 'total design' philosophy and has a strong belief in a multi-disciplinary (design team) approach in a close understanding with many engineering-specialist collaborators worldwide. In their practice, a balanced approach is adopted for each project, reconfiguring progressive design-thinking with practical experience in order to connect a client's building program and budge "t" with design and building solutions.

Their work has won many awards, one of which is the prestigious Aga Khan Award for Architecture in 1996. Their work has also been widely published and exhibited in Europe, Asia and the United States.

天津民航学院

学院总平面根据中文的“人”字形发展而来。沿人字形墙体布置步行通道，并且将基地分成体育、生活和教学三个区。这三个区同时也是三个保安区，在人字形的上下端分别设有检查站，使各区可以独立运作。新旧校园之间有步行天桥相连。天桥和坡道将人流从一层引入各建筑的第三层，在第三层位置设有供聚会用的室外露台。居住区南北向布置以争取冬季的阳光，阳台设有遮阳百叶。在教学综合楼的采光井部分的屋面也采用了百叶装置，在遮阳的同时可以利用自然通风。除此之外，百叶与墙体还具有遮挡附近机场噪音的作用。

Tianjin Civil Aviation School

The master plan is based on Chinese character person" which means human literally. Pedestrian circulation is along the wall of this "person" which demarcates the site into 3 wall secured zones: sports zone, accommodation zone and academic zones. The wall also divides the site in 3-security zone with security checkpoints at the top and bottom of "person". Each area can be operated and accessed independently.

The new campus is linked to the existing school by a pedestrian bridge. The bridge and ramps leads people from the 1st level to the 3rd level of the building which also features open terraces for meeting places. The accommodation is north-south orientated. This maximizes the building to the solar gain from the low-setting winter sun. Sun louvers are provided to protect the balconies from becomming over-heated. The "steel figure" inspired roof scape of the buildings, each "wing" of roof is altered and angled to ventilate, shade and reflects the usage of the building (e.g. sports center). Louvered roof provides double shading to the building and allows natural ventilation to the light well of the teaching complexes. This, together with the wall serves as a noise barrier from the airport nearby.

The proposed total floor area is 148,137 square meters.

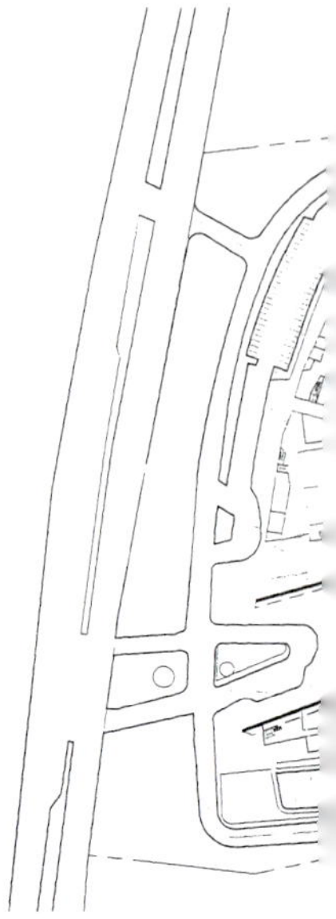

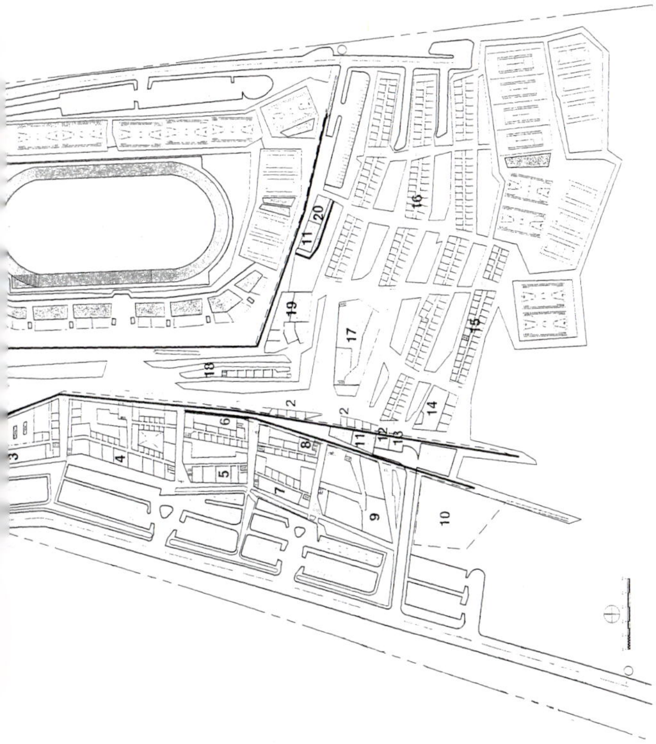

总平面 Master plan

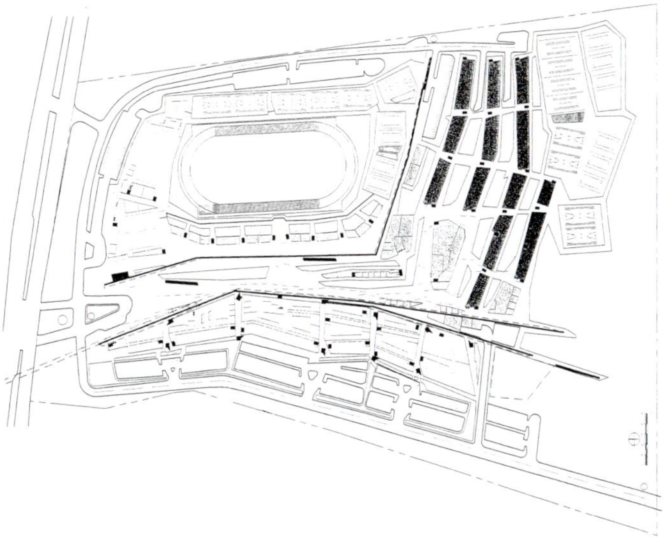

一层平面 Level 1

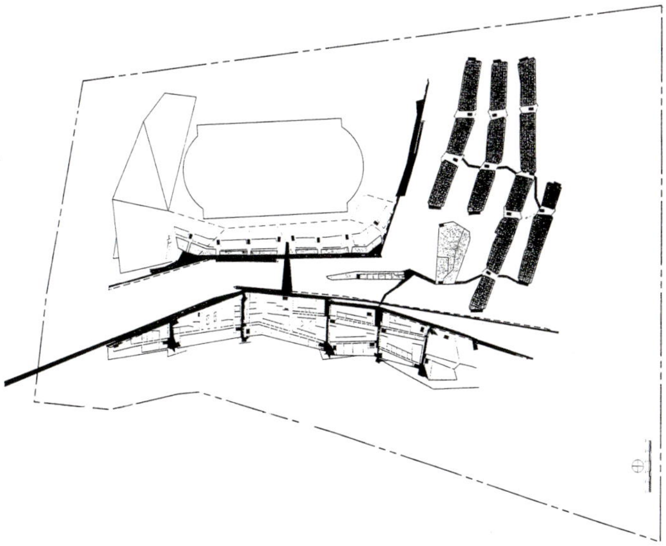

三层平面 Level 3

模型 Model view

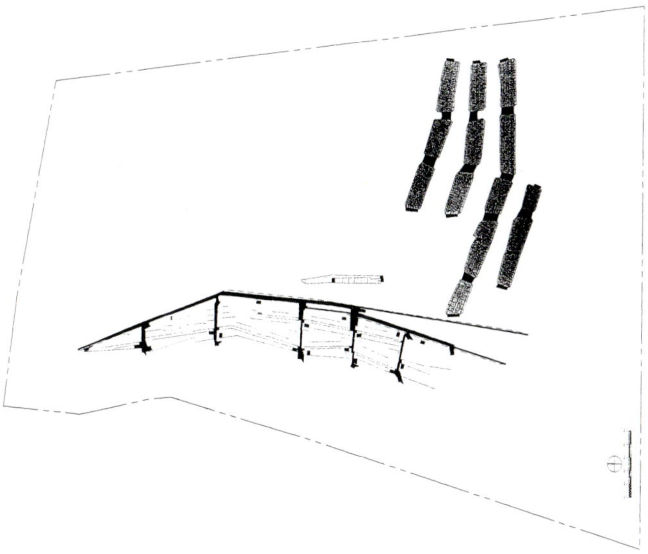

五层平面 Level 5

模型 Model view from north

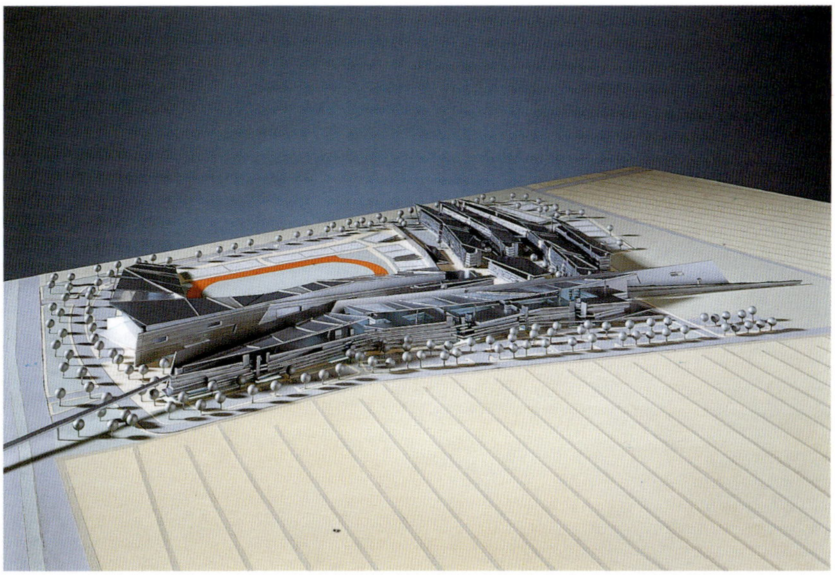

模型 Model view from west

模型 Model view from east

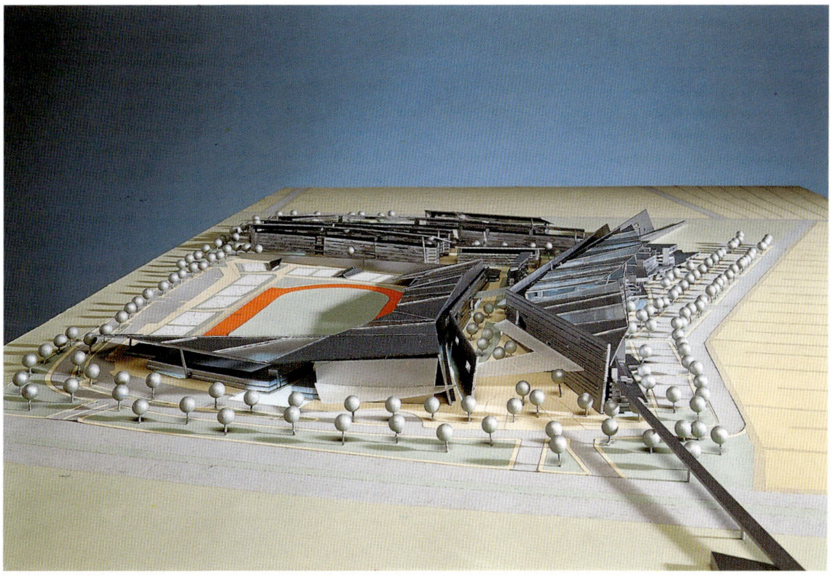

模型 Model view from south

上海军械大厦

这座面积为46000平方米、36层高的大厦运用了一些象征军械的造型元素。外立面大面积金属网犹如古代中国战士的盔甲，顶部舒展的太阳能板表现出战士头盔的造型，挺拔的塔楼如同胜利的火炬，楼梯平面则形似枪的板机。

大厦是一座低能耗、高质量的建筑。在内外建筑功能处理上都利用了生态气候原理，充分开发上海当地海滨气候条件，使使用者在其中能够体验到四季变化。塔楼中某些部位设有空中绿化平台，作为室内外空间的过渡区域，它又是制造氧气的“绿色肺叶”，为建筑及其周边创造出宜人的小气候。建筑外部可调节气候的幕墙成为多功能过滤装置，在抵御外部恶劣气候的同时保证室内具有宽阔无阻的景观面。

Shanghai Armoury Tower

With a total floor area over 46,000 square meters, this 36-storey skyscraper is a symbolic interpretation of components found in military armaments. The sweeping panels of metallic screens on the exterior facade allude to the armor of the Chinese warrior. The curved soaring solar panel atop the building depicts the helmet, while the soaring tower piece is the "victorious torch" The stairs plan suggests the trigger of a gun.

The China Armory Tower is a low-energy high quality building. The external and internal design features use a bio-climatic approach to produce an operationally energy-efficient building that makes the most of the coastal climatic conditions of Shanghai and allows for occupants to experience and be aware of the changing season of the year. Landscaped sky terraces placed at strategic points in the tower represent buffer zones between the inside and outside. In addition they act as oxygen generating "green lungs" which refresh the microclimate of the periphery of the building. The external weather-screen performs as a multi-functional filter against extreme climatic conditions while allowing generous panoramic views of the surrounding urban-space.

总平面 Site plan

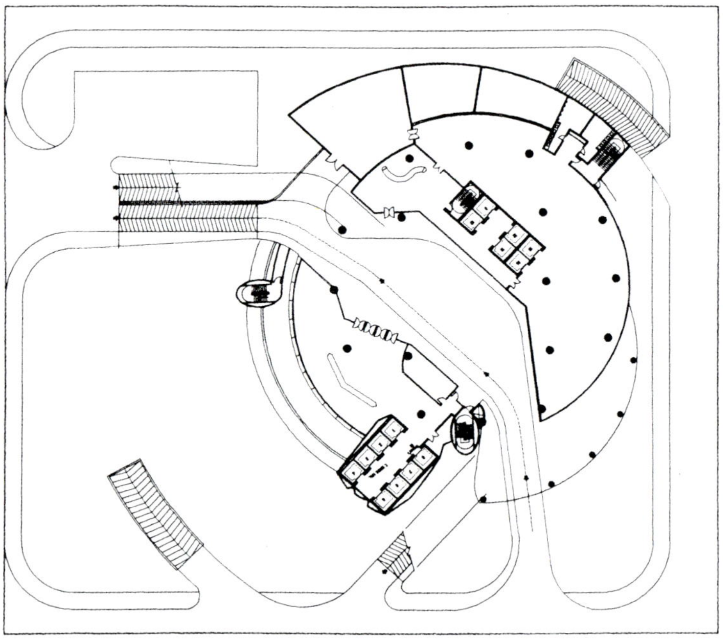

一层平面 First floor

模型 Model view

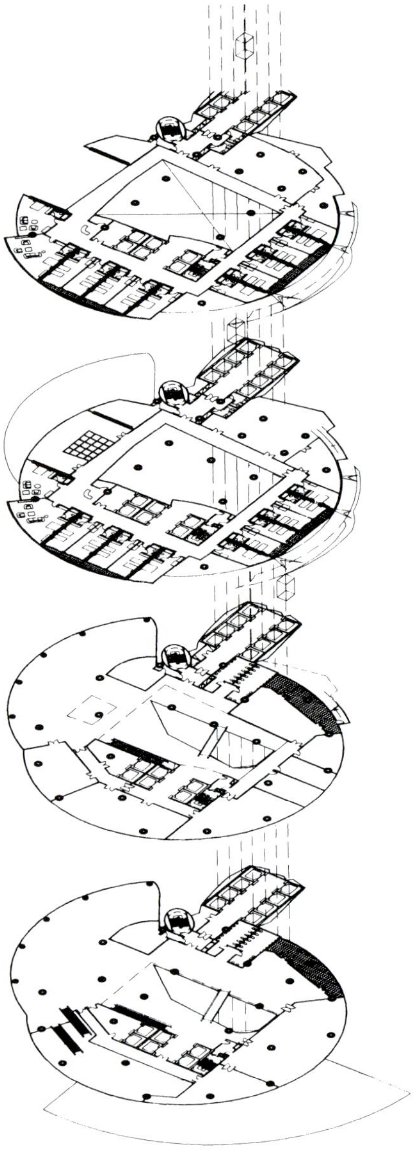

3-6 层平面 Floors 3-6

外观 Mode view

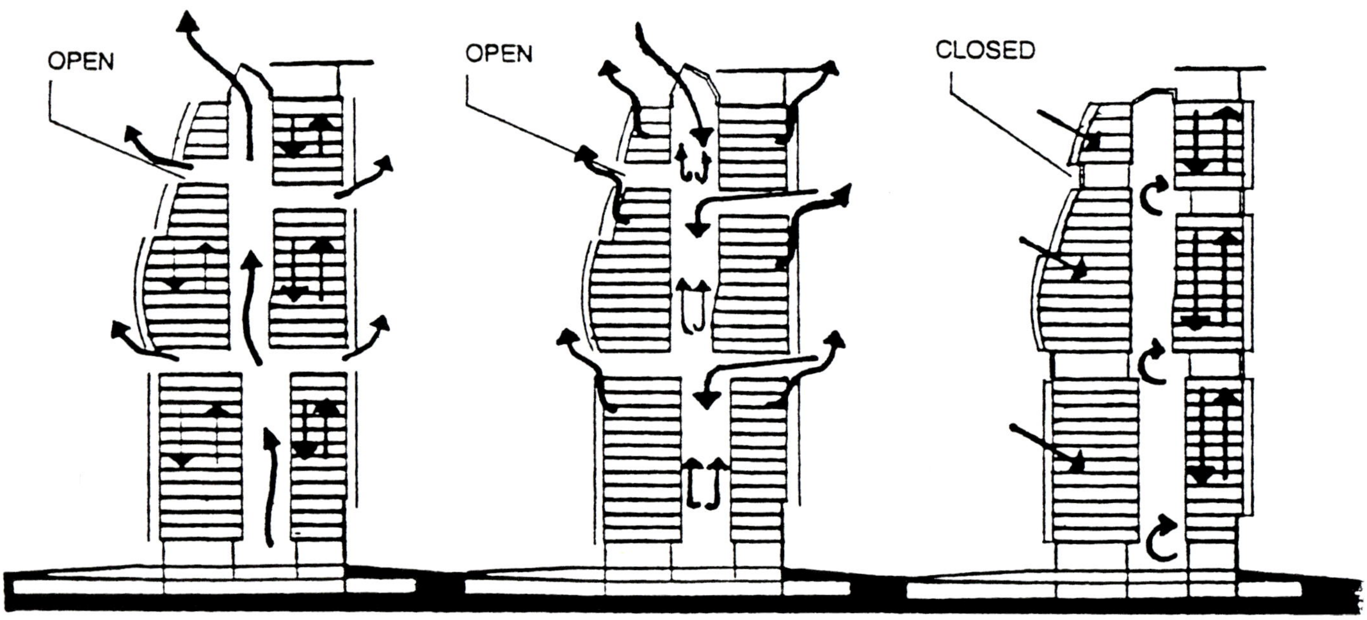

节能分析 Analysis on energy saving

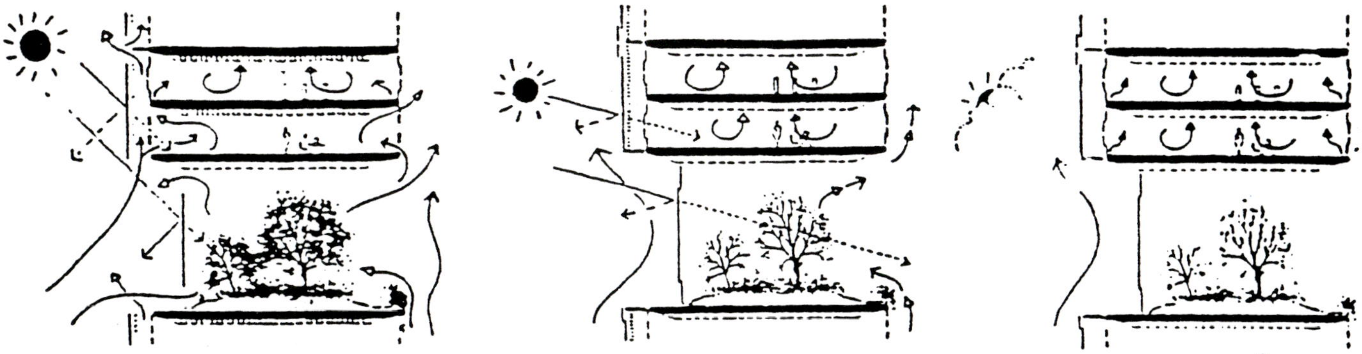

节能分析 Analysis on energy saving

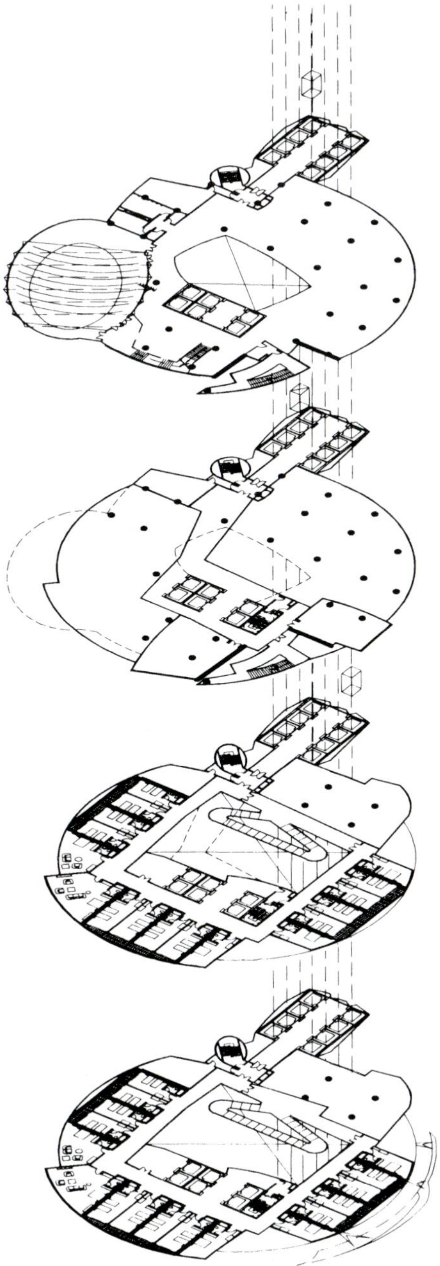

15-18 层平面 Floors 15-18

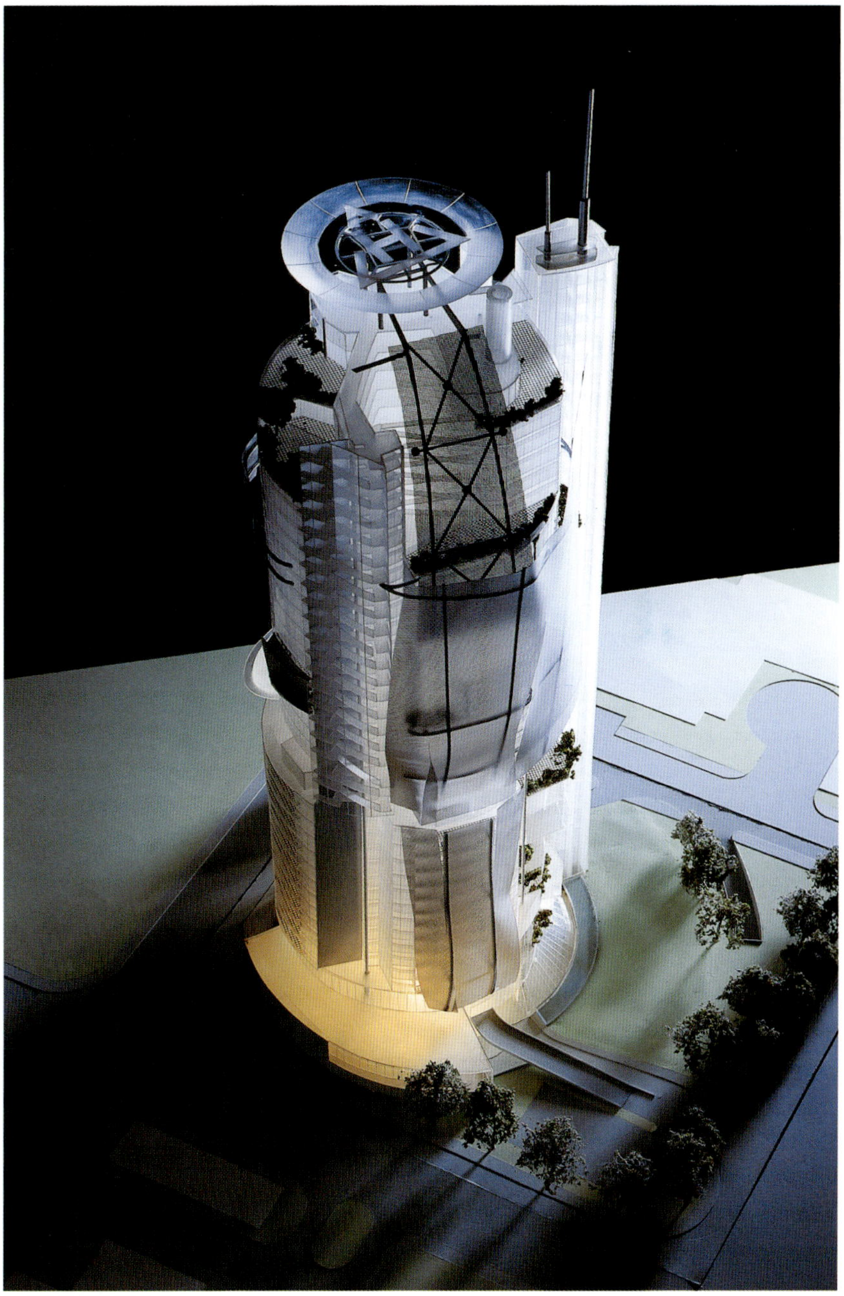

外观 Mode view

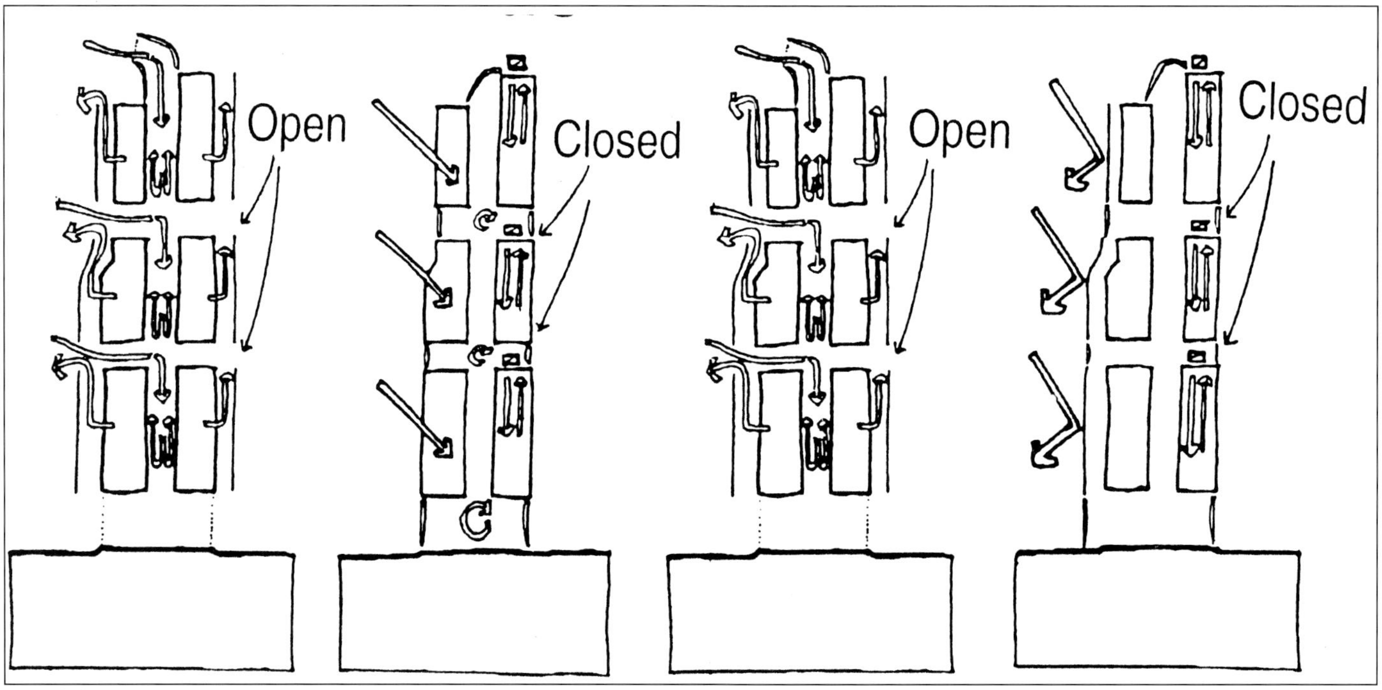

通风分析 Ventilation study

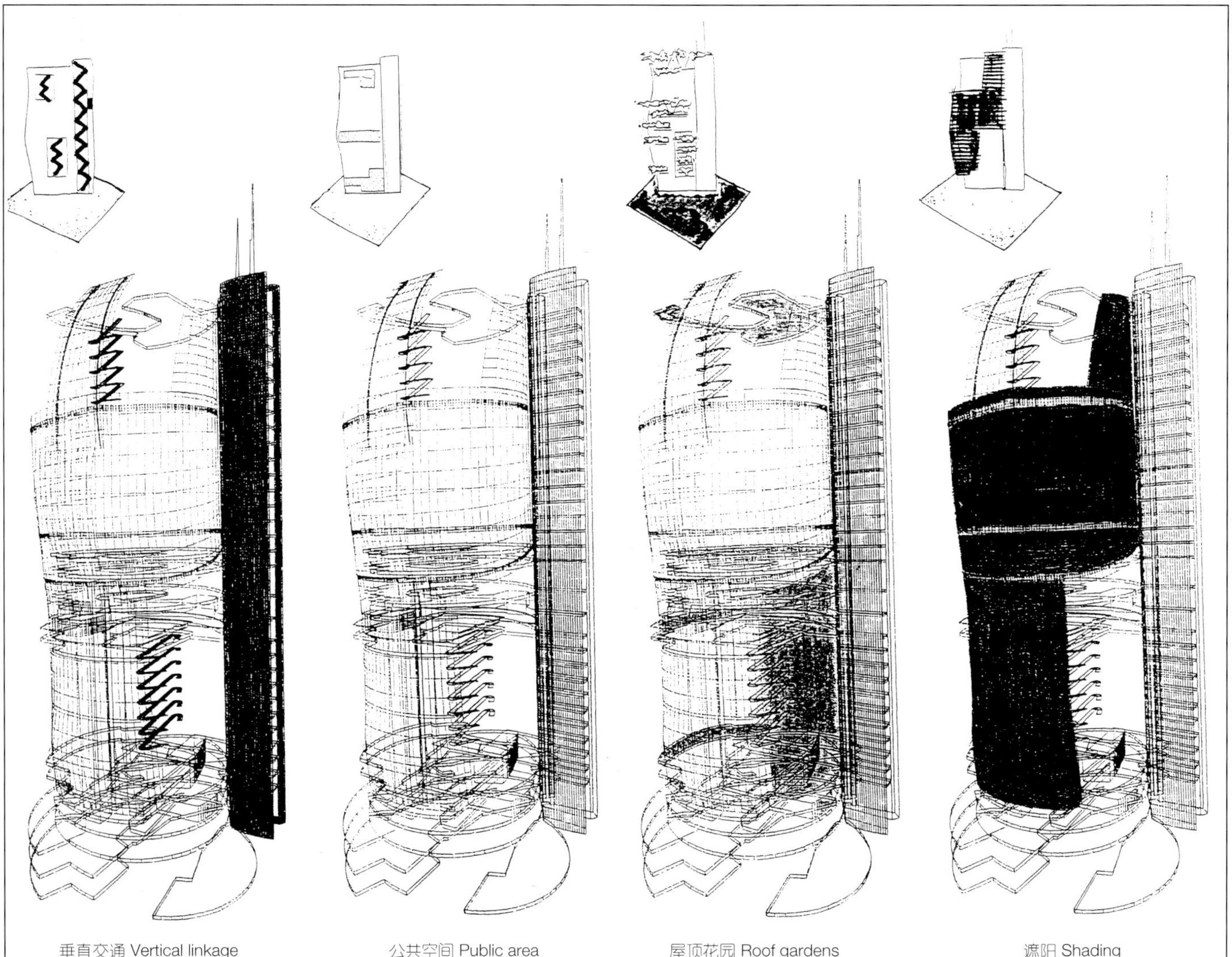

设计分析 Design analysis

外观 Exterior view

海南一号塔楼(旅馆)

业主希望建设一个能够反映热带气候环境特征的五星级酒店。设计将中庭设于椭圆形塔楼的中心，两端间断开启，使日光可以反射到建筑的内部空间。塔楼形状按照空气动力学原理设计，椭圆的顶端朝向主风向，组织屋顶部分的空气流动，调节室内气候。风力由可调节百叶控制，通过外部传感器监视风速。建筑顶部的风动机充分利用周围的风力，制造能量储藏在电池中，为大厦提供热水、采暖以及楼梯和紧急出口照明。中庭顶部有自然采光，楼梯和电梯厅亦全部自然采光通风。总建筑面积34324平方米。

Hainan China Tower #1 (Hotel)

The client wanted a 5-star hotel on the site which acknowledges the tropical character of the locality. The tower is designed as part of the ongoing exploration in the use of wind as an ambient bio-climatic component for design. A central atrium arranged in the middle of oval-shape tower. This atrium is punctuated at both sides by cutout sky-scoops which reflect day-light into the atrium space. The tower is designed to have an aerodynamic shape with tip of oval form pointing generally towards the main wind which are then re-ducted through ceiling plenums to ventilate the inner parts of the building. The wind is controlled by adjustable louvers that are externally sensor-controlled and monitored for the wind-speed. A wind-generator at top of building to make use of the ambient wind to generate free energy which is stored in batteries to supply hot water, heating, lighting to the main and escape stair and to power the emergency lights. A skylight is placed at the top of atrium to bring light down the atrium space. Total floor area for this building is 34, 324 square meters.

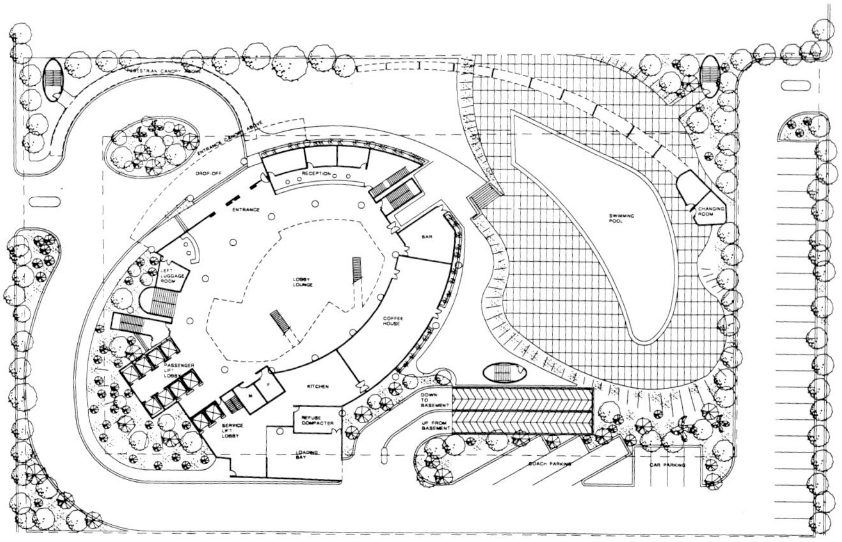
总平面 Site plan

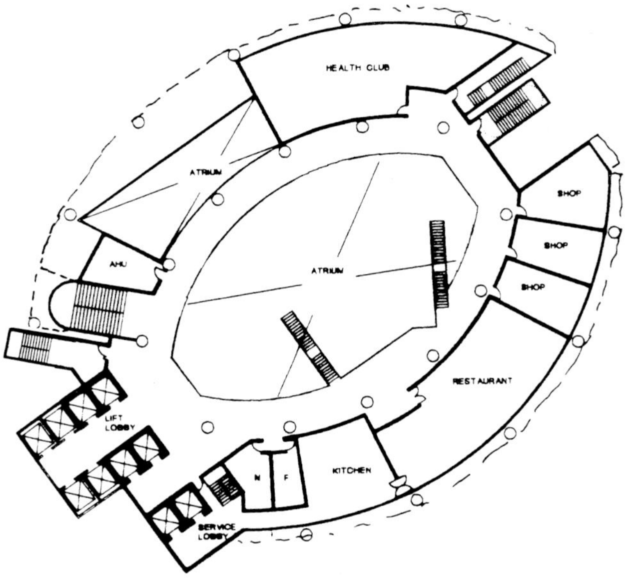

二层平面 Second floor

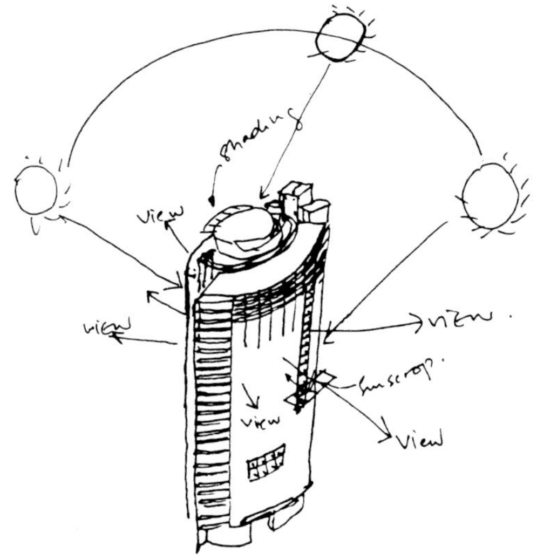
草图 Sketch

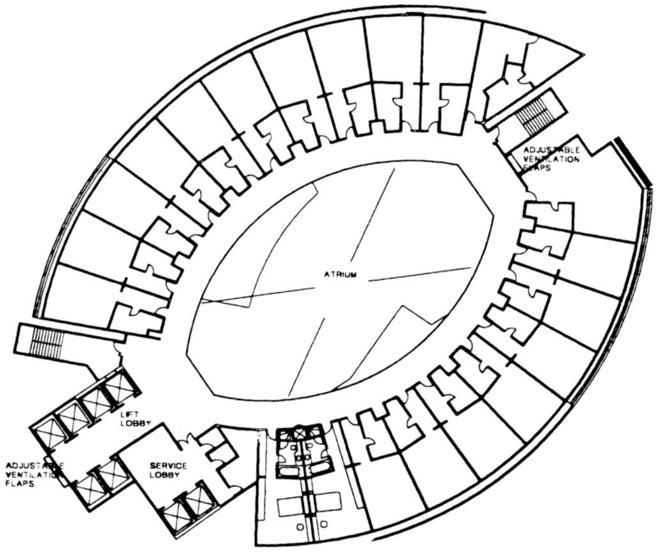

标准层平面 Typical floor

东南外观 Southeast facade

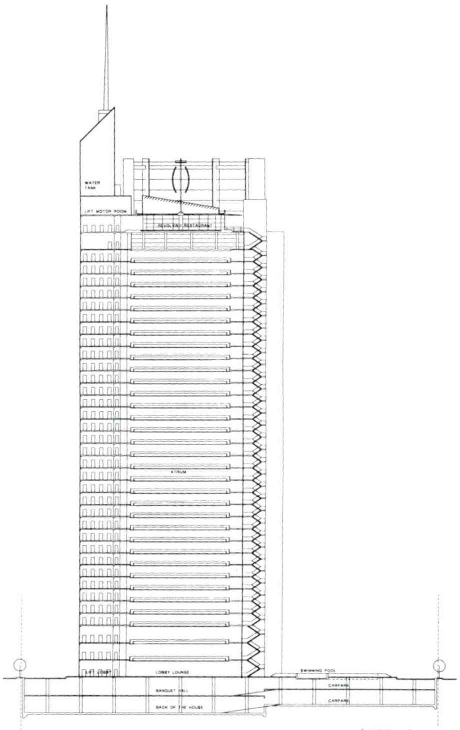

剖面 Section

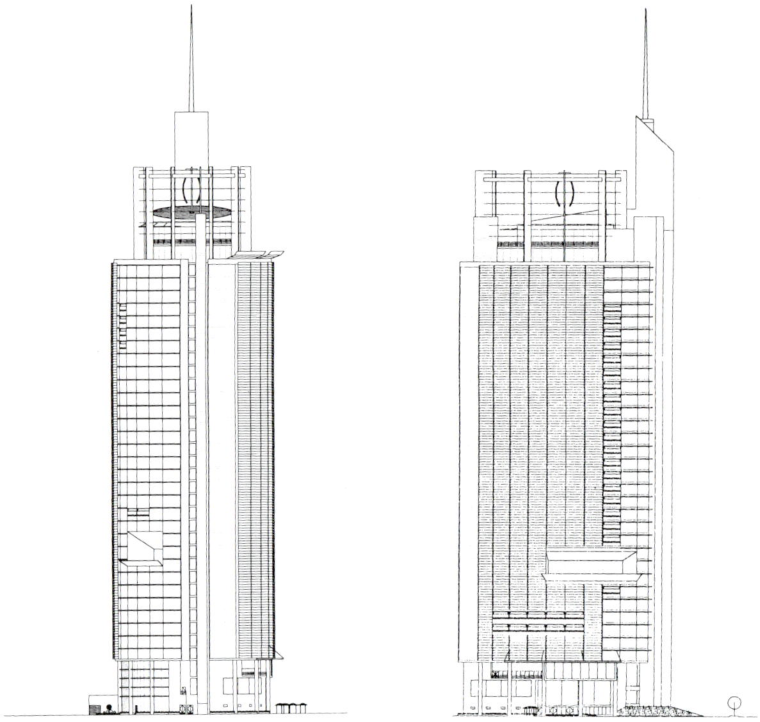

立面 Elevations

西北外观 Northwest facade

总体鸟瞰 Overall view of model

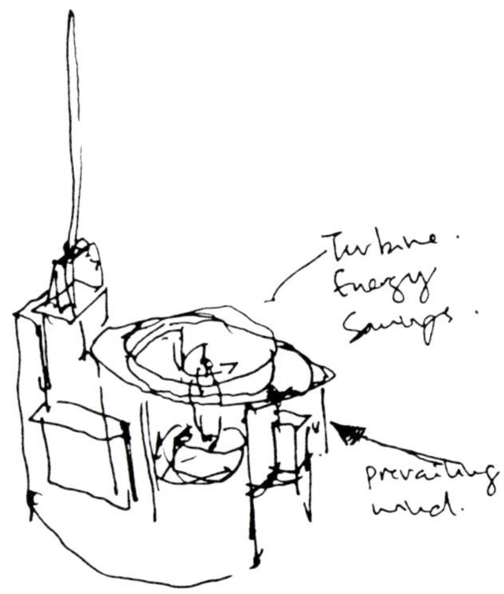

草图 Sketch

侧面外观 Side view

海南二号塔楼(公寓住宅)

项目包含一系列高级海滨公寓和一所乡村俱乐部。地形北侧朝海，南侧面向市区，总建筑面积40000平方米。为了尽可能获得最好的景观，公寓之间互成一定角度排列。塔楼一般为每层四户，而在某些特殊楼层为三户，留出的空间用于布置空中花园。所有户型都有三面外墙，电梯和楼梯厅全部自然采光通风，无机械通风房间。在建筑上部间断布置空中花园，作为建筑中的公共空间。另外，所有户型都有面海的大型阳台，并配有可装卸台风百叶，顶层则设有带泳池的日光平台。

Hainan China Tower #2 (Apartments)

With a total floor area about 40,000 square meters, this proposed development is a complex consisting of up-market apartments combined with a country club that will share its common facilities. The apartment towers are placed at an askew angle to each other to get the best views out towards the sea on the north and the town on the south. The design has the following features: There are four apartment units on each floor except for special floors in which there are three units and the left over space becomes sky-courts and communal spaces-in-the-sky. All apartment units have external-walls ocated on all 3 sides of each unit. The lift-lobby and staircases are naturally ventilated. No rooms are mechanically ventilated. Large skycourts are placed at intermittent upper-parts of the building as communal spaces. All apartment units have large balconies facing the seaward elevation and have moveable typhoon shutters. At the uppermost floor is a sunroof deck with a pool. Wind-generators are located at the uppermost floor.

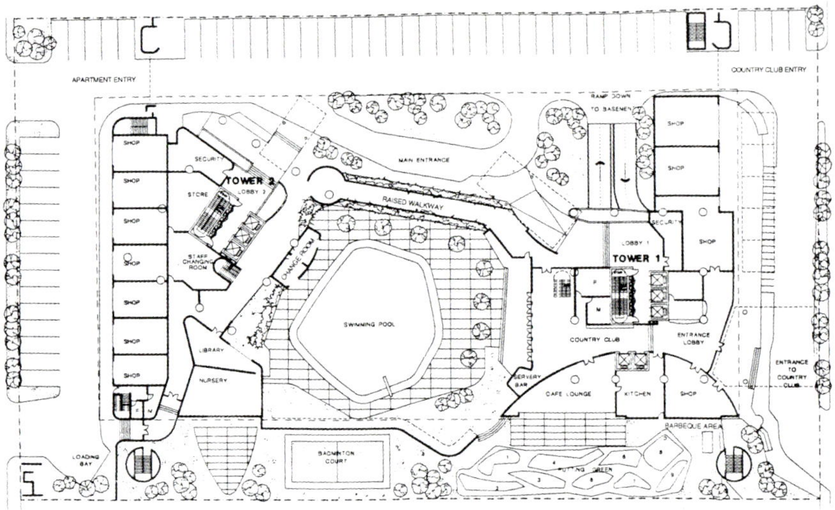

底层平面 First floor

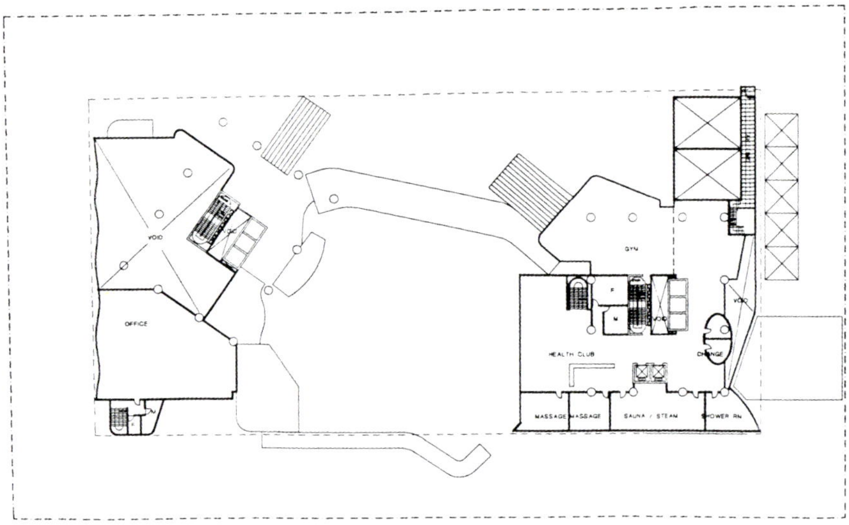

三层平面 Third floor

模型 Model view

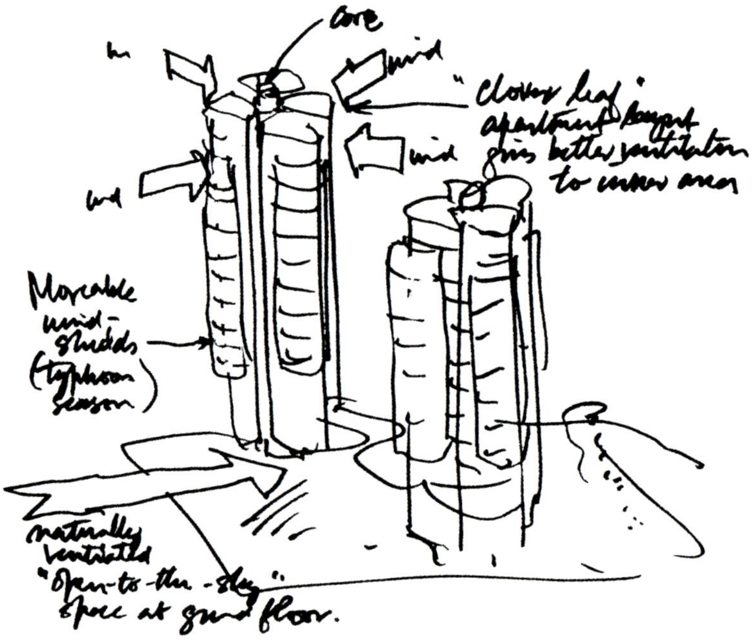

构思草图 Sketch

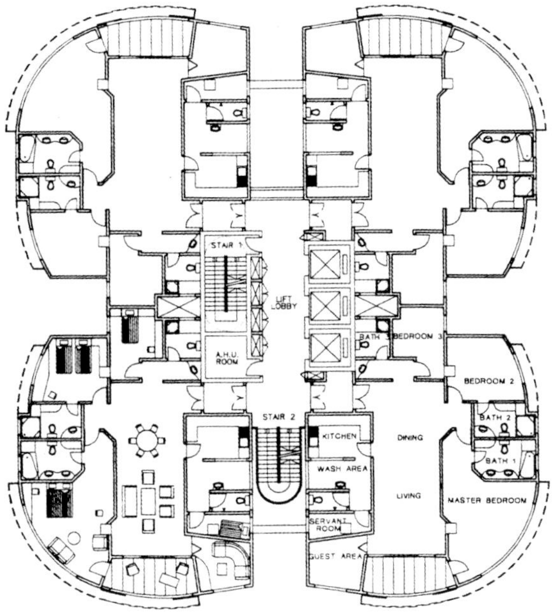

标准层平面 A　Typical floor A

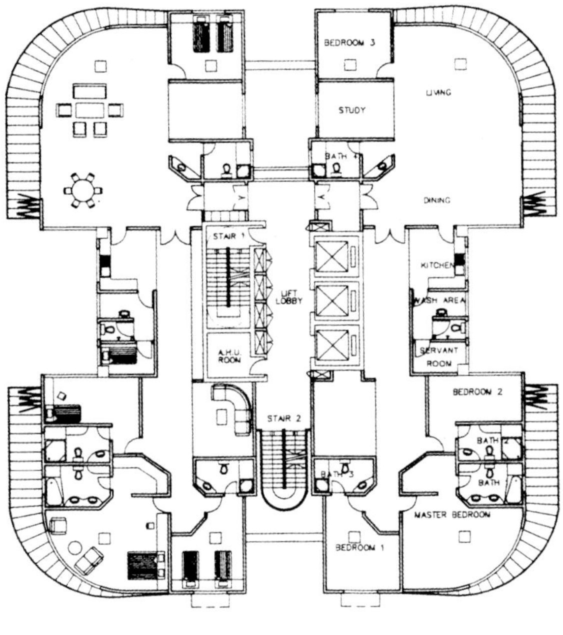

标准层平面 B　Typical floor B

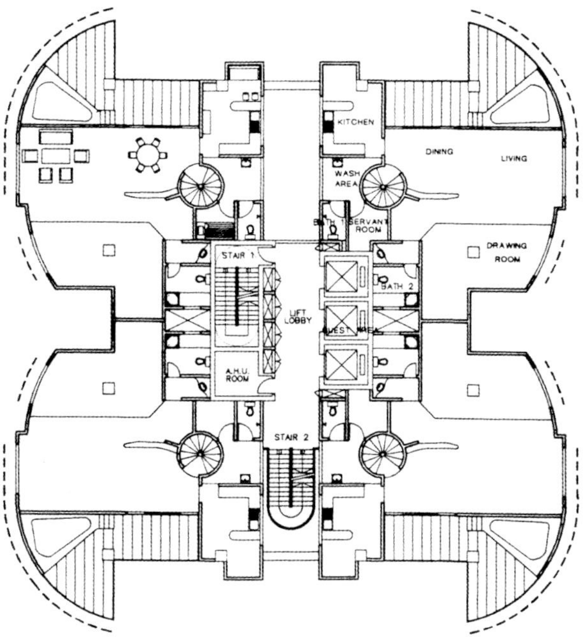

标准层平面 C_1　Typical floor C_1

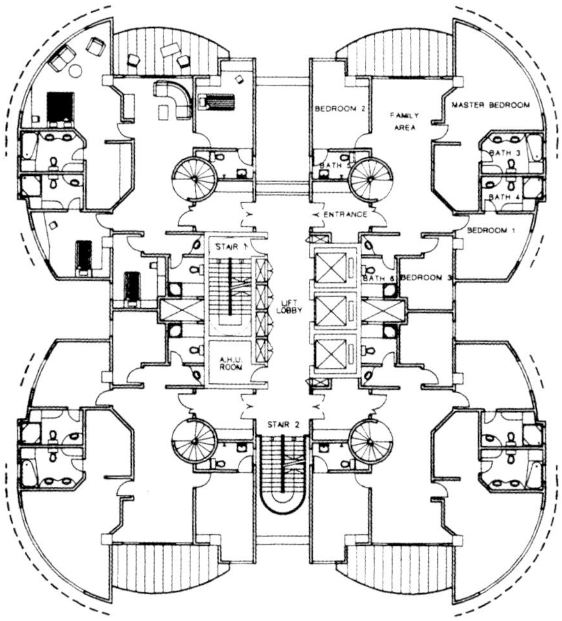

标准层平面 C_2　Typical floor C_2

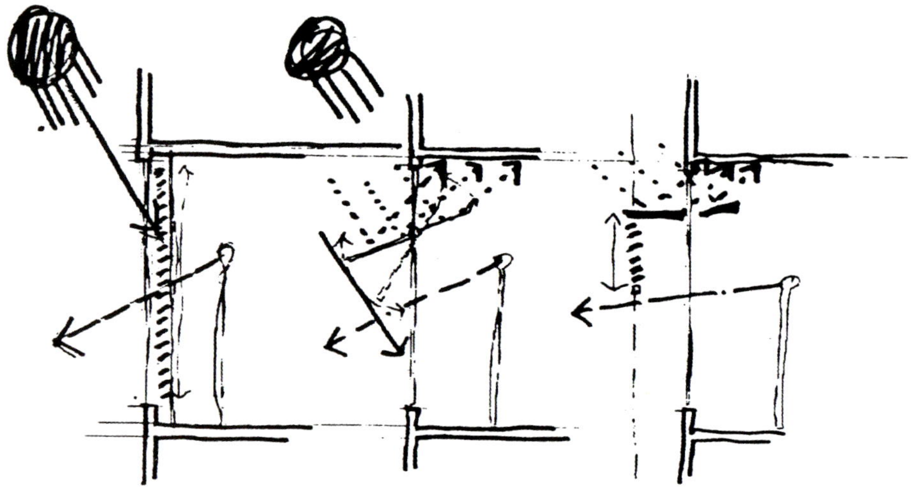

立面遮阳构思 Sketch of shading design

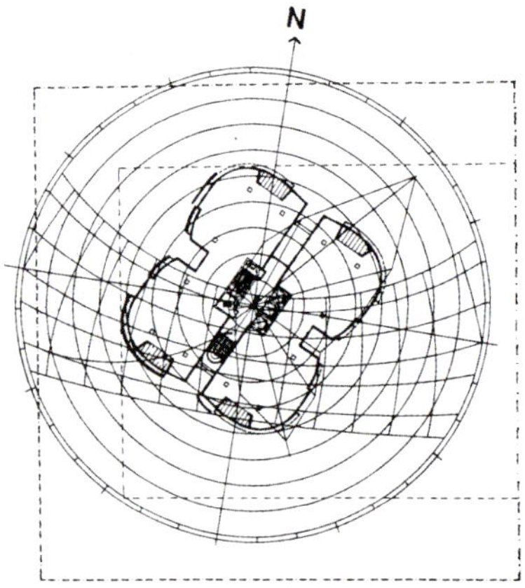

阴影分析 Shading zones

鸟瞰 Overhead view

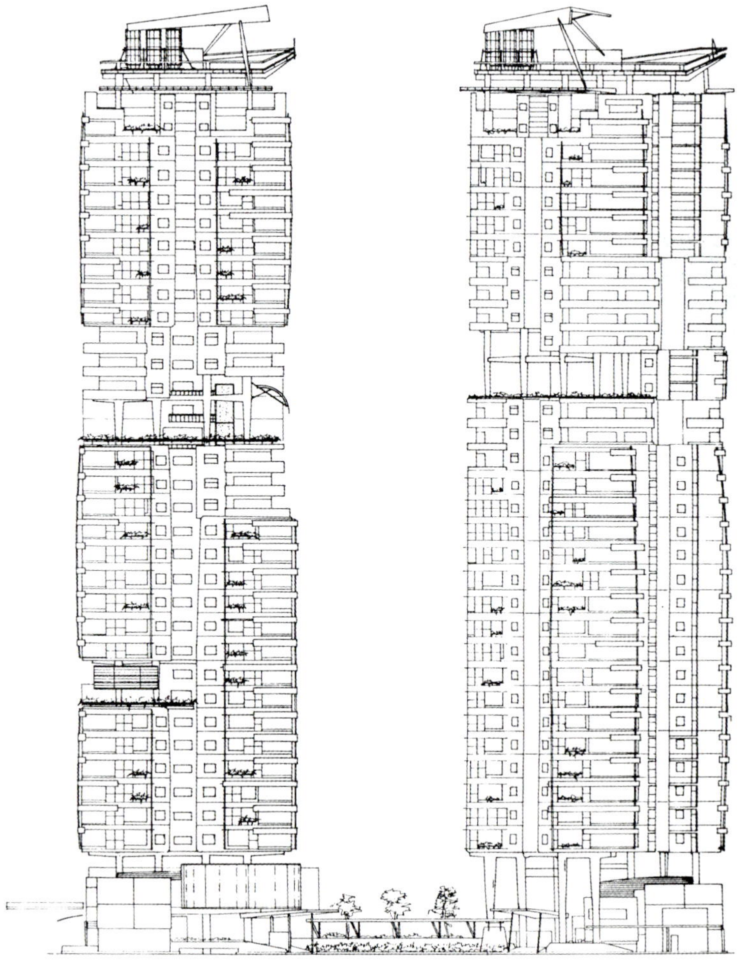

西北立面 Northwest elevation

模型 Model view

海南三号塔楼(办公)

业主希望建设一个具有市场竞争力的高级写字楼。设计具有以下特点：楼梯、电梯厅及卫生间全部自然采光通风。塔楼平面呈椭圆形，面朝主要风向，以便于组织通风。外墙采用光感装置，与弧形墙面成一斜角安装。建筑顶部为旋转餐厅。

Hainan Tower #3 (Office)

The client wanted a top-class office building with Marketing features that would enhance its rental.
The design features are:

Naturally-ventilated and sunlit spaces for the public areas such as lift-lobbies, staircases and toilets.

The tower has an elliptical floor-plate that is oriented to receive wind that is channeled into the building to naturally-ventilate the inner parts of the building and toilet areas. numerous wind-collection devices are adopted.

The external wall design is solar-responsive as it is diagonal and has a curved facade.

At the top of the building is a revolving restauruant.
Total floor area of this building is 40,650 square meters.

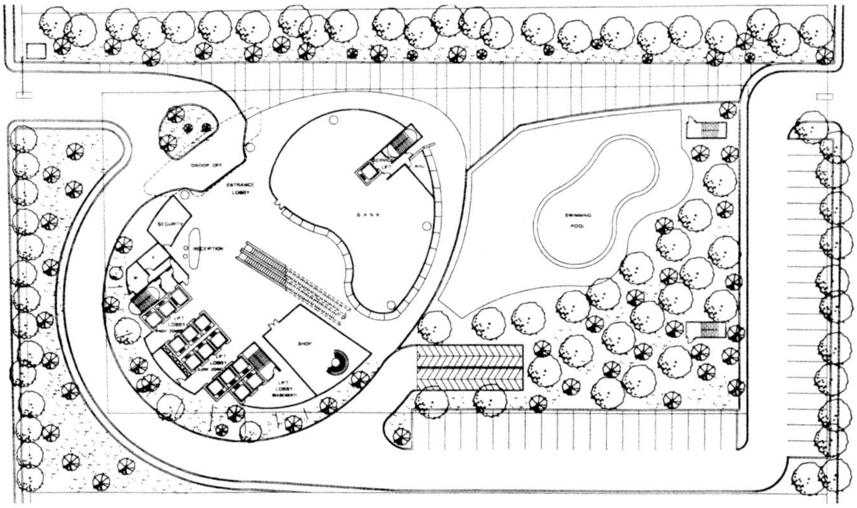

总平面 Site plan

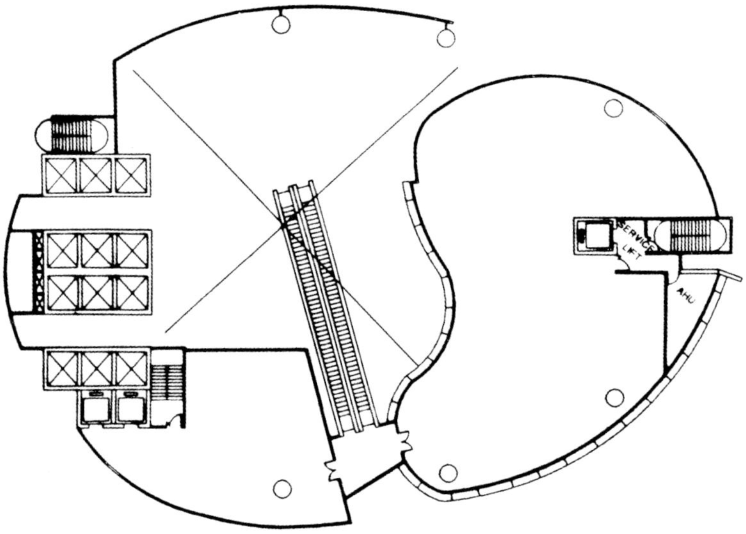

三层平面 Third floor

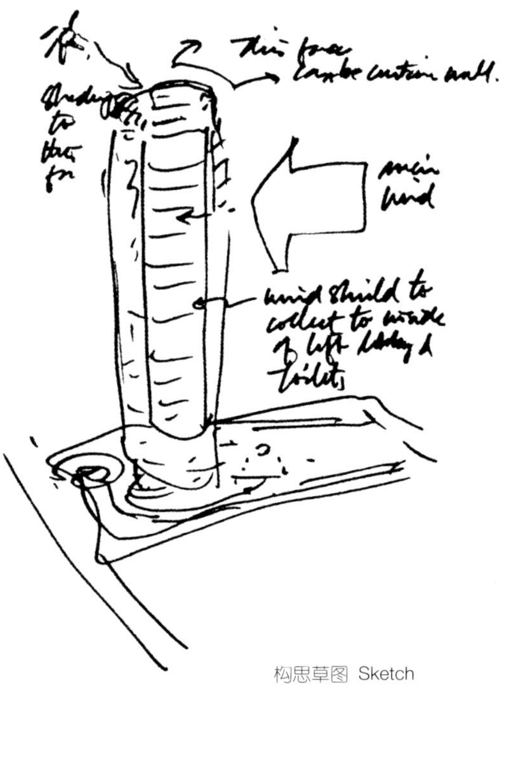

构思草图 Sketch

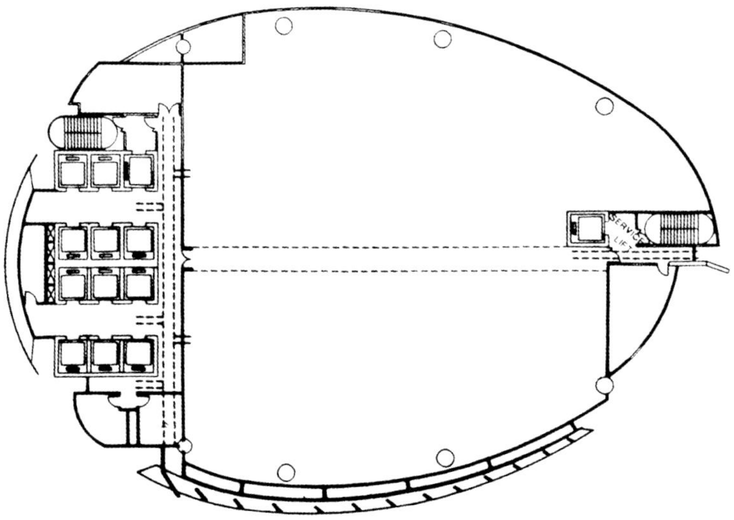

标准层平面 Typical floor

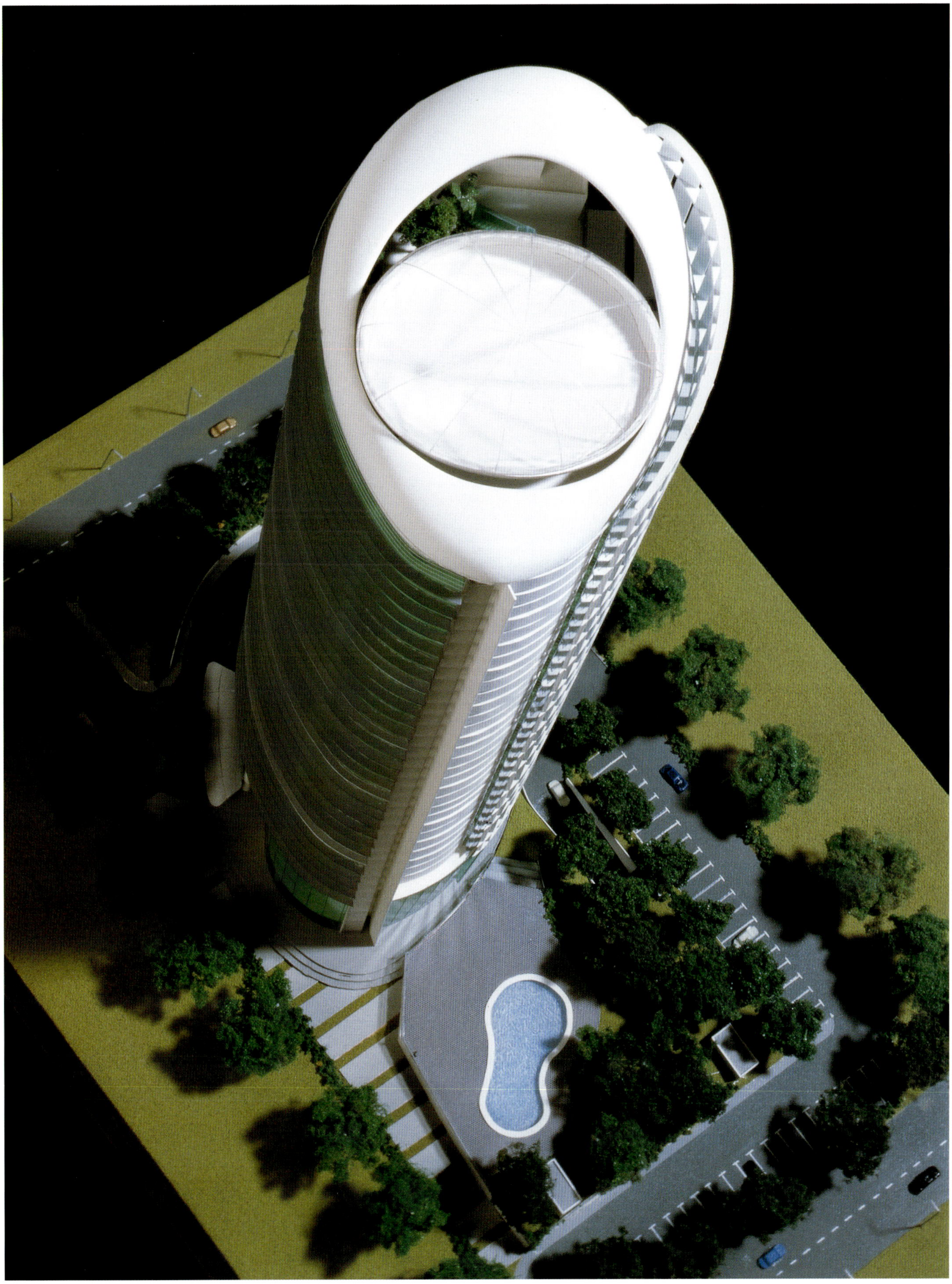

模型鸟瞰 Model view

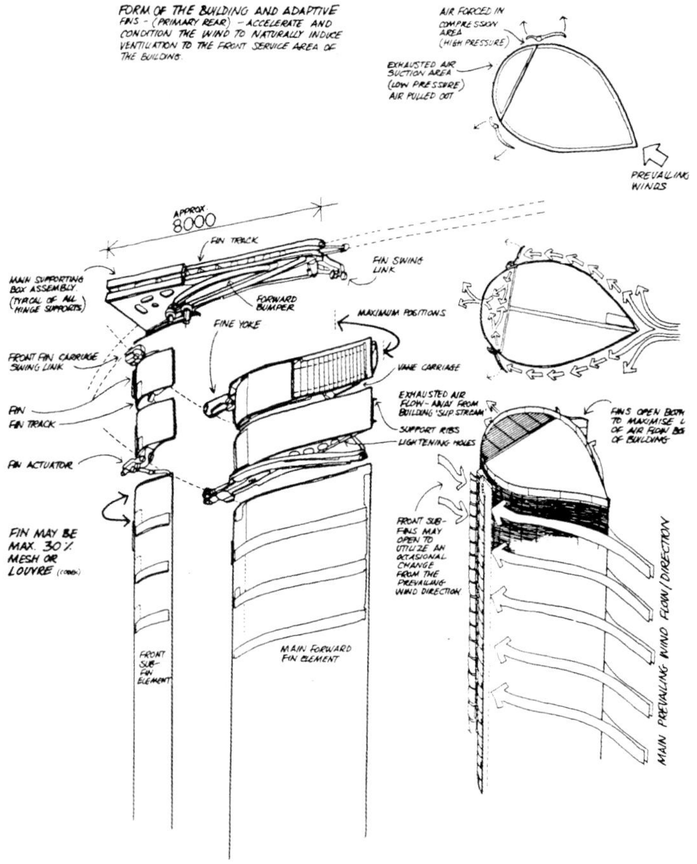

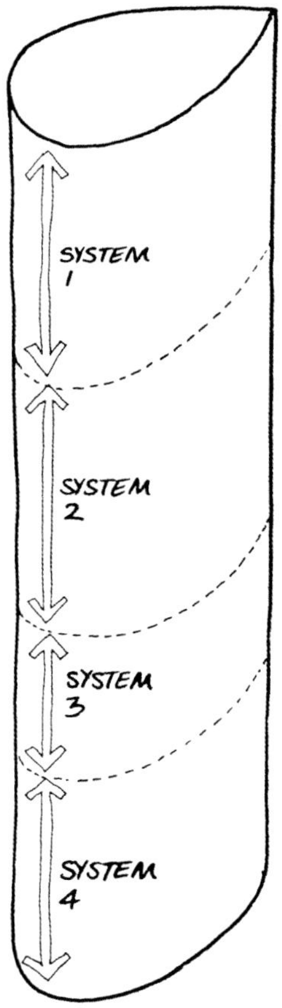

体型分析 Building form analysis

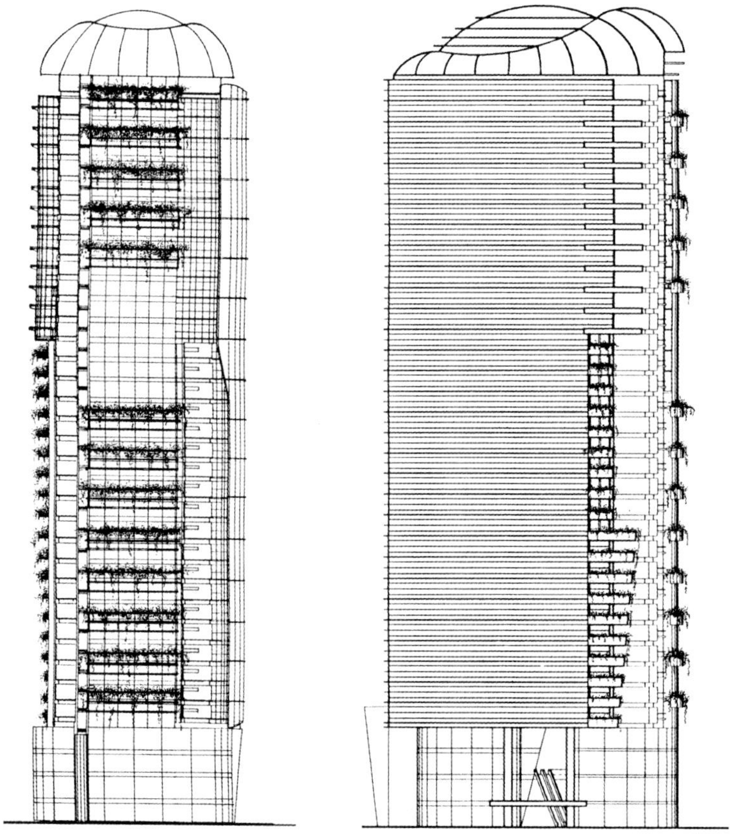

西南立面 South elevation/west elevation

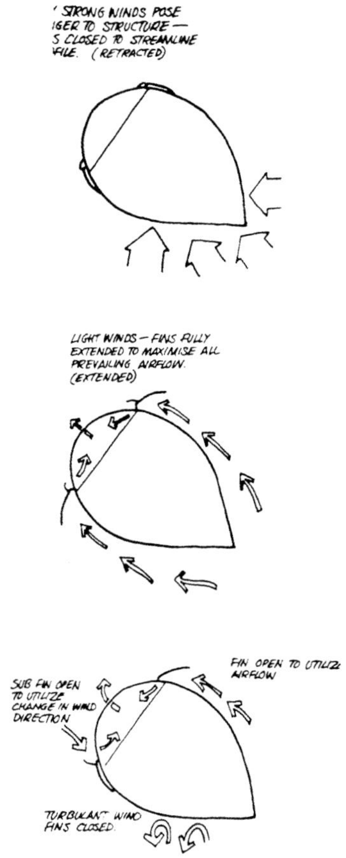

西南外观 Model view from southwestern corner

东侧外观 Model view from east

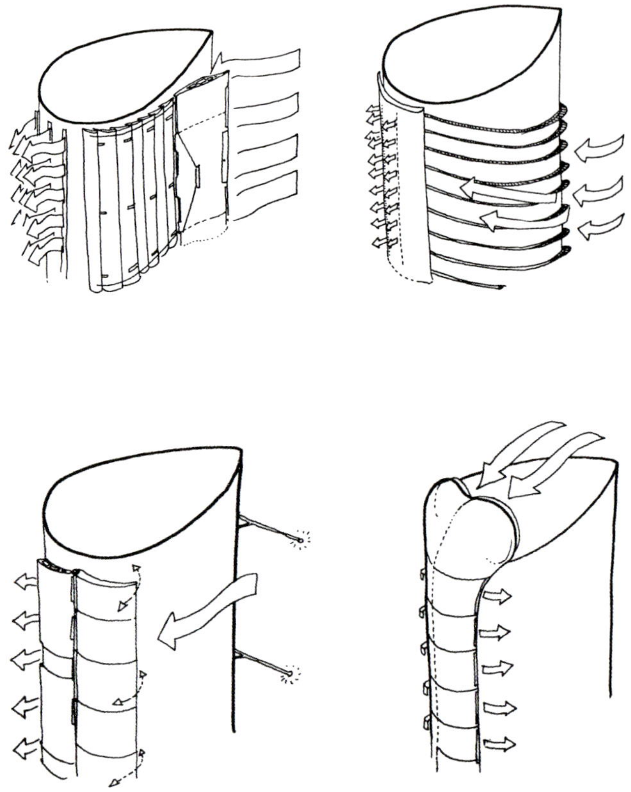

细节研究 Details study

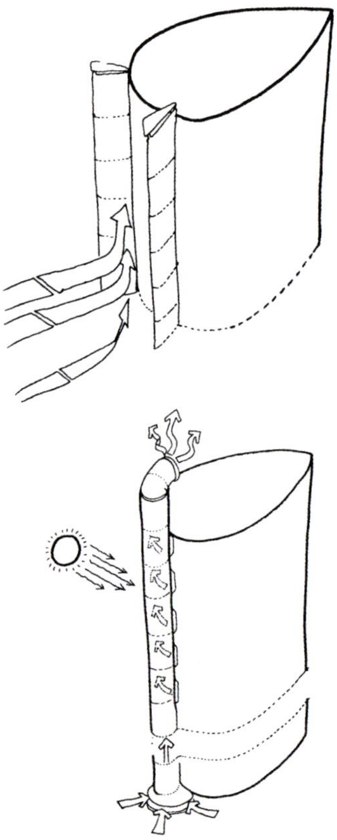

细节研究 Details study

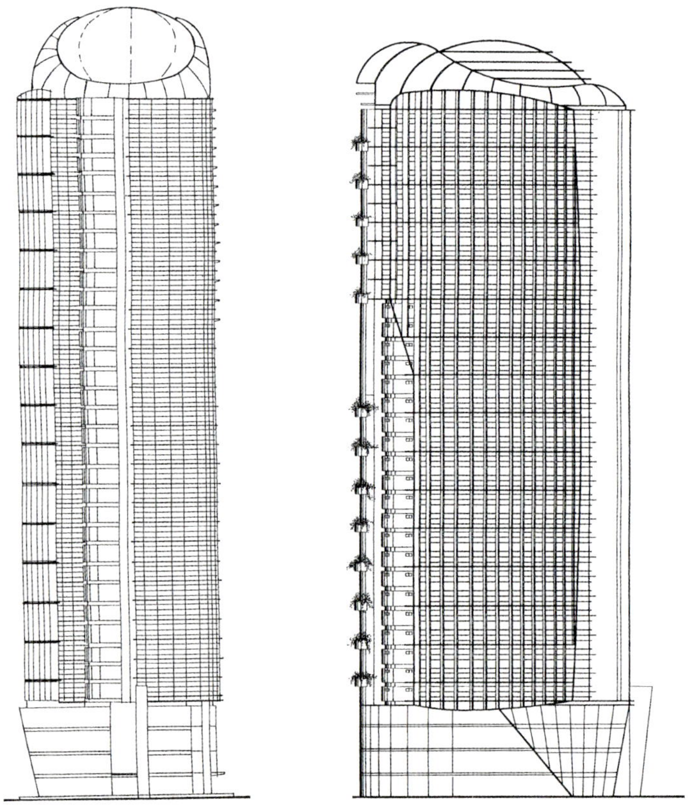

北东立面 North /East elevation

东北侧外观 Model view from northeast

南侧外观 Model view from south

山下和正建筑研究所
KAZUMASA YAMASHITA ARCHITECTS AND ASSOCIATES, INC.

山下和正于1969年设立山下和正建筑研究室。1971年将其改组为有限会社——山下和正建筑研究所，并出任所长。在成功地设计了一系列以住宅为主的小型项目之后，1977年因“FROM Ist”建筑的设计而获得日本建筑学会年度奖，其后又先后于1985年和1987年分别以东京郊区的小山田团地规划设计和神户市西神新城规划设计两次获日本建设大臣奖，设计所亦不断发展壮大，于80年代末已达到有职员15人左右的规模，其中包括设计人员10人以上。到目前为止，设计所的业务范围已扩展到各种规模的住宅、博物馆、餐厅、办公楼、学校、商业设施等的设计及居住小区和大规模城乡开发项目的规划。在设计目标上，强调与社会形成良好关系，改善环境质量，着意营造能让人们亲身感受到生活的丰富多彩的空间，并积极创造能有效地对地区作出贡献的环境构架。

The firm was originally founded by Kazumasa Yamashita in 1969 as Kazumasa Yamashita Studio and in 1971, it was reorganized into Kazumasa Yamashita Architect and Associates Inc. with Yamashita as its president. After a series of successful designs of small-scaled projects, mainly residential ones, Yamashita received an Annual Design Award from the Architectural Institute of Japan in 1977 for his design of "FROM 1st" Building. In 1985 and 1987, Yamashita won a Minister of Construction Award twice for his planning and design of the Oyamada Housing Estate in Suburbs of Tokyo and Seishin New Town in Kobe respectively. The firm had also grown substantially to include a team of around 15 staffs, more than 10 of whom are designers, by the end of 1980's. Up to now, the firm's practice has been diversified into design of residential projects, museums, restaurants, office buildings, schools, commercial complexes & etc. of various size and planning of housing estates and large-scaled urban and rural developments. Their design is aimed at creating good relations with society, improving the quality of the environment, helping to establish a place in which people may live their lives in comfort and with a sense of well-being, and creating an effective framework contributing something really meaningful to a locality.

初步方案外观 Exterior view of preliminary design

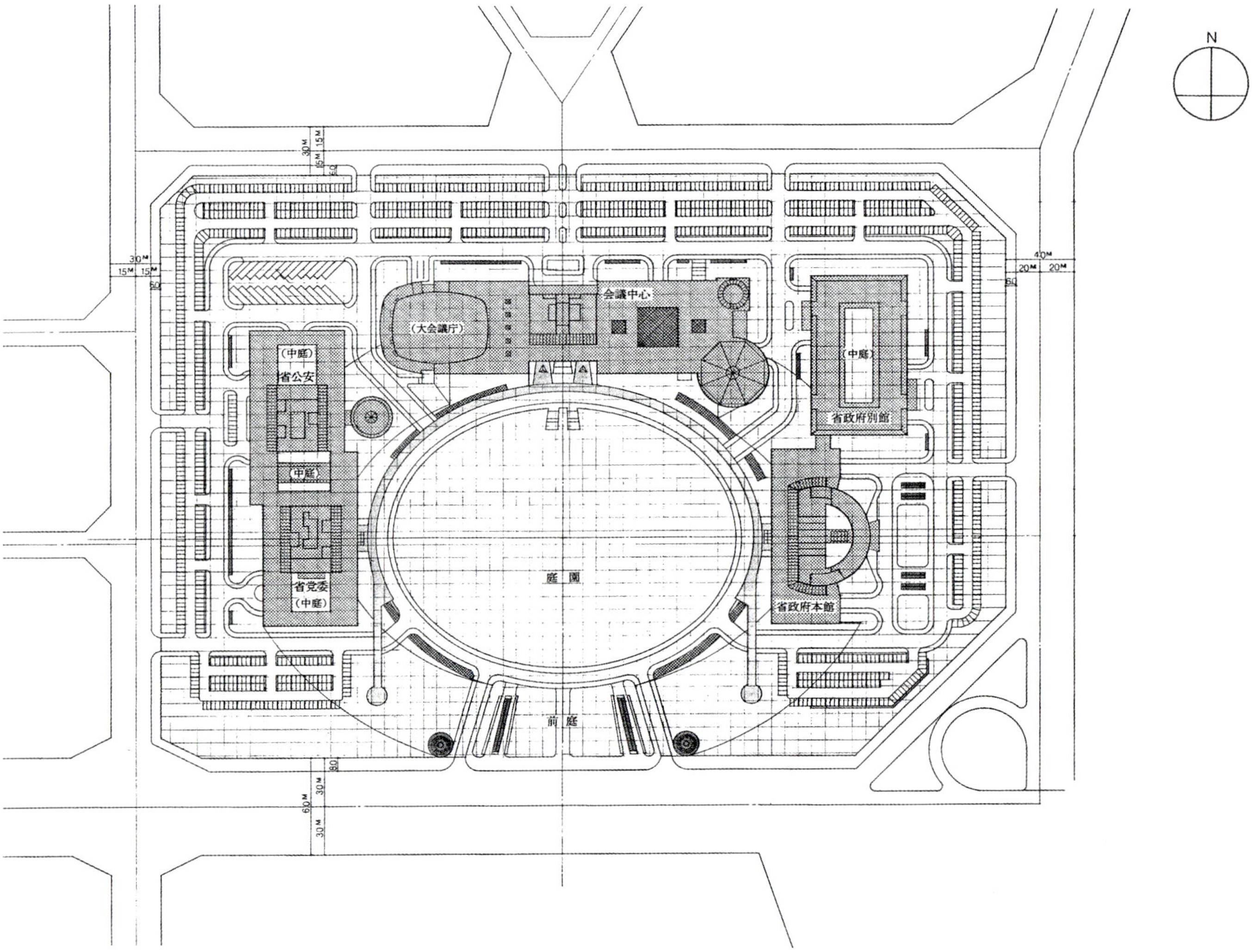

总平面 Site plan

海南广场

广场毗邻海口新机场，包括省委、省政府、省人大、公安厅、法院等行政机构及附属设施。方案采用规整的对称布局，所有建筑围绕中心花园，人大楼居中，省政府楼置于右侧，而其它建筑置于左侧。通过二层的椭圆形环形通道将所有机动交通流线集中，通道底层内侧则形成一个花园，其外侧为商店、餐厅等服务设施，两者之间为步行区域。

Hainan Plaza

Neighbor to the newly planned International Airport at Haikou, the provincial capital of Hainan Province, Hainan Plaza is a group of composite buildings for various provincial government facilities such as Government Offices, the assembly Building, Communist Party Headquarters, Police Headquarters and services. A classical monumental-like layout is adopted, in which all buildings are arranged around a garden similar to the traditional housing form of China, with the Assembly Building in the front, the Government Offices on the right and the other buildings on the left. All the lines of approach to each building for vehicles are brought together in an oval rotary constructed on a mound of earth at second floor level in the center front and form a garden at the first floor level on the inner side. Below the oval rotary, there is a pedestrian precinct with the garden on the inside and all the services such as shops and restaurants are on the outside.

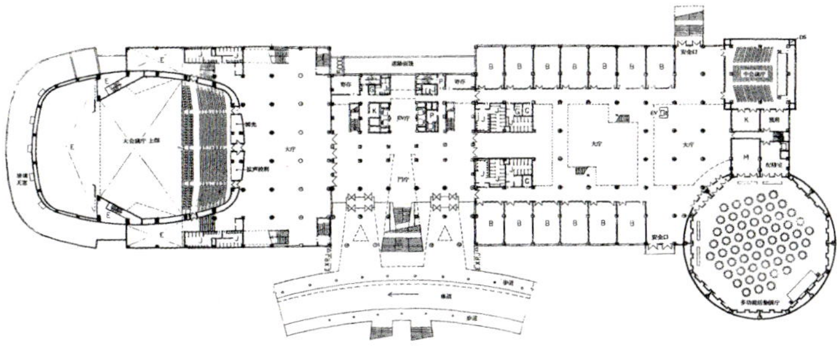
会议中心层平面 Conference center second floor

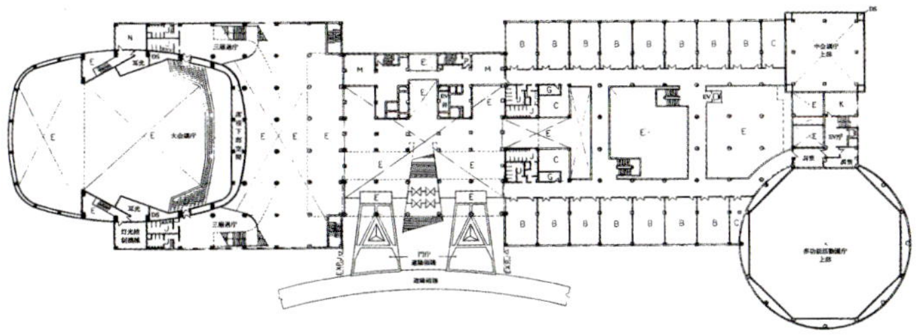
会议中心三层平面 Third floor

会议中心北立面 North elevation

修改方案外观 Exterior view of intermediate scheme

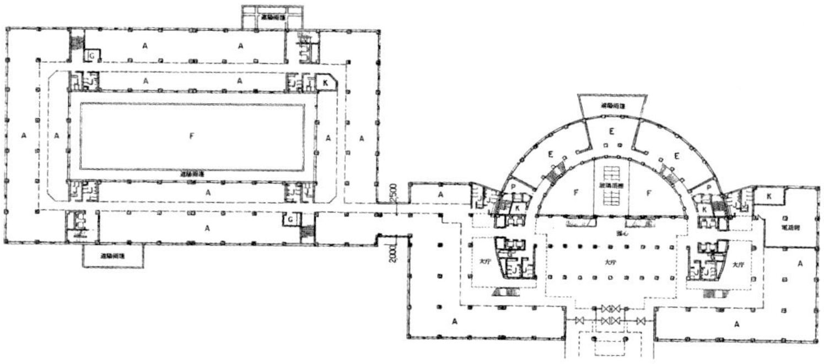

二层平面 Second floor

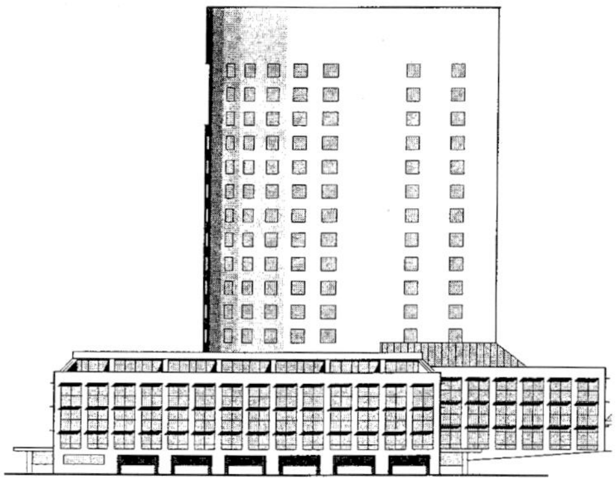

南立面 South elevation

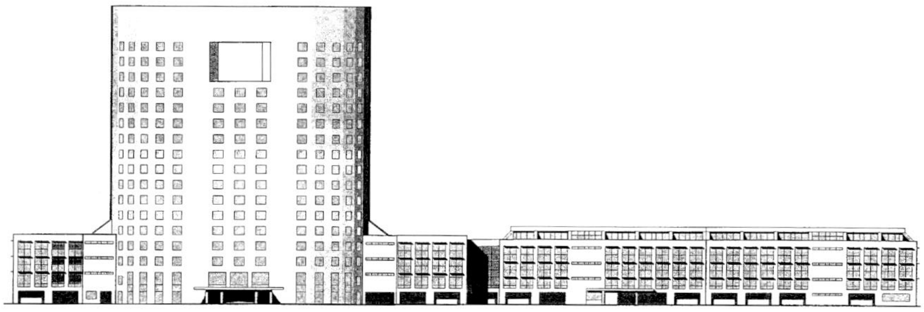

东立面 East elevation
(省委大楼 Building for Provencial Party committe)

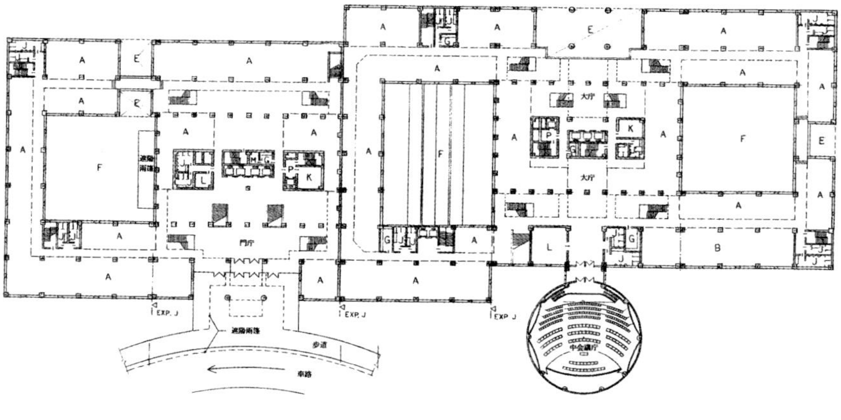

二层平面 Second floor

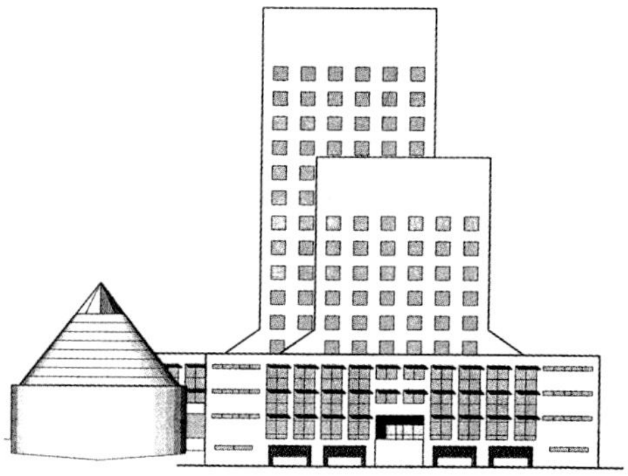

北立面 North elevation

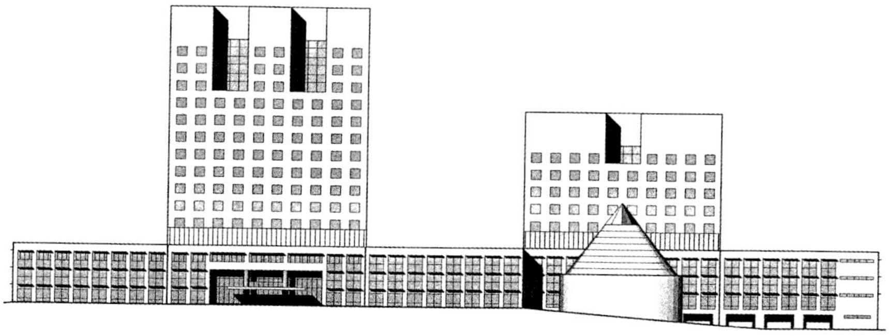

东立面 East elevation
(省政府大楼 Building for Provencial Government)

后　记

《外国建筑师中国作品选》与已出版的《中国当代青年建筑师作品选》及即将出版的《中国当代著名建筑师作品选》形象地记录了80年代以来中国建筑的发展与演变。编者希望通过以上丛书反映这一历史时期中国的建筑实践活动和中外建筑师们的种种努力与探索，这些丰富多彩的作品在城市、建筑、环境设计等多方面为读者展示和提供了广阔的鉴赏、学习、分析及评论的空间。同时在其中也显露出我国社会经济、建筑文化，科学技术及各种观念的发展与变化的进程，以及尚存在的禁锢和局限。书中对作品的介绍尊重设计者的原意和描述。相信各位建筑师的努力和成果能在我国建筑文化发展的长河中起到承前启后、推波助澜的作用。

深切感谢作品提供者和广大读者的支持和帮助，并向一些未能及时来稿或稿件不合编辑和印刷要求而未能直接登刊者表示歉意，衷心希望今后还有继续合作的机会。

编　者
一九九八年十月

Postscript

International Architects in China: Selected Works since 1980, together with Memories and Solutions of Young Architects published earlier and the forthcoming Selected Works of Well-known Chinese Architects, provide a wide range panorama of the architectural practices and endeavors in China since 1980. With this series of publications, the editors intend to reveal changes and developments in society, economy, architecture, science, technology and ideology, as well as extant shackles and limitations. Introduction to the projects is based on the designers' original statement and description, and touches upon issues in urban, architectural, and environmental design. All these have left enough space for the inquiring, analytical scrutiny and even criticizing for the readers. We hope the creative works by these architects can help the reader better understand of the evolution of architecture in China.

We would like to express our most sincere gratitude to those architects who shared their projects with us and to the readers whose support and help are essential for the successful publication of the series. Unfortunately, due to the time and space constraints, we were unable to include all significant works of interest. We do hope, however, that we have a chance review a broader range of projects for inclusion in future editions.

The Editors
October 1998

致谢

在本书编辑与出版过程中，承蒙诸多同行好友的热情帮助与鼓励，在此，我们表示深深谢意。

首先，感谢入选国外建筑师事务所的支持，为本书提供大量作品。并感谢李思贤女士、郑可先生为收集资料所提供的帮助。其次，特别感谢单皓女士、崔悦君博士、黄大田博士、洪勤先生等为本书编辑所付出的辛勤劳动，出版社为本书能尽快与读者见面所作出的努力。

此外，感谢本书的所有照片提供者。由于最后的版面调整，我们十分抱歉不能一一提及每一照片的版权。

Acknowledgments

In the process compiling and producing this book, many groups and individuals have given us generous help and earnest encouragement, for which we would like to express our sincere thanks.

First and foremost, our thanks go to the international architects who provided us with their projects for inclusion in this publication. We also want to thank Ms. Joyce Lee and Mr. Zheng Ke, who helped us in collecting materials for this publication, Ms. Shan Hao, who helped us in translating the English test of the book, and Mr. Hong Qin and Dr. Huang Datian, who also provided editorial support. We are indebted to Dr. Eugene Tsui, who gave final review of the whole English test. We would also like to thank our publisher, who helped bring this book to interested readers.

Finally, we wish to thank all the persons and organizations for their courtesy in allowing us to publish their photographs. At the same time, we sincerely apologize that we could not mention each of the photographic credits due to last minute formatting adjustments required by the publishers.